The Social Theory of W.E.B. Du Bois

The Social Theory of W.E.B. Du Bois

Editor
PHIL ZUCKERMAN
Pitzer College

PINE FORGE PRESS
An Imprint of Sage Publications, Inc.
Thousand Oaks • London • New Delhi

For information:

 Pine Forge Press
A Sage Publications Company
2455 Teller Road
Thousand Oaks, California 91320
E-mail: order@sagepub.com

Sage Publications Ltd.
1 Oliver's Yard
55 City Road
London EC1Y 1SP
United Kingdom

Sage Publications India Pvt. Ltd.
B-42, Panchsheel Enclave
Post Box 4109
New Delhi 110 017 India

Printed in the United States of America

Library of Congress Cataloging-in-Publication Data

Du Bois, W. E. B. (William Edward Burghardt), 1868-1963.
[Essays. Selections]
The social theory of W.E.B. Du Bois / edited and with an introduction by Phil Zuckerman.
    p. cm.
Includes bibliographical references and index.
ISBN 0-7619-2870-7— ISBN 0-7619-2871-5 (pbk.)
    1. Du Bois, W. E. B. (William Edward Burghardt), 1868-1963–Political and social views.
2. Social sciences—United States—Philosophy. 3. African Americans—Social conditions—To 1964. 4. African Americans—Civil rights—History—20th century. 5. United States—Race relations. 6. Social problems—United States—History—20th century. 7. United States—Social conditions—20th century. 8. International relations. I. Zuckerman, Phil. II. Title.

E185.97.D73A25 2004
305.896′073′0092—dc22

                                                            2003024076

04   05   06   10   9   8   7   6   5   4   3   2   1

Acquiring Editor:	Jerry Westby
Editorial Assistant:	Vonessa Vondera
Production Editor:	Diana E. Axelsen
Typesetter:	C&M Digitals (P) Ltd.
Indexer:	David Luljak
Cover Designer:	Edgar Abarca

Contents

Acknowledgments

I would like to thank Benton Johnson, Sandra Barnes, Ernest Allen, and especially Harry Lefever for their critical feedback and input. Appreciation is also extended to the following for all their work and assistance: Frederick Courtright, Amber Carrow, Joanne Zhang, and Elizabeth Shatzer. I would also like to sincerely thank Vonessa Vondera and Jerry Westby at wonderful Pine Forge Press.

Introduction

As an undergraduate majoring in sociology, and subsequently as a graduate student pursuing advanced degrees in the same discipline, I was taught that there were essentially three founders of the discipline—three shapers, three intellectual visionaries, three seminal scholars who forged the theoretical backbone of sociology: Karl Marx (1818–1883) from Germany, Max Weber (1864–1920) from Germany, and Emile Durkheim (1858–1917) from France. These three Europeans who wrote in the latter half of the 19th century and—excluding Marx—into the early decades of the 20th century, unambiguously constituted the "big three." The canonization of Marx, Weber, and Durkheim as comprising the widely recognized "trinity" of sociological theory is well established within various secondary texts (Hurst, 2000; Giddens, 1971; Hadden, 1997; Altschuler, 1998; Pampel, 2000; Gane, 1988), as well as various popular introductory monographs (Berger, 1963; Collins, 1992; Willis, 1996; Charon, 1998, 2002; Kanagy and Kraybill, 1999; Curra, 2003). And in their survey of American professors who teach social theory, Brint and LaValle (2000) found that Marx, Weber, and Durkheim undisputedly constitute the founders of the field, with their names appearing on "virtually every returned survey as theorists who are important to teach in a classical theory course." While the centrality of Marx, Weber, and Durkheim to sociology and social theory is taken for granted, additional scholars are also sometimes included in the canon, such as Vilfred Pareto (1848–1923) of Italy, Georg Simmel (1858–1918) of Germany, and George Herbert Mead (1863–1931) of the United States (see Collins and Makowsky, 1998; Pampel, 2000; Adams and Sydie, 2002; Ritzer, 2000a; Kivisto, 1998). Still others who are occasionally mentioned as significant founders of the sociological enterprise include the Frenchman Auguste Comte (1798–1857), the Englishman Herbert Spencer (1820–1903), and the American Thorstein Veblen (1857–1929).

One might be tempted to conclude that the reason Marx, Weber, and Durkheim—along with some of the additional individuals mentioned above—are so widely recognized as the founding theorists of sociology is simply that they were the first to publish distinctly sociological analyses, and furthermore, that what they published was impressive and insightful in terms of both quantity and quality. However, such a conclusion would be inaccurate and easily challenged by a deeper investigation into the history of sociological scholarship. Canonization, as George Ritzer (2003:5–6) points out, is never a clean, objective process based upon who wrote what first or who wrote what best. Don't misunderstand me; Marx, Weber, and Durkheim were prolific, path-breaking social theorists who added enormously to our understanding of human behavior and its relationship to social institutions. However, there were others. There were other scholars—contemporaries of the big three—who were just as prolific and equally path-breaking in their sociological analyses.

1

Yet their work was largely overlooked because the process of canonization invariably reflects political relations, racial fissures, class differences, national hierarchies, gender biases, and a host of other related imbalances of power, authority, and access to the means of scholarly production, distribution, and recognition. It is only by exposing such dynamics that we can accurately account for the fact that many intellectual contemporaries of the big three were almost completely ignored and wholly excluded—or as Lengermann and Niebrugge-Brantely (1998) argue, literally *erased*—from the canon of classical sociological theory. Charlotte Perkins Gilman (1860–1935) of the United States, Harriet Martineau (1802–1876) of England, and Marianne Weber (1870–1954) of Germany stand out as glaring examples. All three women wrote extensively on social matters of vast theoretical significance, and yet until very recently, were completely ignored within the discipline. Of course, an additional glaring, and perhaps ultimate example of a ground-breaking, prolific, and seminal social theorist whose breath-taking sociological and theoretical output was systematically ignored, excluded, and erased by the academic powers that be, is that of W. E. B. Du Bois of the United States.

Biography

William Edward Burghardt Du Bois[1] (pronounced "Due-Boyss") was born in Great Barrington, Massachusetts, on February 23, 1868. He died in Accra, Ghana, on August 27, 1963. The mere dates of his life span (1868–1963) are cause to pause. He was born just after the Civil War, and he died as the Vietnam War was well under way. He was born when Tchaikovsky was beginning to compose his classical orchestral works, and he died as the Beatles' early hits were topping the pop charts. He was born a few years after the

defeat of slavery, and he died the night before Martin Luther King, Jr., delivered his famous "I Have a Dream" speech at the nation's capital. He was born before the invention of the telephone, and he died when transcontinental airplanes were flying regularly all over the world. He was born before the invention of the electric light bulb, and he died at a time when astronauts were orbiting the earth in space. He was born just after the assassination of Abraham Lincoln, and he died the year of John F. Kennedy's assassination. Few individuals have lived through a greater period of historical, cultural, and technological change.

He married Nina Gomer in 1896, and they had two children: a son, Burghardt (who died a toddler) and a daughter, Yolande. A year after Nina's death in 1950, he married his second wife, Shirley Graham.

Du Bois received a B.A. in 1888 from Fisk University, a second B.A. from Harvard in 1890, and an M.A. from Harvard in 1892. After two years of study at the University of Berlin, he received his Ph.D. from Harvard in 1895. He was Professor of Greek and Latin at Wilberforce University from 1894 to 1896, Assistant Instructor of Sociology at the University of Pennsylvania from 1896 to 1897 (though he was barred from teaching any classes!), and at Atlanta University he was Professor of Economics and History from 1897 to 1910 and Chairman of the Sociology Department there from 1934 to 1944.

Du Bois was a prolific writer, publishing more than twenty books and thousands of essays and articles throughout his life. He wrote regularly for the New York *Age,* the New York *Globe,* the *Chicago Defender,* the New York *Amsterdam News,* and the Springfield *Republican.* He was editor of *The Moon* in 1906, editor of *The Horizon* from 1907 to 1910, editor of *The Crisis* from 1910–1934, and editor of *Phylon* from 1940 to 1944. In addition to his scholarship, he also expressed himself creatively, writing novels as well as poetry. On top of his work as a teacher and scholar, he was a tireless activist for social and racial justice. He was the principal founder of the Niagara Movement and served as its General Secretary. He was a prominent founder of the National Association for the Advancement of Colored People (NAACP) and served as its chairman for many years. He publicly fought against lynching, discrimination, and colonial exploitation. He was a world leader of the Pan-African movement, serving as Secretary of the First Pan-African Congress, and was a leader of many subsequent Pan-African Congresses. A socialist (and later communist),[2] he fought for women's rights, Jewish rights, and workers' rights. Not only was he a principal architect of the civil rights movement, but he also supported the arts and various critical cultural expressions as a founder of the American Negro Academy and one of the supporting pillars of the Harlem Renaissance.

Given such credentials, it comes as no surprise that W. E. B. Du Bois has been recognized by many as an influential cultural and intellectual giant of the 20th century. However, though he has been widely praised as a political leader of the African American community and a noted man of letters, his reputation as a founding sociologist and penetrating social theorist has been distinctly muted.

Sociological Pioneer

Du Bois was never mentioned in a single sociology class during my five years as an undergraduate, nor in my five years of subsequent graduate study in sociology.[3] No books of his were ever assigned, nor a single article, chapter, or essay. He was never referenced in any of my readings as a founding, significant, or noteworthy sociologist or social theorist. And his erasure is evidenced beyond my limited experience; Harry Barnes's (1948) 950-page *An Introduction to the History of Sociology* does not mention his name. His name cannot be found in Maus's (1962) *A Short History of Sociology,* Mitchell's (1968) *A Hundred Years of Sociology,* Swingewood's (1991) *A Short History of Sociological Thought,* Ritzer's (1994) *Sociological Beginnings: On the Origins of Key Ideas in Sociology,* or Levine's (1995) *Visions of the Sociological Tradition.* The *Dictionary of Sociology* on my desk, published by Penguin Books in 1988, doesn't include his name, nor does the 2000 edition I recently perused in a Borders bookstore. Scanning through the relatively dusty shelf where I keep my sociology textbooks, I find his name completely absent from Shepard's (2002) eighth edition, Newman's (2002) fourth edition, Eitzen and Baca Zinn's (2001) ninth edition, Bryjak and Soroka's (2001) fourth edition, Thio's (2000) fourth edition, Giddens's (1991) first edition, and Goode's (1988) second edition. His name and theoretical contributions are wholly omitted in a number of older monographs specifically devoted to summarizing important contributions of social theory (Sorokin, 1928; Borgatta and Meyer, 1956; Abel, 1970; Strasser, 1976; Turner and Beeghley, 1981). Finally, he is excluded from many of the more recently published texts devoted to surveys of social theory (Zeitlin, 2001; Ashley and Orenstein, 2001; Andersen and Kaspersen, 2000; Pampel, 2000; Ritzer, 2000a; Dodd, 1999; Turner, 1998; Cuzzort and King, 1989).

What makes Du Bois's astonishing exclusion from the canon of western sociology so disturbing is that he is arguably one of the most brilliant social theorists this country has ever produced, and without question, he is one of the most imaginative, perceptive, and prolific founders of the sociological discipline—American or otherwise. Although I will frankly admit that ranking sociologists is an indulgent and hazardously subjective activity, given

Du Bois's graceful, impressive, and unparalleled ability to wed poetry with politics, to balance empiricism with theory, to carefully couple objective analysis with personal ideology, and to admirably blend serious scholarship with passionate social activism, a convincing case could easily be made that he is the greatest sociologist this country has ever produced. Consider the following:

Du Bois was a pioneer of urban sociology. Although predated by similar work by Frederick Engels (1994 [1887]), Charles Booth (1892–97), and Jane Addams (1895), Du Bois's (1899a) *The Philadelphia Negro: A Social Study* is, in the words of Charles Lemert (2000:357), "the first great work of American urban ethnography." Julius Lester (1971:32) dubbed it "the first sociological study done in America." While largely ignored at the time of its publication and overlooked ever since—except among black sociologists (Rudwick, 1971; Blackwell and Janowitz, 1974; Anderson, 1999)—it was a study "unique in its intensity of detail on an urban community," marked by "theoretical and methodological sophistication" (Platt, 1996:256). In researching this thorough and impressively empirical analysis of urban life, Du Bois spent a year living among the black population of Philadelphia's Seventh Ward. He spent up to eight hours a day for months on end walking from door to door, visiting over 2,500 dwellings and personally interviewing thousands of individuals, assembling survey data on approximately 10,000 men, women, and children (Katz and Sugrue, 1998; Lewis, 1993:191). The research was exhaustive: He explored matters pertaining to education, literacy, labor, employment, health, family life, income, property holdings, religion, crime, alcoholism, poverty, rents, race relations, suffrage, and more.

Du Bois was a pioneer of rural sociology. Du Bois's work produced *The Negroes of Farmville, Virginia: A Social Study* (1898a), *The Negro in the Black Belt: Some Social Sketches* (1899b), *The Negro Landholder of Georgia* (1901) and *The Negro Farmer* (1904b), which were published as documentary papers by the United States Department of Labor. In these seminal, thorough analyses of small southern towns, Du Bois explored a variety of social issues, including inter- as well as intrarace relations, class divisions, schooling, mortality, family structures, property holdings, sex, the residual impact of slavery, and the effects of growing industrialization on small agricultural communities.

Du Bois was one of the nation's first criminologists (Gabbidon, Greene, and Young, 2002). His sections on crime in *The Philadelphia Negro* (1899a) were empirically impressive; publishing the best available statistical data, he tallied crime rates by specific crimes, by sex, by age, by race and ethnicity, and so on. His analytical assessment of crime was theoretically insightful, forcefully arguing that crime rates are linked to poverty rates, and that the effects of slavery, northern migration, and most important, the concrete manifestations of racism upon the physical and psychological well-being of blacks must be taken into account when assessing levels of criminal activity. In 1904, Du Bois edited and wrote a significant portion of *Notes on Negro Crime Particularly in Georgia;* empirically rich and theoretically path-breaking, it was one of the first sociological monographs devoted to the study of crime ever published in the United States. He further elaborated upon this criminological work in *Morals and Manners Among Negro Americans,* published in 1914.

Du Bois was the first American sociologist of religion (Zuckerman, 2002). He edited and wrote a significant amount of *The Negro Church* (1903a), the first book-length sociological study of religion published in the United States (Zuckerman, Barnes, and Cady, 2003). In addition, he wrote numerous essays, chapters, and articles on religion from a penetrating sociological perspective. "The Problem of Amusement" (1897a), "Of the Faith of the Fathers" (1903b), "Religion in the South" (1907a), and "Will the Church Remove the Color Line?" (1931) are but the tip of the iceberg of his scholarship devoted to the sociological appraisal of American religion (Zuckerman, 2000).

Du Bois was, as David Levering Lewis (2000:550) bluntly puts it, *"the first sociologist of race."* The meaning of race, race relations, racism, race and its connection to other social conflicts and institutions—these topics comprised the heart of Du Bois's scholarly analyses. What class was for Karl Marx and what gender was for Charlotte Perkins Gilman, race was for Du Bois: the most socially significant construct of modernity, the grand fissure of human relations. For Du Bois, "the color line" was the problem of the 20th century, and his entire scholarly output was related in some way to explaining, exploring, and deconstructing that color line.

A pioneer of urban sociology, a pioneer of rural sociology, a pioneer of criminology, the first American sociologist of religion, and the first great social theorist of race— these attributes alone distinguish Du Bois as a seminal pillar of the discipline. Yet his sociological contributions go even further; he wrote an enormous amount—often enough to fill an entire book—on education (Provenzo, 2002; Aldridge, 1999), economics (Jones, 1998; Du Bois, 1899c, 1902, 1907b), American and world history (Gregg, 1998; Byerman, 1994; Wesley, 1970; Du Bois, 1954 [1896], 1962 [1909], 1935), international relations (Du Bois, 1945, 1915), gender (Gilkes, 1996), and the family (Du Bois 1908), not to

mention art and literature (Andrews, 1985; Aptheker, 1989).

Additional Contributions to Sociology

Du Bois was one of the earliest proponents of sociology in the United States, publicly advocating its strengths (Du Bois, 1897b) and establishing a department of sociology at Atlanta University at a time when the discipline was still met with substantial suspicion (Du Bois, 1900, 1903b). He also wrote early works in founding sociology journals, including such articles as "The Study of Negro Problems" (1898b) in *Annals of the American Academy of Political and Social Science,* "Race Friction Between Black and White" (1908a) in the *American Journal of Sociology*— founded only a little over a decade earlier by Albion Small—and "Die Negerfrage in den Vereinigten Staaten [The Negro Question in the United States]" (1906a) in *Archiv fur Socialwissenschaft und Socialpolitik,* a submission written at the request of the journal's editor, Max Weber.

In a short essay published in 1904,[4] a year before he joined the American Sociological Society, Du Bois offered piercing observations and recommendations concerning the neonatal discipline of sociology. Sociology, he argued, cannot be characterized merely as "a science of human action." Nor is it to be understood as simply a field which takes as its subject of study "a certain metaphysical entity called society." Rather, Du Bois asserted, sociologists "seek to know how much of natural law there is in human conduct. Sociology is the science that seeks to measure the limits of chance in human action." A fiercely broad discipline which takes "all human action for [its] province," sociology "endeavors to collate and systematize the facts of human progress and organization." In a speech (1897b) delivered to the American Academy of Political and Social Science delivered in 1897, Du Bois emphasized sociology's concern with social problems; he defined a social problem as "the failure of an organized social group to realize its group ideals, through the inability to adopt a certain desired line of action to given social conditions" (Lester, 1971:230).

Du Bois observed that much of what passed for social science in his day tended to fall into two camps: broad generalizations and theories, on the one hand, or random collections of data comprising a "tangled mass of facts" on the other. Sociology, he insisted, must bridge this chasm between generalizations and facts—it must "bring theory and practice . . . nearer together," and in so doing, discover if indeed "there is rhythm and law in the mass of the deeds of men—and if so how can it best be measured and stated."

Du Bois put his vision of sociology into practice. His courses in sociology at Atlanta University were among the earliest offered in the United States,[5] and in addition to teaching such courses, he organized annual sociological conferences at Atlanta University dedicated to the study of various aspects of black life in the South. Though grossly underfunded and largely ignored by white sociologists (Rudwick, 1974), the Atlanta conferences were groundbreaking, placing Du Bois at "the vanguard of social-science scholarship in America" (Lewis, 1993:225). Du Bois oversaw sixteen of these conferences in the years between 1896 and 1914, and he edited monographs published each year detailing the conferences' findings. Through these conferences and their annual publications, Du Bois "single-handedly initiated serious empirical research on blacks in America" (Rudwick, 1974:46).

Empirical research was of preeminent value for Du Bois (McDaniel, 1998; Green and Driver, 1978:31–39), especially during the years of the Atlanta conferences. In addition to

historically grounding his sociological research, he was determined to "put science into sociology" (Du Bois, 1940:51); he believed that questions of social import could be explored only through the analyses of "facts, any and all facts" and data derived from actual research. Unlike many of the more well-known founding sociologists such as Emile Durkheim, Max Weber, Charles Ellwood, Herbert Spencer, Lester Ward, and Franklin Giddings, Du Bois was not content to limit his scholarship to his office or the library; book-worming and deep thinking did not constitute the sole methods of his sociological inquiry. As McDaniel (1998:155) asserts, Du Bois rejected the grand theorizing that dominated the field in his day, charging the major social theorists of "substituting metaphysical figures from their own imaginations for actual observation of human action." He chastised the "car-window sociologist" (1989 [1903]:107) who draws conclusions about social phenomena without engaging in hands-on research. In a letter written in 1904, he argued that in order to study social problems, you cannot stay "inside of your office," but must "get down here" and live among those people about whom you wish to theorize, studying them "at first hand" (Aptheker, 1973:75). While this volume is dedicated to his theoretical output, which is characterized by broad generalizations and systematic statements concerning matters of macro social significance, it must be stressed that the bulk of Du Bois's sociological work was thickly permeated with original research resulting from participant observation, questionnaire and survey data, ethnographic field work, interviews, and content analyses of archival material, census information, and government documents. Years before the famous studies of the Chicago School, Du Bois's sociological output was characterized by a hands-on, empirical research methodology to a much greater and more respectable degree than that of his more famous contemporaries.

Canonization Imminent

Given the above details of Du Bois's unparalleled, foundational contributions to sociology and social theory, one wonders how his work could have been so blatantly ignored by most sociologists over the last 100 years. The answer is simple: He was a black man writing mostly about black life at a time when most Americans cared little about black men—or women—or their lives (Frazier, 1949; Rudwick, 1974:47–49; Platt, 1996:247). He studied, documented, and theorized about what many would rather ignore or sidestep: racism, that disturbing disease of American culture so readily denied and dismissed by those it infects.

Du Bois's exclusion from the canon of western sociology has been discussed in detail elsewhere (Anderson, 1988; Basu, 2001; Sibley, 1995), and one can bemoan the fact of his exclusion for only so long—I've been bemoaning it myself for many pages now. Enough. What we must emphasize and celebrate henceforth is that his exclusion is unmistakably coming to an end. While black scholars have long since recognized his contributions to sociology (Rudwick, 1969, 1974; Bracey, Meier, and Rudwick, 1971; Jones, 1976), Du Bois is finally gaining the attention of a wider (and whiter) audience. His sociological work is rapidly enjoying the widespread recognition it so rightly deserves. In the survey of American professors who teach social theory mentioned earlier, Brint and LaValle (2000) cited as their most significant finding that Du Bois "is beginning to emerge as a canonical figure." Many recently published texts on social theory have devoted chapters or significant sections to his work (Berger, 2003; Adams and Sydie, 2002; Kivisto, 2000; Farganis, 2000; Ritzer, 2000b; Lemert, 1993), and he is now featured prominently in several introductory textbooks (Stark, 1998; Ferrante, 2000; Macionis, 2001; Giddens and Duneier,

2000; Henslin, 2001). Obviously, this volume itself is part of the effort to further along the process of his canonization.

Relationship to Other Social Theorists

Much has been written elsewhere about the intellectual influences on Du Bois, from his professors in Germany such as Gustav von Schmoller (Broderick, 1958:16), to his mentors at Harvard, such as William James (Zamir, 1995; DeMarco, 1983). What I would like to briefly discuss here is how Du Bois's theoretical contributions relate to the scholarship and orientations of many founding sociologists writing in the late 19th and early 20th centuries. An exhaustive and comprehensive comparison and contrast of the numerous components of his theoretical work with the equally numerous components of the work of other major founding thinkers of the discipline is well beyond the scope of this introduction; however, I will at least highlight some of the more obvious and important areas of similarity and difference.

Similar to Emile Durkheim (1982 [1895]), Du Bois resisted narrow psychological or biological explanations of human behavior, choosing instead to emphasize the enormous impact social institutions and historical circumstances have in shaping individual actions and beliefs (Lester, 1971:187, 499). Durkheim (1951 [1897]) argued that rates of suicide could not be accounted for by looking only at individual psychology or genetic predispositions; rather, they are more accurately explained through analysis of group affiliation and matters of social integration. Similarly, Du Bois argued throughout his writings that racial inequality is not to be explained as a result of innate differences or genetic predispositions, but rather as the result of social, economic, historical, and political forces (Katz and Sugrue, 1998:24). As Collins and Makowsky (1998:199) note, "Du Bois emphasized the preeminence of the environmental approach over genetic doctrine" and despite "the prevailing tendency to stress nature over nurture in the scientific air at the turn of the nineteenth century, Du Bois disallowed any inherent or inherited racial superiority of white over black." When discussing religion, Durkheim (1965 [1915]) emphasized the importance of the social, arguing that religion was an eminently collective enterprise which finds its genesis and sustenance in the effervescent energy of people coming together as a group. In various essays on religion, Du Bois similarly emphasized the social in religious life, stressing the importance of group ties and communal bonding as being central to the religious enterprise (Zuckerman, 2002). Finally, both Durkheim and Du Bois wrote extensively on education as well as socialism.

Like the work of Georg Simmel, Du Bois's writing was often social-psychological in nature (Adams and Sydie, 2002:298). In one of his most famous essays, Simmel (1993 [1908]) contemplated the dynamics of the "stranger" in modern urban life, the city dweller who confronts society in an unusual way, simultaneously composed of "remoteness and nearness, indifference and involvement." The stranger experiences a "peculiar tension" in that he is an organic member of a group, and yet outside it; he is "near and far *at the same time.*" Simmel's words and sentiments in describing the urban stranger are similar to those of Du Bois, who in *The Souls of Black Folk* (1989 [1903]:3), spoke of the peculiar identity of that of a black man in white America:

> . . . a world which yields him no true self-consciousness, but only lets him see himself through the revelation of the other world. It is a peculiar sensation, this double-consciousness, this sense of always looking

at one's self through the eyes of others, of measuring one's soul by the tape of a world that looks on in amused contempt and pity. One ever feels his twoness,—an American, a Negro; two souls, two thoughts, two unreconciled strivings; two warring ideals in one dark body, whose dogged strength alone keeps it from being torn asunder.

"Double-consciousness" is one of Du Bois's most famous concepts, which artfully articulates the notion not only that identity is often fractured by numerous social identities and social roles within one being but also that these social identities and roles can sometimes even be at odds with one another.

Similar to Thorstein Veblen, Du Bois was critical of American capitalism and free enterprise, laissez-faire economic doctrines. Both men saw radical reform of the American economic system as a necessary step toward social justice. As Namasaka (1971:3)—who wrote an entire dissertation comparing the work of Veblen and Du Bois—argues:

> Du Bois and Veblen . . . advocated a planned economy geared to attain social justice. While Du Bois called initially for a voluntary co-operative economy and then for an economy run by the government, Veblen demanded the establishment of a planned economy organized collectively and run by technicians and engineers.

Like Charlotte Perkins Gilman, Du Bois wrote fiction and poetry in addition to social theory, and both Gilman's and Du Bois's critical analyses of society came through explicitly in their novels and short stories (Byerman, 1994:115–137). Both Gilman and Du Bois were fixated on challenging socially constructed systems of inequality and blatant forms of social injustice. Of course, for Gilman, the central fissure was between men and women, whereas for Du Bois it was between blacks and whites. Unfortunately, while Du Bois wrote sympathetically of the plight of women and was a vocal advocate of female suffrage (Du Bois, 1970 [1912]), Gilman wasn't as sympathetic to the plight of blacks in America; in an article published in the *American Journal of Sociology* in 1908, Gilman argued that it was the innate inferiority of black people that best accounted for their poor social conditions. Her racism only got worse as she aged (Lengermann and Niebrugge-Brantley, 1998:112).

Like Vladimir Lenin (1939 [1916]), Du Bois paid particular attention to imperialism as a central pillar of unchecked global capitalist exploitation (DeMarco, 1983:176; Adams and Sydie, 2002:295). Both men wrote extensively on colonialism and its relation to global inequality.

In the tradition of Max Weber, Du Bois infused his sociological writings with detailed historical analysis. Both men took graduate degrees in history, and the bulk of their scholarship was characterized by diligent socioeconomic historical research (Collins and Makowsky, 1998:195). Also, both Weber and Du Bois emphasized the ability of ideas and beliefs to influence and affect social life. Weber (2002 [1904]) focused on the role particular Protestant Calvinist beliefs played in the development of modern Western capitalism. Throughout his work, Du Bois focused on the role racist beliefs and ideas held by the powerful white majority played in the real-life oppressive experiences of blacks. Though irrational and nonempirical (like the Calvinist belief in predestination), the belief that blacks were inferior/subhuman was certainly real in its consequences, lending credence to Weber's theoretical insistence that ideas in and of themselves can and do affect lived social reality, for better or worse. Also, both Weber and Du Bois—though in different contexts and with different areas of focus—wrote about the dynamics of power, stratification, conflict, and domination. Finally, it should be pointed out

that of all the major social theorists, Du Bois had the closest personal relationship with Max Weber.[6] When Du Bois was a graduate student in Germany, he attended lectures by Weber. When Weber came to the United States in 1904, he visited Du Bois in Atlanta and even participated in the conference on crime organized by Du Bois at Atlanta University that year (Lewis, 1993:225). And Weber was so impressed by Du Bois's (1989 [1903]) *The Souls of Black Folk* that he offered to write the introduction to a German translation of the "splendid work" (Aptheker, 1973:106).

The last founding social theorist I wish to mention in relation to Du Bois is Karl Marx. Without question, Du Bois's social theory is directly linked to the work of Marx, usually in explicit and direct ways (Lewis, 2000:304–311). Du Bois learned very little of Marx when in high school, college, or graduate school. He did not discover Marx's theoretical contributions until he was a professor himself, and much of what he found in Marx's writings rang true. He generally agreed with Marx that underlying economic conditions—how people organize themselves in relationship to the means of production and distribution—shape and often determine cultural, political, and other institutional components of a given society (DeMarco, 1983:69–70). Du Bois (1971 [1935]) labeled Karl Marx "one of the greatest philosophers of modern times" and summarized his doctrine thus:

> . . . the wealth which the working masses produce and which is supplied by nature, has been and is being dishonestly taken from them by forced sale of their labor at less than its real value; this reduces the laborer to poverty while the surplus value of their work thus exploited goes to increase the wealth and power of the employing class.

Like Marx, Du Bois believed that a truly just society could be realized only if democracy was extended to the realm of industry; raw materials, tools, technology, land, and natural resources should not be held privately by the few for profit in a system of corporate monopoly, but should be held democratically by all and used to meet "the needs of the mass of men" (Du Bois, 1920:100; see also Du Bois, 1907c; Du Bois, 1920:157–159; Du Bois, 1948; DeMarco, 1983:169). In words still applicable to today's world, Du Bois, (1972 [1931]:380) argued that "political power is curtailed by organized capital in industry and that in this industry, democracy does not prevail; and that until wider democracy does prevail in industry, democracy in government is seriously curtailed and often quite ineffective." Finally, like Marx, Du Bois recognized the important role of class conflict in history and social change (Du Bois, 1935).

Distinct Theoretical Contributions

Despite the similarities between Du Bois and the social theorists mentioned above, there were major differences. Du Bois's sociology was distinct and unique, and as Lemert (2000:357) describes, remarkably "sui generis." The most obvious matter is that of race. Unlike Marx, Durkheim, Weber, Lenin, Gilman, Veblen—or Simmel, Mead, or Comte—Du Bois focused on race. Du Bois recognized that *racial distinctions and racial constructs are supremely important and crucially central to how human beings experience the world,* from health to wealth, from literacy to religion, from crime to politics, from city governance to international relations. Furthermore—and this may be his most important theoretical contribution—Du Bois linked racial analysis with class analysis (Du Bois, 1913, 1935). Nearly a century before hooks (1984) or Collins (2000) discussed interlocking systems of oppression, Du Bois systematically "dealt with the intertwined nature of class and race" (Adams and Sydie, 2002:301). Lemert (2000:257) emphasizes Du Bois's "most

distinctive theoretical conviction: that race never stands alone, apart from the economic realities." One of the most powerful quotes featured by Du Bois in *The Souls of Black Folk* (1989 [1903]:105) comes from the mouth of an old Southern black man, eloquently weaving racism with class exploitation: "White man sit down whole year; Nigger work day and night and make crop; Nigger hardly gits bread and meat; white man sittin' down gits all. *It's wrong.*"

Given Du Bois's theoretical innovation of linking race and class, it becomes apparent that while Du Bois appreciated the heart of Marxist analysis, he saw its shortcomings: raw Marxist class analysis and economic determinism ignored the color line. Du Bois corrected this gross oversight by adding racial dynamics to class dynamics (Du Bois, 1906b; Du Bois, 1995 [1933]). DeMarco (1983:192) notes that

Du Bois's . . . objections to [Marxist] theory and practice involved racial considerations: Blacks formed a special group without a significant class opposition, essentially a proletariat group. Yet blacks were separated from the proletariat movement by racism; the proletariat as an economic class was split on racial lines, an eventuality Du Bois viewed Marxism as incapable of explaining.

Another distinctive element of Du Bois's social theory is his insistence that race is ultimately a social construction, involving matters of economics, history, politics, heritage, and culture much more than simple biology or physicality (Du Bois, 1939). Antedating the work of Montagu (1997 [1942]) and Omi and Winant (1994) by numerous decades, Du Bois was the first sociologist to argue explicitly that race could not be reduced to merely a scientific category or biological determinant (Du Bois, 1920:98; Du Bois, 1915:13,232; Holt, 1998; Winant, 2000:181). In addition, Du Bois—"one of the first of the great decolonizing thinkers" (Lemert, 2000:362)—was one of the earliest social theorists to link class and race to globalization (Adams and Sydie, 2002:295; Du Bois, 1945). Long before the important contributions of Memmi, (1959), Fanon (1963), and Wallerstein (1979), Du Bois offered piercing, systematic analyses of the colonial world system, noting how the color line played itself out on an international scale, with economic exploitation girded to that color line in every nation and colony (Lemert, 1998; Du Bois, 1940, 1979 [1947]).

Du Bois's distinct theoretical contributions go beyond the color line. For instance, concerning crime, he argued that individual criminal behavior is always related to "a lack of harmony with social surroundings" (Du Bois, 1899a:235); criminal behavior must be understood as a result of certain social conditions and institutional dynamics, rather than a result of genetic predisposition (Du Bois, 1971 [1932]). Concerning religion, Du Bois stressed the communal role of churches as centers of social bonding and refuge, illustrating the degree to which religion provides not only other-worldly rewards but this-worldly benefits in the form of social spaces and social centers for marginalized communities (Zuckerman, 2002). His analysis of war and its relationship to class/business was prophetic; this passage, written in 1950, still rings true over half a century later in the wake of President George W. Bush's 2003 invasion of Iraq:

> War is Big Business and a business immensely profitable to a few, but of measureless disaster and death of dreams to many. Big business wants war in order to keep your mind off social reform; it would rather spend your taxes for atom bombs than for schools because in this way it makes more money; it would rather have your sons dying in Korea than studying in America and asking awkward questions . . . (quoted in Lewis, 1995:769).

He offered a plethora of theoretical insights into labor, economics, class, politics, gender, education, and so on. But there is no need for me to go on summarizing in further detail; this volume contains numerous excerpts of the writings on these matters from the sage himself, which, in their directness and eloquence, require little additional elaboration.

Conclusion

Like every sociologist/social theorist, Du Bois certainly had his faults and blind spots. His early research was often plagued by poorly constructed surveys and ambiguous sampling methodologies, and when describing his subjects, he often employed such terms as "ignorant," "intelligent" or "immoral," which today appear unempirical and improper. His theoretical assertions were often stated implicitly, rather than explicitly; that is, his major theoretical insights were often developed and articulated through detailed historical illustrations and ethnographic analyses, rather than succinct statements or exact theoretical declarations.[7] Though "one of the most militant male feminists of the early twentieth century" (Lewis, 1995:289), he didn't always incorporate gender into his analysis to a degree we might expect of a social theorist today (Carby, 1998).[8] His shortcomings as a father and husband were pronounced (Lewis, 2000). Toward the end of his life, his bitterness toward American racism, militarism, and McCarthyism led him to embrace the very worst of Soviet communism; Du Bois (1995 [1953]:796) publicly praised Joseph Stalin— one of the most evil despots of the 20th century—lauding him as a "great man." That Du Bois could embrace the Soviet Union's most lethal dictator is testimony to the fact that even the most brilliant and perceptive among us are only human, and therefore, fallible.

Yet, despite these shortcomings, Du Bois remains a sociological beacon. He was, in the words of Martin Luther King, Jr. (1968), "a tireless explorer and gifted discoverer of social truths." As David Levering Lewis (2000:228) argues, his "profound understanding of the human condition was often matchless." In *The Sociological Imagination* (1959), C. Wright Mills offered the ideal portrait of a sociologist. The ideal sociologist is one who consistently recognizes the intersections of biography within history and society. The ideal sociologist is one who avoids grand theorizing for the mere sake of grand theorizing, and who resists conveying his or her thoughts in obtuse, obscure language. The ideal sociologist is one who avoids abstract empiricism—collecting facts and figures outside of a critical theoretical framework. The work of the ideal sociologist is comparative, historical, and interdisciplinary. The ideal sociologist utilizes empirical data within a clear theoretical vision marked by an ever-present sensitivity to social justice. The ideal sociologist is one who, through a careful coupling of research and theory, strives to make the world a better place. Du Bois fits Mills's ideal perfectly. As Du Bois (1907b) wrote in the introduction of the monograph of the 1907 Atlanta conference, *Economic Cooperation Among Negro Americans*:

> The object of these studies is primarily scientific—a careful search for truth conducted as thoroughly, broadly, and honestly as the material resources and mental equipment at command will allow; but this is not our sole object: we wish not only to make the Truth clear but to present it in such shape as will encourage and help social reform.

Notes

1. There is no consensus on whether W. E. B. 's last name should be written as "Du Bois" (with a space) or as "DuBois" (with no space). I have seen it appear both ways in a variety of texts and sources. For instance, *The Philadelphia Negro* (1899) and *The Gift of Black Folk* (1924) spell the author's name as "DuBois" but *Economic Cooperation Among Negroes* (1907b), *The Negro* (1915), and *Darkwater* (1920) spell the author's name as "Du Bois." I have chosen to follow David Levering Lewis (1995) by going with the "Du Bois" (spaced) spelling.

2. The difference between "socialist" and "communist" in this instance refers to one's position regarding (1) parliamentary democracy and (2) the Soviet Union. Socialists favored political democracy in their quest for economic justice and were hostile to the government of the Soviet Union for its dictatorial, antidemocratic regime, with its violations of basic civil and human rights. Communists favored the Leninist-Stalinist political approach (vanguard party leads the people, any political opposition brutally repressed), and were loyal to the Soviet dictators, supporting and following whatever directives were issued from Moscow. For most of his life, Du Bois was for socialism and democracy; only toward the end did he embrace Soviet-style communism.

3. What is even more incredible about this is that I took several courses, undergraduate as well as graduate, specifically analyzing race and ethnicity. A colleague of mine here at Pitzer, who received his Ph.D. in sociology from UCLA, had a similar experience wherein Du Bois was never mentioned in any graduate sociology classes.

4. "The Atlanta Conferences," reprinted in Green and Driver (1978): 53-60.

5. While teaching at Wilberforce University in 1895, Du Bois sought to offer a course in sociology, but the administration refused his request. Had his request been granted, his would have been among the very first sociology courses ever taught in the United States (Green and Driver, 1978:9).

6. Du Bois also had a close professional relationship with social activist Jane Addams; he visited her Hull House numerous times, and she participated in his 1908 Atlanta Conference on the family.

7. Most social theory is written in a similar vein, with Emile Durkheim being a notable example. He did offer clear, succinct theoretical statements, for example, "suicide varies inversely with the degree of integration of religious ... domestic ... and political society" (Durkheim, (1951 [1895]:208).

8. However, it must be pointed out that he did address the concerns of women and was sensitive to gender inequality to a degree unparalleled by his peers (see Gilkes, 1996).

Bibliography

Abel, Theodore. 1970. *The Foundation of Sociological Theory*. New York: Random House.

Adams, Bert and R.A. Sydie. 2002. *Classical Sociological Theory*. Thousand Oaks, CA: Pine Forge Press.

Addams, Jane. 1895. *Hull House Maps and Papers: A Presentation of Nationalities and Wages in a Congested District of Chicago*. New York: T.Y. Crowell.

Aldridge, Derrick. 1999. "Conceptualizing a Du Boisian Philosophy of Education: Toward a Model for African-American Education," *Educational Theory* 49(3):359–80.

Altschuler, Richard. 1998. *The Living Legacy of Marx, Durkheim, and Weber, Vols. 1 and 2*. New York: Gordian Knot Books.

Andersen, Heine and Lars Bo Kaspersen. 2000. *Classical and Modern Social Theory*. Malden, MA: Blackwell.

Anderson, Elijah. 1999. *Code of the Street: Decency, Violence, and the Moral Life of the Inner City*. New York: W. W. Norton.

Anderson, T. 1988. "Black Encounters of Racism and Elitism in White Academe: A Critique of the System." *Journal of Black Studies* 18: 259–72.

Andrews, William. 1985. *Critical Essays on W. E. B. Du Bois*. Boston: G.K. Hall.

Aptheker, Herbert (Ed). 1973. *The Correspondence of W. E. B. Du Bois, Vol. 1, Selection, 1877–1934*. Amherst, MA: University of Massachusetts Press.

———. 1989. *The Literary Legacy of W. E. B. Du Bois*. Millwood, NY: Kraus International Publishers.

Ashley, David and David Michael Orenstein. 2001. *Sociological Theory: Classical Statements*. Boston: Allyn and Bacon.

Barnes, Harry Elmer. 1948. *An Introduction to the History of Sociology*. Chicago: University of Chicago Press.

Basu, Dipa. 2001. "Sociology and the Color Line" in *The Politics of Social Science Research: Race, Ethnicity, and Social Change*, edited by Peter Ratcliffe. New York: Palgrave.

Berger, Arthur Asa. 2003. *Durkheim is Dead!* Walnut Creek, CA: AltaMira Press.

Berger, Peter. 1963. *Invitation to Sociology*. New York: Anchor.

Blackwell, James and Morris Janowitz. 1974. *Black Sociologists: Historical and Contemporary Perspectives*. Chicago: Chicago University Press.

Booth, Charles. 1892–1897. *Life and Labour of the People of London*. London and New York: Macmillan.

Borgatta, Edgar and Henry Meyer. 1956. *Sociological Theory: Present Day Sociology From the Past*. New York: Alfred Knopf.

Bracey, John, August Meier, and Elliott Rudwick. 1971. *The Black Sociologists: The First Half Century*. Belmont, CA: Wadsworth.

Brint, Steven and James LaValle. 2000. "Du Bois Ascendant! And Other Results From the Brint-LaValle Theory Sections Survey" in *Perspectives*, 22(1): 1.

Broderick, Francis, 1958. "The Academic Training of W. E. B. Du Bois." *Journal of Negro Education* 27 (Winter):10–16.

Bryjak, George and Michael Soroka. 2001. *Sociology: Changing Societies in a Diverse World*, 4th edition. Boston: Allyn and Bacon.

Byerman, Keith. 1994. *Seizing the World: History, Art, and Self in the Work of W. E. B. Du Bois*. Athens, GA: University of Georgia Press.

Carby, Hazel. 1998. *Race Men*. Cambridge, MA: Harvard University Press.

Charon, Joel. 1998. *Ten Questions: A Sociological Perspective*. Belmont, CA: Wadsworth.

———. 2002. *The Meaning of Sociology*. Upper Saddle River, NJ: Prentice Hall.

Collins, Patricia Hill. 2000. *Black Feminist Thought*. New York: Routledge.

Collins, Randall. 1992. *Sociological Insight: An Introduction to Non-Obvious Sociology*. New York: Oxford University Press.

Collins, Randall and Michael Makowsky. 1998. *The Discovery of Society*. Boston: McGraw Hill.

Curra, John. 2003. *The Human Experience: Insights From Sociology*. Boston: Allyn and Bacon.

Cuzzort, R. P. and E. W. King. 1989. *Twentieth Century Social Thought*. Fort Worth: Holt, Rinehart, and Winston, Inc.

DeMarco, Joseph. 1983. *The Social Thought of W. E. B. Du Bois*. Lanham, MD: University Press of America.

Dodd, Nigel. 1999. *Social Theory and Modernity*. Malden, MA: Blackwell.

Du Bois, W. E. B. 1897a. "The Problem of Amusement." Reprinted in *Du Bois on Religion,* edited by Phil Zuckerman, 2000. Walnut Creek, CA: Alta Mira Press.

——. 1897b. "A Program for a Sociological Society." Manuscript of speech given at Atlanta University. Du Bois Papers, University of Massachusetts, Amherst.

——. 1898a. "The Negroes of Farmville, Virginia: A Social Study." *Bulletin of the Department of Labor* 3 (January):1–38.

——. 1898b. "The Study of Negro Problems." *Annals of the American Academy of Political and Social Science*, XI (Jan):1–23.

——. 1899a. *The Philadelphia Negro: A Social Study*. New York: Benjamin Blom.

——. 1899b. "The Negro in the Black Belt: Some Social Sketches." *Bulletin of the Department of Labor* 4 (May):401–17.

——. (Ed.). 1899c. *The Negro in Business*. Atlanta, GA: Atlanta University Press.

——. 1900. "Post Graduate Work in Sociology at Atlanta University." Speech delivered in Athens, GA, ca. 1900. Du Bois Papers, University of Massachusetts, Amherst.

——. 1901. "The Negro Landholder of Georgia." *Bulletin of the Department of Labor* 6 (July): 647–777.

——. (Ed.). 1902. *The Negro Artisan: A Social Study*. Atlanta, GA: Atlanta University Press.

——. (Ed.). 1903a. *The Negro Church*. Atlanta, GA: Atlanta University Press.

——. 1903b. "Of the Faith of the Fathers." Reprinted in *Du Bois on Religion*, edited by Phil Zuckerman, 2000. Walnut Creek, CA: AltaMira Press.

——. 1903c. "The Laboratory in Sociology at Atlanta University." *The Annals of American Academy of Political and Social Science* 21 (May): 503–5.

——. (Ed.). 1904a. *Notes on Negro Crime Particularly in Georgia*. Atlanta, GA: The Atlanta University Press.

——. 1904b. "The Negro Framer." Department of Commerce and Labor, Bureau of the Census, Bulletin, no. 8, 69-68, Washington, D.C.

——. 1906a. "Die Negerfrage in den Vereinignen Staaten" [The Negro Question in the United States]. *Archiv for Socialwissenschaft un Socialpolitik* 22:21–79.

——. 1906b. "The Economic Future of the Negro." *Publications of the American Economic Association,* VII:219–42.

Du Bois, W. E. B. 1907a. "Religion in the South." Reprinted in *Du Bois on Religion,* edited by Phil Zuckerman, 2000. Walnut Creek, CA: AltaMira Press.

——. (Ed.). 1907b. *Economic Cooperation Among Negro Americans*. Atlanta, GA: The Atlanta University Press.

——. 1907c. "Socialist of the Path" in *The Horizon*, 1(2) Feb:7–8.

——. 1908a. "Race Friction Between Black and White." *American Journal of Sociology* 12 (May):834–38.

——. (Ed.). 1908b. The Negro American Family. Atalnat, Georgia: Atlanta University Press.

——. 1913. "Socialism and the Negro Problem." *The New Review,* January:138–41.

——. Editor. 1914. *Morals and Manners Among Negro Americans*. Atlanta, GA: Atlanta University Press.

——. 1915. *The Negro*. New York: Henry Holt .

——. 1920. *Darkwater*. New York: Harcourt, Brace, and Howe.

——. 1931. "Will the Church Remove the Color Line?" Reprinted in *Du Bois on Religion,* edited by Phil Zuckerman, 2000. Walnut Creek, CA: AltaMira Press.

——. 1935. *Black Reconstruction in America*. New York: S.A. Russell Company.

——. 1939. *Black Folk: Then and Now: An Essay in the History and Sociology of the Negro Race*. New York: Holt, Rinehart, and Winston.

——. 1940. *Dusk of Dawn: an essay Toward an Autobiography of a Race Concept*. New York: Harcourt, Brace.

——. 1945. *Color and Democracy: Colonies and Peace*. New York: Harcourt, Brace.

Du Bois, W. E. B. 1948. "Socialism." *Chicago Defender*, February 14.

——. 1954 [1896]. *The Suppression of the African Slave-Trade to the United States 1638–1870*. New York: The Social Science Press.

——. 1962 [1909]. *John Brown*. New York: International Publishers.

——. 1970 [1912]. "Disfranchisement," in *W.E.B. Du Bois Speaks: Speeches and Addresses 1890–1919*, 230-238, edited by Philip Foner. New York: Pathfinder Press.

——. 1971 [1932]." Courts and Jails" in *An ABC of Color*. New York: International Publishers.

——. 1971 [1935]. "The Present Economic Problem of the American Negro," in *A W. E. B. Du Bois Reader*, edited by Andrew Paschal, 1971. New York: Macmillan.

——. 1972 [1931]. "The American Worker" in *W. E. B. Du Bois: The Crisis Writings*, 380, edited by Daniel Walden. Greenwich, CT: Fawcett Publications.

——. 1979 [1947]. *The World and Africa*. New York: International Publishers.

——. 1989 [1903]. *The Souls of Black Folk*. New York: Bantam Books.

——. 1995 [1953]. "On Stalin." In *W. E. B. Du Bois: A Reader*, edited by David Levering Lewis, New York: Henry Holt.

——. 1995 [1933]. "Marxism and the Negro Problem." In *W. E. B. Du Bois: A Reader*, edited by David Levering Lewis, New York: Henry Holt.

Durkheim, Emile. 1951 [1897]. *Suicide*. New York: The Free Press.

——. 1965 [1915]. *The Elementary Forms of the Religious Life*. New York: The Free Press.

——. 1982 [1895]. *The Rules of Sociological Method*. New York: The Free Press.

Eitzen, D. Stanley and Maxine Baca Zinn. 2001. *In Conflict and Order: Understanding Society*. Boston: Allyn and Bacon.

Engels, Frederick. 1994 [1887]. *The Condition of the Working Class in England*. Chicago: Academy Chicago Publishers.

Fanon, Frantz. 1963. *The Wretched of the Earth*. New York: Grove Press.

Farganis, James. 2000. *Readings in Social Theory: The Classic Tradition to Post-Modernism*. Boston: McGraw Hill.

Ferrante, Joan. 2000. *Sociology: The United States in a Global Community*. Belmont, CA: Wadsworth.

Frazier, E. Franklin. 1949. "Race Contacts and the Social Structure," *American Sociological Review* XIV (February):1–11.

Gabbidon, Shaun, Helen Greene, and Verneta Young (Eds.). 2002. *African American Classics in Criminology and Criminal Justice*. Thousand Oaks, CA: Sage Publications.

Gane, Mike, 1988. *On Durkheim's The Rules of Sociological Method*. New York: Routledge.

Giddens, Anthony. 1971. *Capitalism and Modern Social Theory: An Analysis of the Writings of Marx, Durkheim, and Weber*. London: Cambridge University Press.

——. 1991. *Introduction to Sociology*. New York: W.W. Norton.

Giddens, Anthony and Mitchell Duneier. 2000. *Introduction to Sociology*. New York: W.W. Norton.

Gilkes, Cheryl Townsend. 1996. "The Margin as the Center of a Theory of History: African-American Women, Social Change, and the Sociology of W. E. B. Du Bois," in *W. E. B. Du Bois on Race and Culture*, edited by Bernard Bell, Emily Grosholz, and James Stewart, New York: Routledge.

Gilman, Charelotte Perkins. 1908. "A Suggestion on the Negro Problem." *American Journal of Sociology* 14:78–85.

Goode, Erich. 1998. *Sociology*, 2nd ed. Englewood Cliffs, NJ: Prentice Hall.

Green, Dan and Edwin Driver. 1978. *W. E. B. Du Bois on Sociology and the Black Community*. Chicago: University of Chicago Press.

Gregg, Robert. 1998. "Giant Steps: W. E. B. Du Bois and the Historical Enterprise" in *W. E. B. Du Bois, Race, and the City*, edited by Michael Katz and Thomas Sugrue. Philadelphia: University of Pennsylvania Press.

Hadden, Richard. 1997. *Sociological Theory: An Introduction to the Classical Tradition*. Ontario, Canada: Broadview Press.

Henslin, James. 2001. *Sociology: A Down to Earth Approach*. Boston: Allyn and Bacon.

Holt, Thomas. 1998. "W. E. B. Du Bois's Archeology of Race." In *W. E. B. Du Bois, Race, and the City*, edited by Michael Katz and Thomas Sugrue. Philadelphia: University of Philadelphia Press.

hooks, bell. 1984. *Feminist Theory: From Margin to Center*. Boston: South End Press.

Hurst, Charles. 2000. *Living Theory: The Applications of Classical Social Theory to Contemporary Life*. Boston: Allyn and Bacon.

Jones, Atlas Jack. 1976. "The Sociology of W. E. B. Du Bois." *The Black Sociologist* 6(1):4–15.

Jones, Jacqueline. 1998. "'Lifework' and Its Limits" in *W. E. B. Du Bois, Race, and the City*, edited by Michael Katz and Thomas Sugrue. Philadelphia: University of Philadelphia Press.

Kanagy, Conrad and Donald Kraybill. 1999. *The Riddles of Human Society*. Thousand Oaks, CA: Pine Forge Press.

Katz, Michael and Thomas Sugrue (Eds.). 1998. W. E. B. Du Bois, Race, and the City. Philadelphia, Penn: University of Pennsylvania Press.

King, Jr., Martin Luther. 1968. "Honoring Dr. Du Bois." *Freedomways*, Spring:104–11.

Kivisto, Peter. 1998. *Illuminating Social Life: Classical and Contemporary Theory Revisited*. Thousand Oaks, CA: Pine Forge Press.

——. 2000. *Social Theory: Roots and Branches*. Los Angeles, CA: Roxbury.

Lemert, Charles. 1993. *Social Theory: The Multicultural and Classic Readings*. Boulder, CO: Westview.

——. 2000. "W. E. B. Du Bois." *The Blackwell Companion to Major Social Theorists*, edited by George Ritzer. Malden, MA: Blackwell.

Lengermann, Patricia Madoo and Jil Niebrugge-Brantley. (1998). *The Women Founders: Sociology and Social Theory 1830–1930*. Boston: McGraw-Hill.

Lenin, Vladimir. 1939 [1916]. *Imperialism: the Highest Form of Capitalism (vol. XIX)*. New York: International Publishers.

Lester, Julius. 1971. *The Seventh Son: The Thought and Writings of W. E. B. Du Bois, Volume One*. New York: Vintage Books.

Levine, Donald. 1995. *Visions of the Sociological Tradition*. Chicago: University of Chicago Press.

Lewis, David Levering. 1993. *W. E. B. Du Bois: Biography of a Race, 1868–1919*. New York: Henry Holt.

——. 1995. *W. E. B. Du Bois: A Reader*. New York: Henry Holt.

Lewis, David Levering. 2000. *W. E. B. Du Bois: The Fight For Equality and the American Century, 1919–1963*. New York: Henry Holt.

Macionis, John. 2001. *Sociology*. Upper Saddle River, NJ: Prentice Hall.

Maus, Heinz. 1962. *A Short History of Sociology*. New York: Philosophical Library.

McDaniel, Antonio. 1998. "The 'Philadelphia Negro' Then and Now." In *W. E. B. DuBois, Race, and the City*, edited by Michael Katz and Thomas Sugrue. Philadelphia: University of Philadelphia Press.

Memmi, Albert. 1959. The Colonizer and the Colonized. Boston: Beacon Press.

Mills, C. Wright. 1959. *The Sociological Imagination*. New York: Oxford University Press.

Mitchell, G. Duncan. 1968. *A Hundred Years of Sociology*. Chicago: Aldine.

Montagu, Ashely. 1997 [1942]. *Man's Most Dangerous Myth*. Walnut Creek, CA: Alta Mira Press.

Namasaki, Boaz Nalika. 1971. *William E. B. Du Bois and Thorstein B. Veblen: Intellectual Activists of Progressivism, a Comparative Study, 1900–1930*. Unpublished doctoral dissertation. Claremont, CA: Claremont Graduate School.

Newman, David. 2002. *Sociology: Exploring the Architecture of Everyday Life*, 4th edition. Thousand Oaks, CA: Pine Forge Press.

Omi, Michael and Howard Winant. 1994. *Racial Formation in the United States*. New York: Routledge.

Pampel, Fred. 2000. *Sociological Lives and Ideas: An Introduction to the Classical Theorists*. New York: Worth.

Platt, Jennifer. 1996. *A History of Sociological Research Methods in America 1920–1960*. New York: Cambridge University Press.

Provenzo, Eugene F., Jr. 2002. *Du Bois on Education*. Walnut Creek, CA: AltaMira Press.

Ritzer, George. 1994. *Sociological Beginnings: On the Origins of Key Ideas in Sociology*. New York: McGraw-Hill.

——. 2000a. *Classical Sociological Theory*. Boston: McGraw Hill.

——. 2000b. *The Blackwell Companion to Social Theorists*. Lamden, MA: Blackwell.

Ritzer, George. 2003. *Contemporary Sociological Theory and Its Classical Roots: The Basics.* Boston: McGraw-Hill.

Rudwick, Elliott. 1969. "Note on a Forgotten Black Sociologist: W. E. B. Du Bois and the Sociological Profession." *The American Sociologist* 4 (4):303–06.

——. 1974. "W. E. B. Du Bois as Sociologist." In *Black Sociologists: Historical and Contemporary Perspectives,* edited by James Blackwell and Morris Janowitz. Chicago: Chicago University Press.

Shepard, Jon. 2002. *Sociology,* 8th edition. Belmont, CA: Wadsworth.

Sibley, D. 1995. *Geographies of Exclusion.* New York: Routledge.

Simmel, Georg. 1993 [1908]. "The Stranger." In *Social Theory: The Multicultural and Classic Readings,* edited by Charles Lemert. Boulder, CO: Westview Press.

Sorokin, Pitrim. 1928. *Contemporary Sociological Theories: Through the First Quarter of the Twentieth Century.* New York: Harper and Row.

Stark, Rodney. 1998. *Sociology.* Belmont, CA: Wadsworth.

Strasser, Hermann. 1976. *The Normative Structure of Sociology.* London, UK: Routledge and Kegan Paul.

Swingewood, Alan. 1991. *A Short History of Sociological Thought.* New York: St. Martin's Press.

Thio, Alex. 2000. *Sociology: A Brief Introduction,* 4th ed. Boston: Allyn and Bacon.

Turner, Jonathan. 1998. *The Structure of Sociological Theory.* Belmont, CA: Wadsworth.

Turner, Jonathan and Leonard Beeghley. 1981. *The Emergence of Sociological Theory.* Homewood, IL: Dorsey Press.

Wallerstein, Immanuel. 1979. *The Capitalist World-Economy.* New York: Cambridge University Press.

Weber, Max. 2002 [1904]. *The Protestant Ethic and the Spirit of Capitalism.* Los Angeles, CA: Roxbury.

Wesley, Charles. 1970. "W. E. B. Du Bois: the Historian." *In Black Titan: W. E. B. Du Bois,* edited by John Henrik Clarke. Boston: Beacon Press.

Willis, Evan. 1996. *The Sociological Quest: An Introduction to the Study of Social Life.* New Brunswick, NJ: Rutgers University Press.

Winant, Howard. 2000. "The Theoretical Status of the Concept of Race." In *Theories of Race and Racism,* edited by Les Back and John Solomos. New York: Routledge.

Zamir, Shamoon. 1995. *Dark Voices: W. E. B. Du Bois and American Thought, 1888–1903.* Chicago: The University of Chicago Press.

Zeitlin, Irving. 2001. *Ideology and the Development of Sociological Theory.* Upper Saddle River, NJ: Prentice Hall.

Zuckerman, 2002. (Ed.). 2000. *Du Bois on Religion.* Walnut Creek, CA: Alta Mira Press.

——. "The Sociology of Religion of W. E. B. Du Bois." *Sociology of Religion* 63 (2):239–53.

Zuckerman, Phil, Sandra Barnes, and Daniel Cady. 2003. "The Negro Church: An Introduction," in *The Negro Church,* edited by W. E. B. Du Bois. Walnut Creek, CA: AltaMira Press.

Chapter 1

On the Meaning of Race

"Race" is one of those concepts that almost everyone takes for granted as being clear and simple. But race is neither; comparative historical analysis and sociological insight reveal that race is actually a contested and nebulous construct. While in an early essay "The Conservation of Races" (1897) Du Bois declared that "human beings are divided into races" and that this division is related to "common blood," he simultaneously asserted that a scientific definition of race is impossible because race is never limited to—indeed, it clearly transcends—the mere physical. His scholarship on the meaning of race would continue in this latter vein, arguing against essentialist, biological race differences. In *Dusk of Dawn* (1940) he emphasized "social heritage" as the distinguishing component of the black race over any "physical bond." Indebted to the anthropological work of Franz Boas, Du Bois's deconstruction of race as a scientific, rigid system of classification was groundbreaking. Equally groundbreaking was his analysis of whiteness in *Darkwater* (1920), with its emphasis upon racial construction and its direct relationship to the exploitation of human labor and natural resources.

1. "The Conservation of Races"

Published in 1897 in
the *Occasional Papers* of
the American Negro Academy

The American Negro has always felt an intense personal interest in discussions as to the origins and destinies of races: primarily because back of most discussions of race with which he is familiar, have lurked certain assumptions as to his natural abilities, as to his political, intellectual and moral status, which he felt were wrong. He has, consequently, been led to deprecate and minimize race distinctions, to believe intensely that out of one blood God created all nations, and to speak of human brotherhood as though it were the possibility of an already dawning to-morrow.

Nevertheless, in our calmer moments we must acknowledge that human beings are divided into races; that in this country the two most extreme types of the world's races have met, and the resulting problem as to the future relations of these types is not only of intense and living interest to us, but forms an epoch in the history of mankind.

It is necessary, therefore, in planning our movements, in guiding our future development, that at times we rise above the pressing, but smaller questions of separate schools and cars, wage-discrimination and lynch law, to survey the whole question of race in human philosophy and to lay, on a basis of broad knowledge and careful insight, those large lines of policy and higher ideals which may form our guiding lines and boundaries in the practical difficulties of every day. For it is certain that all human striving must recognize the hard limits of natural law, and that any striving, no matter how intense and earnest, which is against the constitution of the world, is vain. The question, then, which we must seriously consider is this: What is the real meaning of Race; what has, in the past, been the law of race development, and what lessons has the past history of race development to teach the rising Negro people?

When we thus come to inquire into the essential difference of races we find it hard to come at once to any definite conclusion. Many criteria of race differences have in the past been proposed, as color, hair, cranial measurements and language. And manifestly, in each of these respects, human beings differ widely. . . . All these physical characteristics are patent enough, and if they agreed with each other it would be very easy to classify mankind. Unfortunately for scientists, however, these criteria of race are most exasperatingly intermingled. Color does not agree with texture of hair, for many of the dark races have straight hair; nor does color agree with the breadth of the head, for the yellow Tartar has a broader head than the German; nor, again, has the science of language as yet succeeded in clearing up the relative authority of these various and contradictory criteria. The final word of science, so far, is that we have at least two, perhaps three, great families of human beings—the whites and Negroes, possibly the yellow race. . . .

Although the wonderful developments of human history teach that the grosser physical differences of color, hair and bone go but a short way toward explaining the different roles which groups of men have played in Human Progress, yet there are differences—subtle, delicate and elusive, though they may be—which have silently but definitely separated men into

groups. While these subtle forces have generally followed the natural cleavage of common blood, descent and physical peculiarities, they have at other times swept across and ignored these. At all times, however, they have divided human beings into races, which, while they perhaps transcend scientific definition, nevertheless, are clearly defined to the eye of the Historian and Sociologist.

If this be true, then the history of the world is the history, not of individuals, but of groups, not of nations, but of races, and he who ignores or seeks to override the race idea in human history ignores and overrides the central thought of all history. What, then, is a race? It is a vast family of human beings, generally of common blood and language, always of common history, traditions and impulses, who are both voluntarily and involuntarily striving together for the accomplishment of certain more or less vividly conceived ideals of life. . . .

We find upon the world's stage today eight distinctly differentiated races, in the sense in which History tells us the word must be used. They are, the Slavs of eastern Europe, the Teutons of middle Europe, the English of Great Britain and America, the Romance nations of Southern and Western Europe, the Negroes of Africa and America, the Semitic people of Western Asia and Northern Africa, the Hindoos of Central Asia and the Mongolians of Eastern Asia. There are, of course, other minor race groups, as the American Indians, the Esquimaux and the South Sea Islanders; . . .

The question now is: What is the real distinction between these nations? Is it the physical differences of blood, color and cranial measurements? Certainly we must all acknowledge that physical differences play a great part, and that, with wide exceptions and qualifications, these eight great races of to-day follow the cleavage of physical race distinctions; . . . But while race differences have followed mainly physical race lines, yet no mere physical distinctions would really define or explain the deeper differences—the cohesiveness and continuity of these groups. The deeper differences are spiritual, psychical, differences—undoubtedly based on the physical, but infinitely transcending them. The forces that bind together the Teuton nations are, then, first, their race identity and common blood; secondly, and more important, a common history, common laws and religion, similar habits of thought and a conscious striving together for certain ideals of life. The whole process which has brought about these race differentiations has been a growth, and the great characteristic of this growth has been the differentiation of spiritual and mental differences between great races of mankind and the integration of physical differences.

The age of nomadic tribes of closely related individuals represents the maximum of physical differences. They were practically vast families, and there were as many groups as families. As the families came together to form cities the physical differences lessened, purity of blood was replaced by the requirement of domicile, and all who lived within the city bound became gradually to be regarded as members of the group; i.e., there was a slight and slow breaking down of physical barriers. This, however, was accompanied by an increase of the spiritual and social differences between cities. This city became husbandmen, this, merchants, another warriors, and so on. The *ideals of life* for which the different cities struggled were different. When at last cities began to coalesce into nations there was another breaking down of barriers which separated groups of men. The larger and broader differences of color, hair and physical proportions were not by any means ignored, but myriads of minor differences disappeared, and the sociological and historical races of men began to approximate the present division of races as indicated by physical researches. At the same time the spiritual and physical differences of race groups which constituted the nations became deep and decisive. . . . striving, each in its own way, to develop for civilization its particular massage, its particular ideal, which shall help to guide the world nearer and nearer that perfection of human life for which we all long, that

"one far off Divine event."

This has been the function of race differences up to the present time. What shall be its function in the future? Manifestly some of the great races of today—particularly the Negro race—have not as yet given to civilization the full spiritual message which they are capable of giving. I will not say that the Negro race has as yet given no message to the world, for it is still a mooted question among scientists as to just how far Egyptian civilization was Negro in its origin; if it was not wholly Negro, it was certainly very closely allied. Be that as it may, however, the fact still remains that the full, complete Negro message of the whole Negro race has not as yet been given to the world: That the messages and ideal of the yellow race have not been completed, and that the striving of the mighty Slavs has but begun. The question is, then: How shall this message be delivered; how shall these various ideals be realized? The answer is plain: By the development of these race groups, not as individuals, but as races. . . . We cannot reverse history; we are subject to the same natural laws as other races, and if the Negro is ever to be a factor in the world's history—if among the gaily-colored banners that deck the broad ramparts of civilization is to hang one uncompromising black, then it must be placed there by black hands, fashioned by black heads and hallowed by the travail of 200,000,000 black hearts beating in one glad song of jubilee.

For this reason, the advance guard of the Negro people—the 8,000,000 people of Negro blood in the United States of America—must soon come to realize that if they are to take their just place in the van of Pan-Negroism, then their destiny is *not* absorption by the white Americans. That if in America it is to be proven for the first time in the modern world that not only Negroes are capable of evolving individual men like Toussaint, the Saviour, but are a nation stored with wonderful possibilities of culture, then their destiny is not a servile imitation of Anglo-Saxon culture, but a stalwart originality which shall unswervingly follow Negro ideals.

It may, however, be objected here that the situation of our race in America renders this attitude impossible; that our sole hope of salvation lies in our being able to lose our race identity in the commingled blood of the nation; and that any other course would merely increase the friction of races which we call race prejudice, and against which we have so long and so earnestly fought.

Here, then, is the dilemma, and it is a puzzling one, I admit. No Negro who has given earnest thought to the situation of his people in America has failed, at some time in life, to find himself at these cross-roads; has failed to ask himself at some time: What, after all, am I? Am I an American or am I a Negro? Can I be both? Or is it my duty to cease to be a Negro as soon as possible and be an American? If I strive as a Negro, am I not perpetuating the very cleft that threatens and separates Black and White America? Is not my only possible practical aim the subduction of all that is Negro in me to the American? Does my black blood place upon me any more obligation to assert my nationality than German, or Irish or Italian blood would?

It is such incessant self-questioning and the hesitation that arises from it, that is making the present period a time of vacillation and contradiction for the American Negro; combined race action is stifled, race responsibility is shirked, race enterprises languish, and the best blood, the best talent, the best energy of the Negro people cannot be marshalled to do the bidding of the race. They stand back to make room for every rascal and demagogue who chooses to cloak his selfish deviltry under the veil of race pride.

Is this right? Is it rational? Is it good policy? Have we in America a distinct mission as a race—a distinct sphere of action and an opportunity for race development, or is self-obliteration the highest end to which Negro blood dare aspire?

If we carefully consider what race prejudice really is, we find it, historically, to be nothing but the friction between different groups of people; it is the difference in aim, in feeling, in ideals of two different races; if, now, this difference exists touching territory, laws, language, or even religion, it is manifest that these people cannot live in the same territory without fatal collision; but if, on the other hand, there is substantial agreement in laws, language and religion; if there is a satisfactory adjustment of economic life, then there is no reason why, in the same country and on the same street, two or three great national ideals might not thrive and develop, that men of different races might not strive together for their race ideals as well, perhaps even better, than in isolation. Here, it seems to me, is the reading of the riddle that puzzles so many of us. We are Americans, not only by birth and by citizenship, but by our political ideals, our language, our religion. Farther than that, our Americanism does not go. At that point, we are Negroes, members of a vast historic race that from the very dawn of creation has slept, but half awakening in the dark forests of its African fatherland. We are the first fruits of this new nation, the harbinger of that black to-morrow which is yet destined to soften the whiteness of the Teutonic to-day. We are that people whose subtle sense of song has given America its only American music, its only American fairy tales, its only touch of pathos and humor amid its mad money-getting plutocracy. As such, it is our duty to conserve our physical powers, our intellectual endowments, our spiritual ideals; as a race we must strive by race organization, by race solidarity, by race unity to the realization of that broader humanity which freely recognizes differences in men, but sternly deprecates inequality in their opportunities of development. . . .

2. *"Of Our Spiritual Strivings"*

Published in 1903 in
The Souls of Black Folk

Between me and the other world there is ever an unasked question: unasked by some through feelings of delicacy; by others through the difficulty of rightly framing it. All, nevertheless, flutter round it. They approach me in a half-hesitant sort of way, eye me curiously or compassionately, and then, instead of saying directly, How does it feel to be a problem? they say, I know an excellent colored man in my town; or, I fought at Mechanicsville; or, Do not these Southern outrages make your blood boil? At these I smile, or am interested, or reduce the boiling to a simmer, as the occasion may require. To the real question, How does it feel to be a problem? I answer seldom a word.

And yet, being a problem is a strange experience,—peculiar even for one who has never been anything else, save perhaps in babyhood and in Europe. It is in the early days of rollicking boyhood that the revelation first bursts upon one, all in a day, as it were. I remember well when the shadow swept across me. I was a little thing, away up in the hills of New England, where the dark Housatonic winds between Hoosac and Taghkanic to the sea. In a wee wooden schoolhouse, something put it into the boys' and girls' heads to buy gorgeous visiting-cards—ten cents a package—and exchange. The exchange was merry, till one

girl, a tall newcomer, refused my card,—refused it peremptorily, with a glance. Then it dawned upon me with a certain suddenness that I was different from the others; or like, mayhap, in heart and life and longing, but shut out from their world by a vast veil. I had thereafter no desire to tear down that veil, to creep through; I held all beyond it in common contempt, and lived above it in a region of blue sky and great wandering shadows. That sky was bluest when I could beat my mates at examination-time, or beat them at a foot-race, or even beat their stringy heads. Alas, with the years all this fine contempt began to fade; for the worlds I longed for, and all their dazzling opportunities, were theirs, not mine. But they should not keep these prizes, I said; some, all, I would wrest from them. Just how I would do it I could never decide: by reading law, by healing the sick, by telling the wonderful tales that swam in my head,—some way. With other black boys the strife was not so fiercely sunny: their youth shrunk into tasteless sycophancy, or into silent hatred of the pale world about them and mocking distrust of everything white; or wasted itself in a bitter cry, Why did God make me an outcast and a stranger in mine own house? The shades of the prison-house closed round about us all: walls strait and stubborn to the whitest, but relentlessly narrow, tall, and unscalable to sons of night who must plod darkly on in resignation, or beat unavailing palms against the stone, or steadily, half hopelessly, watch the streak of blue above.

After the Egyptian and Indian, the Greek and Roman, the Teuton and Mongolian, the Negro is a sort of seventh son, born with a veil, and gifted with second-sight in this American world,—a world which yields him no true self-consciousness, but only lets him see himself through the revelation of the other world. It is a peculiar sensation, this double-consciousness, this sense of always looking at one's self through the eyes of others, of measuring one's soul by the tape of a world that looks on in amused contempt and pity. One ever feels his two-ness,—an American, a Negro; two souls, two thoughts, two unreconciled strivings; two warring ideals in one dark body, whose dogged strength alone keeps it from being torn asunder.

The history of the American Negro is the history of this strife,—this longing to attain self-conscious manhood, to merge his double self into a better and truer self. In this merging he wishes neither of the older selves to be lost. He would not Africanize America, for America has too much to teach the world and Africa. He would not bleach his Negro soul in a flood of white Americanism, for he knows that Negro blood has a message for the world. He simply wishes to make it possible for a man to be both a Negro and an American, without being cursed and spit upon by his fellows, without having the doors of Opportunity closed roughly in his face.

This, then, is the end of his striving: to be a co-worker in the kingdom of culture, to escape both death and isolation, to husband and use his best powers and his latent genius. These powers of body and mind have in the past been strangely wasted, dispersed, or forgotten. The shadow of a mighty Negro past flits through the tale of Ethiopia the Shadowy and of Egypt the Sphinx. Throughout history, the powers of single black men flash here and there like falling stars, and die sometimes before the world has rightly gauged their brightness. Here in America, in the few days since Emancipation, the black man's turning hither and thither in hesitant and doubtful striving has often made his very strength to lose effectiveness, to seem like absence of power, like weakness. And yet it is not weakness,—it is the contradiction of double aims. The double-aimed struggle of the black artisan—on the one hand to escape white contempt for a nation of mere hewers of wood and drawers of water, and on the other hand to plough and nail and dig for a poverty-stricken horde—could only

result in making him a poor craftsman, for he had but half a heart in either cause. By the poverty and ignorance of his people, the Negro minister or doctor was tempted toward quackery and demagogy; and by the criticism of the other world, toward ideals that made him ashamed of his lowly tasks. The would-be black *savant* was confronted by the paradox that the knowledge his people needed was a twice-told tale to his white neighbors, while the knowledge which would teach the white world was Greek to his own flesh and blood. The innate love of harmony and beauty that set the ruder souls of his people a-dancing and a-singing raised but confusion and doubt in the soul of the black artist; for the beauty revealed to him was the soul-beauty of a race which his larger audience despised, and he could not articulate the message of another people. This waste of double aims, this seeking to satisfy two unreconciled ideals, has wrought sad havoc with the courage and faith and deeds of ten thousand thousand people,— has sent them often wooing false gods and invoking false means of salvation, and at times has even seemed about to make them ashamed of themselves. . . .

In those sombre forests of his striving his own soul rose before him, and he saw himself,—darkly as through a veil; and yet he saw in himself some faint revelation of his power, of his mission. He began to have a dim feeling that, to attain his place in the world, he must be himself, and not another. For the first time he sought to analyze the burden he bore upon his back, that dead-weight of social degradation partially masked behind a half-named Negro problem. He felt his poverty; without a cent, without a home, without land, tools, or savings, he had entered into competition with rich, landed, skilled neighbors. To be a poor man is hard, but to be a poor race in a land of dollars is the very bottom of hardships. He felt the weight of his ignorance,—not simply of letters, but of life, of business, of the humanities; the accumulated sloth and shirking and awkwardness of decades and centuries shackled his hands and feet. Nor was his burden all poverty and ignorance. The red stain of bastardy, which two centuries of systematic legal defilement of Negro women had stamped upon his race, meant not only the loss of ancient African chastity, but also the hereditary weight of a mass of corruption from white adulterers, threatening almost the obliteration of the Negro home.

A people thus handicapped ought not to be asked to race with the world, but rather allowed to give all its time and thought to its own social problems. But alas! while sociologists gleefully count his bastards and his prostitutes, the very soul of the toiling, sweating black man is darkened by the shadow of a vast despair. Men call the shadow prejudice, and learnedly explain it as the natural defence of culture against barbarism, learning against ignorance, purity against crime, the "higher" against the "lower" races. To which the Negro cries Amen! and swears that to so much of this strange prejudice as is founded on just homage to civilization, culture, righteousness, and progress, he humbly bows and meekly does obeisance. But before that nameless prejudice that leaps beyond all this he stands helpless, dismayed, and well-nigh speechless; before that personal disrespect and mockery, the ridicule and systematic humiliation, the distortion of fact and wanton license of fancy, the cynical ignoring of the better and the boisterous welcoming of the worse, the all-pervading desire to inculcate disdain for everything black, from Toussaint to the devil,—before this there rises a sickening despair that would disarm and discourage any nation save that black host to whom "discouragement" is an unwritten word.

But the facing of so vast a prejudice could not but bring the inevitable self-questioning, self-disparagement, and lowering of ideals which ever accompany repression and breed in an atmosphere of contempt and hate. Whisperings and portents came borne upon the four winds: Lo! we are diseased and dying, cried the dark hosts; we cannot write, our voting is vain; what need of education, since we must always cook and serve? And the Nation echoed and enforced this self-criticism, saying: Be content to be servants, and nothing more; what need of higher culture for half-men? Away with the black man's ballot, by force or fraud,—and behold the suicide of a race! Nevertheless, out of the evil came something of good,—the more careful adjustment of education to real life, the clearer perception of the Negroes' social responsibilities, and the sobering realization of the meaning of progress.

So dawned the time of *Sturm und Drang*: storm and stress to-day rocks our little boat on the mad waters of the world-sea; there is within and without the sound of conflict, the burning of body and rending of soul; inspiration strives with doubt, and faith with vain questionings. The bright ideals of the past,—physical freedom, political power, the training of brains and the training of hands,—all these in turn have waxed and waned, until even the last grows dim and overcast. Are they all wrong,—all false? No, not that, but each alone was oversimple and incomplete,—the dreams of a credulous race-childhood, or the fond imaginings of the other world which does not know and does not want to know our power. To be really true, all these ideals must be melted and welded into one. The training of the schools we need to-day more than ever,—the training of deft hands, quick eyes and ears, and above all the broader, deeper, higher culture of gifted minds and pure hearts. The power of the ballot we need in sheer self-defence,—else what shall save us from a second slavery? Freedom, too, the long-sought, we still seek,—the freedom of life and limb, the freedom to work and think, the freedom to love and aspire. Work, culture, liberty,—all these we need, not singly but together, not successively but together, each growing and aiding each, and all striving toward that vaster ideal that swims before the Negro people, the ideal of human brotherhood, gained through the unifying ideal of Race; the ideal of fostering and developing the traits and talents of the Negro, not in opposition to or contempt for other races, but rather in large conformity to the greater ideals of the American Republic, in order that some day on American soil two world-races may give each to each those characteristics both so sadly lack. We the darker ones come even now not altogether empty-handed: there are to-day no truer exponents of the pure human spirit of the Declaration of Independence than the American Negroes; there is no true American music but the wild sweet melodies of the Negro slave; the American fairy tales and folk-lore are Indian and African; and, all in all, we black men seem the sole oasis of simple faith and reverence in a dusty desert of dollars and smartness. Will America be poorer if she replace her brutal dyspeptic blundering with light-hearted but determined Negro humility? or her coarse and cruel wit with loving jovial good-humor? or her vulgar music with the soul of the Sorrow Songs?

Merely a concrete test of the underlying principles of the great republic is the Negro Problem, and the spiritual striving of the freedmen's sons is the travail of souls whose burden is almost beyond the measure of their strength, but who bear it in the name of an historic race, in the name of this the land of their fathers' fathers, and in the name of human opportunity. . . .

"The First Universal Races Congress"

Presented in 1911 at
a conference in London

Of the two thousand international meetings that have taken place in the last seventy-five years there have been few that have so touched the imagination as the Universal Races Congress of this summer.

Such a meeting may be viewed in many lights: as a meeting of widely separated men, as a reunion of East and West, as a glance across the color line or as a sort of World Grievance Committee. Perhaps it was in part something of each of these. There was, however, one thing that this congress could do of inestimable importance. Outside the discussion of racial problems, it could make clear the present state of scientific knowledge concerning the meaning of the term "race."

This the congress did and this was its most important work. There were practically no reports of new anthropological knowledge. There were, however, several reviews and restatements in popular terms of the present *dicta* of the science in the matter of human races, exprest with a clearness, force and authority that deserve especial mention.

The scientific men who contributed papers to the congress, and who were with few exceptions there in person to take part in the discussions, were, many of them, of the first rank: Von Luschan and Von Ranke, of Germany; Sergi, of Italy; Myers, Lyde and Hadden, of England, and Boas, of America, are all well known; among the other speakers were the Indian scholar, Seal; Lacerda, of Brazil; Fino of France, and Reinsch, of America. All those mentioned, save Boas, were present in person.

To realize the full meaning of the statements made by these men one must not forget the racial philosophy upon which America has long been nursed. The central idea of that philosophy has been that there are vast and, for all practical purposes, unbridgeable differences between the races of men, the whites representing the higher nobler stock, the blacks the lower meaner race. Between the lowest races (who are certainly undeveloped and probably incapable of any considerable development) and the highest, range the brown and yellow peoples with various intermediate capacities.

The proofs of these assumptions have been repeatedly pointed out; the high civilization of the whites, the lack of culture among the blacks, the apparent incapacity for self-rule in many non-Europeans, and the stagnation of Asia. The reasons for this condition were variously stated: some assumed separate development for each race, while others spoke as tho the various races represented different stages in the same general development, with thousands of years between, the Negro remaining nearest the ape, the whites furthest from the common ancestor.

Had these assumptions remained merely academic opinions it would not be necessary to recall them, but they have become the scientific sanction for wide-spread and decisive political action—like the disfranchisement of American Negroes, the subjection of India and the partition of Africa. Under the aegis of this philosophy strong arguments have justified human slavery and peonage, conquest, enforced ignorance, the dishonoring of women and the exploitation of children. It was divine to enslave Negroes; Mexican peonage is the only remedy for laziness; powerful nations must rule the mass of men who are not fit and cannot be fitted to rule themselves; colored women must not be expected to be treated like white, and if commerce is arranged so as to make the dark world toil for the luxury and ease of the white, this is but the law of nature.

As I sat in the great hall of the University of London, I wondered how many of those audiences of five, six and seven hundred who daily braved the sweltering heat of a midsummer meeting realized how epoch-making many of the words quietly spoken there were, and how far they went toward undermining long and comfortably cherished beliefs.

The anthropologists were not rash in statement. They spoke with full realization of the prevalent attitude of Europeans toward other races. Some, like Von Luschan, took pains to emphasize separate racial development for the sake of the "hassenkampf," but he began with the sweeping assertion that "mankind is one":

"Fair and dark races, long and short-headed, intelligent and primitive, all come from one stock. Favorable circumstances and surroundings, especially a good environment . . . caused one group to advance more quickly than another."

Moreover both he and Von Ranke, Sergi and others ridiculed the possibility of a "science" of race, or, indeed, of the possibility or desirability of drawing complete racial lines: "The question of the number of human races," said Von Luschan, "has quite lost its *raison d'être,* and has become a subject of philosophical speculation, rather than of scientific research. It is of no more importance to know how many races there are than to know how many angels dance on the point of a needle!"

Especial insistence was made against regarding races as unchangeable accomplished facts; they were, in the words of Boas and Seal, "growing developing entities" and "the old idea of the absolute stability of racial types must evidently be given up; and with it the belief in the hereditary superiority of certain types over others."

This brought the discussion to the crucial point, for granted that human beings form a family thru which it is difficult to draw absolute lines, yet does not the present advancement of the various groups of men correspond on the whole with their physical characteristics? No proposition was more emphatically denied than this. In physique, said Seal, quoting Weisbach, "each race has its share of the characteristics of inferiority," and it is impossible to arrange the main groups of men in an ascending scale of physical development. Lyde, of Oxford, added that even color, which is today made the greatest of racial barriers, is with little doubt "entirely a matter of climatic control."

Nevertheless there are tremendous differences in the present condition of the various groups of men—whence do they arise and how permanent are they? Practically every anthropologist present laid the chief stress on environment in explaining these differences; not simply physical environment but the even more important social environment in which the individual is educated. Von Luschan traced dark-skinned primitive man from Southern Asia to the Negro and Negroid toward the Northwest, the Indo-European toward the North and the Mongol toward the Northeast. "We have thus the three chief varieties of mankind," he said, "all branching off the same primitive stock, diverging from each other for thousands of years, but all three forming a complete unity, intermarrying in all directions without the slightest decrease of fertility." Sir Harry Johnston emphasized this early interpenetration of primitive races and found traces of Negro blood from Asia to Ireland. Others like Reinsch showed that the differences that arose among the scattered branches of men were due at first to physical environment, and pointed out the way in which the contrasting geography of Greece and Africa, and Europe and Asia, had influenced the history of their inhabitants.

Had not this long difference of environment left traces in the characters of races so ingrained as to be today practically ineradicable? Myers, of Oxford, asserted, in answer to this, that the mental characteristics of the majority of Europe were today essentially the same as those of the primitive peoples of the earth; that such differences as exist are due to present social and physical environment and that therefore "the progressive development of all primitive people must be conceded if the environment can be appropriately changed."

From the papers submitted to the congress and from his own studies, Gustav Spiller, the secretary, stated that a fair interpretation of the scientific evidence would support these propositions:

1. It is not legitimate to argue from differences in physical characteristics to difference in mental characteristics.

2. Physical and mental characteristics of races are not permanent, nor are they modifiable only thru long ages. On the contrary they are capable of being profoundly modified in a few generations by changes in education, public sentiment and environment generally.

3. The status of a race at any particular time offers no index as to its innate or inherited capacities.

As to race mixture all the anthropologists said that there were no "pure" races and that modern peoples were all more or less mixt. Nevertheless while many of these mixtures were obviously beneficial, it was not clear whether all racial mixtures would be. Certainly it was unscientific to assert that mulattoes and Eurasians were degenerate in the absence of all scientific data. Lacerda, of Brazil, showed the high proportion of mulattoes in the population of Brazil and the leading role they had played in emancipating the slaves, in establishing the republic and in the literary and political life of the day. Sir Charles Bruce and Sir Sidney Olivier made somewhat similar statements concerning the West Indies.

It would be too much to say that all anthropologists today would subscribe to the main conclusions of those who attended the Races Congress or that the doctrine of inevitable race superiority is dead. On the other hand there is good reason to affirm with Finot, in the brochure which he gave to the congress:

The conception of races as of so many watertight compartments into which human beings can be crammed as if they were so many breeds of horses or cattle, has had its day. The word race will doubtless long survive, even tho it may have lost all meaning. From time immemorial men have taken far more pains to damn their souls than would have sufficed to save them. Hence they will be certain to preserve this most scientific term which incites to hatred and unjustifiable contempt for our fellow men, instead of replacing it by some word implying the brotherhood of man.

The congress itself recorded its judgment on the matter of race differences by

> urging the vital importance at this juncture of history of discountenancing race prejudice, as tending to inflict on humanity incalculable harm, and as based on generalizations unworthy of an enlightened and progressive age.

4. "Does Race Antagonism Serve Any Good Purpose?"

Published in 1914 in *The Crisis*

There are four classes of reasons usually given in defense of race antagonism.

1. It is an instinctive repulsion from something harmful and is, therefore, a subtle condition of ultimate survival.

The difficulty with this theory is that it does not square with the facts: race antipathy is not instinctive but a matter of careful education. Black and white children play together gladly and know no prejudice until it is implanted precept upon precept and by strong social pressure; and when it is so implanted it is just as strong in cases where there is no physical difference as it is where physical differences are striking. The racial repulsion in the Balkans among peoples of practically the same blood is today greater than it was between whites and blacks on the Virginia plantations.

2. Racial antagonism, whether instinctive or not, is a reasonable measure of self-defense against undesirable racial traits.

This second proposition is the one which usually follows careful examination of the first. After all, it is admitted "instinct" is an unimportant fact. Instincts are simply accumulated reasons in the individual or in the race. The reasons for antagonizing inferior races are clear and may be summed up as follows:

Poor health and stamina.

Low ability.

Harmful ideals of life.

We are now on surer ground because we can now appeal to facts. But no sooner do we make this appeal than we are astonished to find that there are surprising little data: Is it true that the Negro as a physical animal is inferior to the white man or is he superior? Is the high death rate of the Indian a proof of his poor physique or is it proof of wretched conditions of life which would long ago have killed off a weaker people? And, again, is spiritual superiority always in direct proportion to physical strength in races any more than in individuals? Connected with this matter of health comes the question of physical beauty, but surely, if beauty were to become a standard of survival how small our world population would be!

It is argued, however, that it may be granted that the physical stamina of all races is probably approximately the same and that physical comeliness is rather a matter of taste and selection than of absolute racial difference. However, when it comes to intellectual ability the races differ so enormously that superior races must in self-defense repel the inferior sternly, even brutally. Two things, however, must be said in answer to this: First, the prejudice against the Jews, age long and worldwide is surely not based on inferior ability. We have only to name Jeremiah, Disraeli and Jesus Christ to set our minds at rest on that point. Moreover, if we compare the intellectual ability of Teuton and Chinese which is inferior? Or, if we take Englishman and Bantu, is the difference a difference of native ability or of training and environment? The answer to this is simple: we do not know. But arguing from all known facts and analogies we must certainly admit in the words of the secretary of the First International Races Congress, that "an impartial investigator would be inclined to look upon the various important peoples of the world as, to all intents and purposes, essentially equals in intellect, enterprise, morality and physique."

3. Racial antipathy is a method of race development.

We may admit so far as physique and native ability go, that as Ratzel says: "There is only one species of man; the variations are numerous, but do not go deep." At the same time it is plain that Europe has outstripped China in civilization, and China has outstripped Africa. Here at least are plain facts. Is not racial antipathy a method of maintaining the European level of culture? But is it necessary for the runner to hate and despise the man he is outdistancing? Can we only maintain culture in one race by increasing barbarism in others? Does it enhance the "superiority" of white men to allow them to steal from yellow men and enslave black men and reduce colored women to concubinage and prostitution? Surely not. Admitting that in the world's history again and again this or that race has outstripped another in culture, it is impossible to prove that inherent racial superiority was the cause or that the level of culture has been permanently raised in one race by keeping other races down.

4. Race antipathy is a method of group specialization.

This argument admits the essential equality of races but insists on the difference in gifts and argues that antipathy between races allows each to develop its own peculiar gifts and aptitudes. Does it? That depends on the "antipathy." If antipathy means the enslaving of the African, the exploitation of the Chinese, the peonage of Mexicans, and the denial of schools to American Negroes then it is hard to see where the "encouragement" comes in. If it means the generous encouragement of all men according to their gifts and ability then why

speak of race "antipathy" or encourage it? Let us call it human uplift and universal brotherhood and be done with it.

Such are the arguments. Most persons use all four at once and skillfully skip from one to the other. Each argument has in other days been applied to individuals and social classes, but we have outgrown that. We apply it today to "races" because race is a vague, unknown term which may be made to cover a multitude of sins. After all, what is a "race" and how many races are there? Von Luschan, one of the greatest of modern anthropologists, says: "The question of the number of human races has quite lost its *raison d'être*, and has become a subject rather of philosophic speculation than of scientific research." What we have on earth is men. Shall we help them or hinder them? Shall we hate and kill them or love and preserve and uplift them? Which method will do us most good? This is the real question of "Race" antipathy.

"Africa and the Slave Trade"

Published in 1915 in *The Negro*

... The modern world, in contrast, knows the Negro chiefly as a bond slave in the West Indies and America. Add to this the fact that the darker races in other parts of the world have, in the last four centuries, lagged behind the flying and even feverish footsteps of Europe, and we face to-day a widespread assumption throughout the dominant world that color is a mark of inferiority.

The result is that in writing of this, one of the most ancient, persistent, and widespread stocks of mankind, one faces astounding prejudice. That which may be assumed as true of white men must be proven beyond peradventure if it relates to Negroes. One who writes of the development of the Negro race must continually insist that he is writing of a normal human stock, and that whatever it is fair to predicate of the mass of human beings may be predicated of the Negro. It is the silent refusal to do this which has led to so much false writing on Africa and of its inhabitants. Take, for instance, the answer to the apparently simple question "What is a Negro?" We find the most extraordinary confusion of thought and difference of opinion. There is a certain type in the minds of most people which, as David Livingstone said, can be found only in caricature and not in real life. When scientists have tried to find an extreme type of black, ugly, and woolly-haired Negro, they have been compelled more and more to limit his home even in Africa. At least nine-tenths of the African people do not at all conform to this type, and the typical Negro, after being denied a dwelling place in the Sudan, along the Nile, in East Central Africa, and in South Africa, was finally given a very small country between the Senegal and the Niger, and even there was found to give trace of many stocks. As Winwood Reade says, "The typical Negro is a rare variety even among Negroes."

As a matter of fact we cannot take such extreme and largely fanciful stock as typifying that which we may fairly call the Negro race. In the case of no other race is so narrow a definition attempted. A "white" man may be of any color, size, or facial conformation and have endless variety of cranial measurement and physical characteristics. A "yellow" man is perhaps an even vaguer conception.

In fact it is generally recognized to-day that no scientific definition of race is possible. Differences, and striking differences, there are between men and groups of men, but they fade into each other so insensibly that we can only indicate the main divisions of men in broad outlines. As Von Luschan says, "The question of the number of human races has quite lost its *raison d'être* and has become a subject rather of philosophic speculation than of scientific research. It is of no more importance now to know how many human races there are than to know how many angels can dance on the point of a needle. Our aim now is to find out how ancient and primitive races developed from others and how races changed or evolved through migration and inter-breeding."

The mulatto (using the term loosely to indicate either an intermediate type between white and black or a mingling of the two) is as typically African as the black man and cannot logically be included in the "white" race, especially when American usage includes the mulatto in the Negro race.

It is reasonable, according to fact and historic usage, to include under the word "Negro" the darker peoples of Africa characterized by a brown skin, curled or "frizzled" hair, full and sometimes everted lips, a tendency to a development of the maxillary parts of the face, and a dolichocephalic head. This type is not fixed or definite. The color varies widely; it is never black or bluish, as some say, and it becomes often light brown or yellow. The hair varies from curly to a wool-like mass, and the facial angle and cranial form show wide variation.

It is as impossible in Africa as elsewhere to fix with any certainty the limits of racial variation due to climate and the variation due to intermingling. In the past, when scientists assumed one unvarying Negro type, every variation from that type was interpreted as meaning mixture of blood. To-day we recognize a broader normal African type which, as Palgrave says, may best be studied "among the statues of the Egyptian rooms of the British Museum; the larger gentle eye, the full but not over-protruding lips, the rounded contour, and the good-natured, easy, sensuous expression. This is the genuine African model." To this race Africa in the main and parts of Asia have belonged since prehistoric times.

The color of this variety of man, as the color of other varieties, is due to climate. Conditions of heat, cold, and moisture, working for thousands of years through the skin and other organs, have given men their differences of color. This color pigment is a protection against sunlight and consequently varies with the intensity of the sunlight. Thus in Africa we find the blackest men in the fierce sunlight of the desert, red pygmies in the forest, and yellow Bushmen on the cooler southern plateau.

Next to the color, the hair is the most distinguishing characteristic of the Negro, but the two characteristics do not vary with each other. Some of the blackest of the Negroes have curly rather than woolly hair, while the crispest, most closely curled hair is found among the yellow Hottentots and Bushmen. The difference between the hair of the lighter and darker races is a difference of degree, not of kind, and can be easily measured. If the hair follicles of a Chinaman, a European, and a Negro are cut across transversely, it will be found that the diameter of the first is 100 by 77 to 85, the second 100 by 62 to 72, while that of the Negro is 100 by 40 to 60. This elliptical form of the Negro's hair causes it to curl more or less tightly.

There have been repeated efforts to discover, by measurements of various kinds, further and more decisive differences which would serve as really scientific determinants of race. Gradually these efforts have been given up. To-day we realize that there are no hard and fast racial types among men. Race is a dynamic and not a static conception, and the typical races are continually changing and developing, amalgamating and differentiating. In this little book, then, we are studying the history of the darker part of the human family, which is separated from the rest of mankind by no absolute physical line, but which nevertheless forms, as a mass, a social group distinct in history, appearance, and to some extent in spiritual gift. . . .

6. *"The Souls of White Folk"*

Published in 1920 in *Darkwater*

. . . The discovery of personal whiteness among the world's peoples is a very modern thing,—a nineteenth and twentieth century matter, indeed. The ancient world would have laughed at such a distinction. The Middle Age regarded skin color with mild curiosity; and even up into the eighteenth century we were hammering our national manikins into one, great, Universal Man, with fine frenzy which ignored color and race even more than birth. Today we have changed all that, and the world in a sudden, emotional conversion has discovered that it is white and by that token, wonderful!

This assumption that of all the hues of God whiteness alone is inherently and obviously better than brownness or tan leads to curious acts; even the sweeter souls of the dominant world as they discourse with me on weather, weal, and woe are continually playing above their actual words an obligato of tune and tone, saying:

"My poor, un-white thing! Weep not nor rage. I know, too well, that the curse of God lies heavy on you. Why? That is not for me to say, but be brave! Do your work in your lowly sphere, praying the good Lord that into heaven above, where all is love, you may, one day, be born—white!"

I do not laugh. I am quite straight-faced as I ask soberly:

"But what on earth is whiteness that one should so desire it?" Then always, somehow, some way, silently but clearly, I am given to understand that whiteness is the ownership of the earth forever and ever, Amen!

Now what is the effect on a man or a nation when it comes passionately to believe such an extraordinary dictum as this? That nations are coming to believe it is manifest daily. Wave on wave, each with increasing virulence, is dashing this new religion of whiteness on the shores of our time. Its first effects are funny: the strut of the Southerner, the arrogance of the Englishman amuck, the whoop of the hoodlum who vicariously leads your mob. Next it appears dampening generous enthusiasm in what we once counted glorious; to free the slave is discovered to be tolerable only in so far as it freed his master! Do we sense somnolent writhings in black Africa or angry groans in India or triumphant banzais in Japan? "To your tents, O Israel!" These nations are not white!

After the more comic manifestations and the chilling of generous enthusiasm come subtler, darker deeds. Everything considered, the title to the universe claimed by White Folk is faulty. It ought, at least, to look plausible. How easy, then, by emphasis and omission to make children believe that every great soul the world ever saw was a white man's soul; that every great thought the world ever knew was a white man's thought; that every great deed the world ever did was a white man's deed; that every great dream the world ever sang was a white man's dream. In fine, that if from the world were dropped everything that could not fairly be attributed to White Folk, the world would, if anything, be even greater, truer, better than now. And if all this be a lie, is it not a lie in a great cause?

Here it is that the comedy verges to tragedy. The first minor note is struck, all unconsciously, by those worthy souls in whom consciousness of high descent brings burning desire to spread the gift abroad,—the obligation of nobility to the ignoble. Such sense of duty assumes two things: a real possession of the heritage and its frank appreciation by the humble-born. So long, then, as humble black folk, voluble with thanks, receive barrels of old clothes from lordly and generous whites, there is much mental peace and moral satisfaction. But when the black man begins to dispute the white man's title to certain alleged

bequests of the Fathers in wage and position, authority and training; and when his attitude toward charity is sullen anger rather than humble jollity; when he insists on his human right to swagger and swear and waste,—then the spell is suddenly broken and the philanthropist is ready to believe that Negroes are impudent, that the South is right, and that Japan wants to fight America.

After this the descent to Hell is easy. On the pale, white faces which the great billows whirl upward to my tower I see again and again, often and still more often, a writing of human hatred, a deep and passionate hatred, vast by the very vagueness of its expressions. Down through the green waters, on the bottom of the world, where men move to and fro, I have seen a man—an educated gentleman—grow livid with anger because a little, silent, black woman was sitting by herself in a Pullman car. He was a white man. I have seen a great, grown man curse a little child, who had wandered into the wrong waiting-room, searching for its mother: "Here, you damned black—" He was white. In Central Park I have seen the upper lip of a quiet, peaceful man curl back in a tigerish snarl of rage because black folk rode by in a motor car. He was a white man. We have seen, you and I, city after city drunk and furious with ungovernable lust of blood; mad with murder, destroying, killing, and cursing; torturing human victims because somebody accused of crime happened to be of the same color as the mob's innocent victims and because that color was not white! We have seen,—Merciful God! in these wild days and in the name of Civilization, Justice, and Motherhood,—what have we not seen, right here in America, of orgy, cruelty, barbarism, and murder done to men and women of Negro descent.

Up through the foam of green and weltering waters wells this great mass of hatred, in wilder, fiercer violence, until I look down and know that today to the millions of my people

no misfortune could happen,—of death and
pestilence, failure and defeat—that would not
make the hearts of millions of their fellows
beat with fierce, vindictive joy! Do you doubt
it? Ask your own soul what it would say if the
next census were to report that half of black
America was dead and the other half dying.

Unfortunate? Unfortunate. But where is
the misfortune? Mine? Am I, in my blackness,
the sole sufferer? I suffer. And yet, somehow,
above the suffering, above the shackled anger
that beats the bars, above the hurt that crazes
there surges in me a vast pity,—pity for a
people imprisoned and enthralled, hampered
and made miserable for such a cause, for such
a phantasy!

Conceive this nation, of all human peoples,
engaged in a crusade to make the "World Safe
for Democracy"! Can you imagine the United
States protesting against Turkish atrocities in
Armenia, while the Turks are silent about mobs
in Chicago and St. Louis; what is Louvain compared with Memphis, Waco, Washington,
Dyersburg, and Estill Springs? In short, what
is the black man but America's Belgium, and
how could America condemn in Germany that
which she commits, just as brutally, within her
own borders?

A true and worthy ideal frees and uplifts a
people; a false ideal imprisons and lowers. Say
to men, earnestly and repeatedly: "Honesty is
best, knowledge is power; do unto others as
you would be done by." Say this and act it and
the nation must move toward it, if not to it.
But say to a people: "The one virtue is to be
white," and the people rush to the inevitable
conclusion, "Kill the 'nigger'!"

Is not this the record of present America? Is
not this its headlong progress? Are we not
coming more and more, day by day, to making
the statement "I am white," the one fundamental tenet of our practical morality? Only
when this basic, iron rule is involved is our
defense of right nation-wide and prompt.
Murder may swagger, theft may rule and

prostitution may flourish and the nation gives
but spasmodic, intermittent and lukewarm
attention. But let the murderer be black or the
thief brown or the violator of womanhood
have a drop of Negro blood, and the righteousness of the indignation sweeps the world.
Nor would this fact make the indignation less
justifiable did not we all know that it was
blackness that was condemned and not crime.

In the awful cataclysm of World War,
where from beating, slandering, and murdering us the white world turned temporarily
aside to kill each other, we of the Darker
Peoples looked on in mild amaze. . . .

The European world is using black and
brown men for all the uses which men know.
Slowly but surely white culture is evolving the
theory that "darkies" are born beasts of burden for white folk. It were silly to think otherwise, cries the cultured world, with stronger
and shriller accord. The supporting arguments
grow and twist themselves in the mouths of
merchant, scientist, soldier, traveler, writer,
and missionary: Darker peoples are dark in
mind as well as in body; of dark, uncertain,
and imperfect descent; of frailer, cheaper stuff;
they are cowards in the face of mausers and
maxims; they have no feelings, aspirations,
and loves; they are fools, illogical idiots,—
"half-devil and half-child."

Such as they are civilization must, naturally,
raise them, but soberly and in limited ways.
They are not simply dark white men. They are
not "men" in the sense that Europeans are
men. To the very limited extent of their shal-
low capacities lift them to be useful to whites,
to raise cotton, gather rubber, fetch ivory, dig
diamonds,—and let them be paid what men
think they are worth—white men who know
them to be well-nigh worthless.

Such degrading of men by men is as old as
mankind and the invention of no one race or
people. Ever have men striven to conceive of
their victims as different from the victors, endlessly different, in soul and blood, strength and

cunning, race and lineage. It has been left, however, to Europe and to modern days to discover the eternal world-wide mark of meanness,—color!

Such is the silent revolution that has gripped modern European culture in the later nineteenth and twentieth centuries. Its zenith came in Boxer times: White supremacy was all but world-wide, Africa was dead, India conquered, Japan isolated, and China prostrate, while white America whetted her sword for mongrel Mexico and mulatto South America, lynching her own Negroes the while. Temporary halt in this program was made by little Japan and the white world immediately sensed the peril of such "yellow" presumption! What sort of a world would this be if yellow men must be treated "white"? Immediately the eventual overthrow of Japan became a subject of deep thought and intrigue, from St. Petersburg to San Francisco, from the Key of Heaven to the Little Brother of the Poor.

The using of men for the benefit of masters is no new invention of modern Europe. It is quite as old as the world. But Europe proposed to apply it on a scale and with an elaborateness of detail of which no former world ever dreamed. The imperial width of the thing,—the heaven-defying audacity—makes its modern newness.

The scheme of Europe was no sudden invention, but a way out of long-pressing difficulties. It is plain to modern white civilization that the subjection of the white working classes cannot much longer be maintained. Education, political power, and increased knowledge of the technique and meaning of the industrial process are destined to make a more and more equitable distribution of wealth in the near future. The day of the very rich is drawing to a close, so far as individual white nations are concerned. But there is a loophole. There is a chance for exploitation on an immense scale for inordinate profit, not simply to the very rich, but to the middle class and to the laborers. This chance lies in the exploitation of darker peoples. It is here that the golden hand beckons. Here are no labor unions or votes or questioning onlookers or inconvenient consciences. These men may be used down to the very bone, and shot and maimed in "punitive" expeditions when they revolt. In these dark lands "industrial development" may repeat in exaggerated form every horror of the industrial history of Europe, from slavery and rape to disease and maiming, with only one test of success,—dividends!

This theory of human culture and its aims has worked itself through warp and woof of our daily thought with a thoroughness that few realize. Everything great, good, efficient, fair, and honorable is "white"; everything mean, bad, blundering, cheating, and dishonorable is "yellow"; a bad taste is "brown"; and the devil is "black." The changes of this theme are continually rung in picture and story, in newspaper heading and moving-picture, in sermon and school book, until, of course, the King can do no wrong,—a White Man is always right and a Black Man has no rights which a white man is bound to respect.

There must come the necessary despisings and hatreds of these savage half-men, this unclean *canaille* of the world—these dogs of men. All through the world this gospel is preaching. It has its literature, it has its priests, it has its secret propaganda and above all— it pays!

There's the rub,—it pays. Rubber, ivory, and palm-oil; tea, coffee, and cocoa; bananas, oranges, and other fruit; cotton, gold, and copper—they, and a hundred other things which dark and sweating bodies hand up to the white world from their pits of slime, pay and pay well, but of all that the world gets the black world gets only the pittance that the white world throws it disdainfully.

Small wonder, then, that in the practical world of things-that-be there is jealousy and strife for the possession of the labor of dark millions, for the right to bleed and exploit the colonies of the world where this golden stream may be had, not always for the asking, but surely for the whipping and shooting. It was this competition for the labor of yellow, brown, and black folks that was the cause of the World War. . . .

As to the darkest and weakest of peoples there was but one unanimity in Europe,—that which Herr Dernberg of the German Colonial Office called the agreement with England to maintain white "prestige" in Africa,—the doctrine of the divine right of white people to steal.

Thus the world market most wildly and desperately sought today is the market where labor is cheapest and most helpless and profit is most abundant. This labor is kept cheap and helpless because the white world despises "darkies." If one has the temerity to suggest that these workingmen may walk the way of white workingmen and climb by votes and self-assertion and education to the rank of men, he is howled out of court. They cannot do it and if they could, they shall not, for they are the enemies of the white race and the whites shall rule forever and forever and everywhere. Thus the hatred and despising of human beings from whom Europe wishes to extort her luxuries has led to such jealousy and bickering between European nations that they have fallen afoul of each other and have fought like crazed beasts. Such is the fruit of human hatred.

But what of the darker world that watches? Most men belong to this world. With Negro and Negroid, East Indian, Chinese, and Japanese they form two-thirds of the population of the world. A belief in humanity is a belief in colored men. If the uplift of mankind must be done by men, then the destinies of this world will rest ultimately in the hands of darker nations.

What, then, is this dark world thinking? It is thinking that as wild and awful as this shameful war was, *it is nothing to compare with that fight for freedom which black and* *brown and yellow men must and will make unless their oppression and humiliation and insult at the hands of the White World cease. The Dark World is going to submit to its present treatment just as long as it must and not one moment longer.*

Let me say this again and emphasize it and leave no room for mistaken meaning: The World War was primarily the jealous and avaricious struggle for the largest share in exploiting darker races. As such it is and must be but the prelude to the armed and indignant protest of these despised and raped peoples. Today Japan is hammering on the door of justice, China is raising her half-manacled hands to knock next, India is writhing for the freedom to knock, Egypt is sullenly muttering, the Negroes of South and West Africa, of the West Indies, and of the United States are just awakening to their shameful slavery. Is, then, this war the end of wars? Can it be the end, so long as sits enthroned, even in the souls of those who cry peace, the despising and robbing of darker peoples? If Europe hugs this delusion, then this is not the end of world war,—it is but the beginning!

We see Europe's greatest sin precisely where we found Africa's and Asia's,—in human hatred, the despising of men; with this difference, however: Europe has the awful lesson of the past before her, has the splendid results of widened areas of tolerance, sympathy, and love among men, and she faces a greater, an infinitely greater, world of men than any preceding civilization ever faced.

It is curious to see America, the United States, looking on herself, first, as a sort of natural peace-maker, then as a moral protagonist in this terrible time. No nation is less fitted for this rôle. For two or more centuries America has marched proudly in the van of human hatred,—making bonfires of human flesh and laughing at them hideously, and making the insulting of millions more than a matter of dislike,—rather a great religion, a world war-cry: Up white, down black; to your tents, O white folk, and world war with black and parti-colored mongrel beasts! . . .

7. "Social Equality and Racial Intermarriage"

Published in 1922 in *World Tomorrow*

There is no doubt but that at the bottom of the race problem in the United States is the question of "Social Equality": and the kernel of the "Social Equality" question is the question of intermarriage.

These questions moreover are made almost impossible of rational discussion because of the intense bitterness and hatred which their mere mention gives rise to: one party hotly begins the discussion by intimating in plain terms that blacks are degenerates and prostitutes, commerce with whom on any plane is monstrous. The other party retorts with a record of millions of mulattoes and mixed bloods, the deliberate degradation of black womanhood and the criminal lust of the white race the world over. With such beginnings there is no rational end of discussion, no reasonable enlightenment.

Let us here, however, seek to forget a moment the hateful and hurtful and set down in cold phrase the main elements of the problem.

1. The sexual intermingling of race groups and more particularly of the lightest and darkest races is regarded by many folk as physically monstrous.

As a scientific dictum this is false. From earliest records racial mixture has been the rule and not the exception and there are today no pure races and no scientific line can be drawn between races. There is no scientific proof that the intermingling of any and all of the branches of the present human family does not produce normal human beings.

2. It is, however, believed by many that while race mixture is not physically monstrous, nevertheless certain strains of blood are superior to others; that the darker races have a larger number of inferior strains and that the preservation of the best human culture calls for the survival of the white race in as pure a state as possible.

There is undoubtedly vast difference in heredity, strains of blood leading to the rise of individuals of great ability here and others of criminal and degenerative tendencies there. It is also undoubtedly a great human duty to improve the human stock by rational breeding and by eliminating the unfit and dangerous. But our knowledge of human heredity is at present extremely vague and inexact and it is a monstrous perversion of our proven scientific knowledge to assume that the white race is the physical, mental and moral superior of other races, and that it has a right to secure its own survival and the death of the majority of men by any and all methods. It is quite possible that science will eventually show just as many superior strains in black and yellow as in white peoples, and just as much innate degeneracy in Europe as in Asia and Africa.

3. Racial intermingling, while neither monstrous nor necessarily deleterious, is regarded by many as at present inadvisable:

(a) because of widespread and deep seated racial antagonisms and hatreds.

(b) because of the necessity of group solidarity as a means of transmitting human culture.

(c) because of the value of the group in initiating human culture.

(d) because of differences of taste as to human types of efficiency and beauty.

Here we come to a much more reasonable basis for agreement. Humanity always has worked in groups and while these groups have gradually increased in size from the patriarchal family to the nation and even to the "empire" and the race, there is little likelihood that in the next millennium race lines will wholly disappear and we shall emerge as one undifferentiated humanity. Undoubtedly groups and races can and will do much to initiate culture and to transmit tradition. Moreover racial repulsions and antagonisms, within bounds, have their uses and incentives. No one can envisage a dead level of sameness in human types. There are the blue and blonde beauty of the Nordic race; the golden glory of the yellow world; the soft and sensuous allure of the brown people and the starry midnight beauty of the blacks; outside of the mere physical appeal there is every shade of method and conception and thought in differing groups of human hearts and minds, and the preservation and development of this interesting and stimulating variety in mankind is a great human duty.

But how are racial variety and human differentiation to be encouraged?

1. Some think that races can be kept from mingling only by force; that force should take the form of law even if this involves the prostitution of women of the darker races.

This cost is too great. If the only method of keeping races from intermingling is to force them into degradation and inferiority then it is far better to let them intermingle indiscriminately.

2. Some folk would depend on slander and gossip to discourage intermarriage. They would spread the rumor that dark races are diseased and abnormal, make impossible mates and so should be avoided.

This is simply a campaign of lies and again is socially too costly to maintain.

3. Most people depend on social exclusion— the denial of social equality to those with whom intermarriage is for any reason undesirable.

8. "Should the Negro Be Encouraged to Seek Cultural Equality?"

From a speech delivered in 1929 in Chicago

. . . If you were not familiar with the race problem in the United States or in the modern world, you would ask: Why should you not encourage Negroes or anybody else in the wide world to seek cultural equality? Is not this the aim of civilization? Is it not the ideal for which all men yearn? What could you conceive as better than a world in which all citizens were not only encouraged to cultural equality but accomplished their aim? Would not this be the best conceivable sort of world?

And yet you who know America, know perfectly well that large numbers of people have always denied to the Negro even the chance to try to reach such a goal. This denial has taken two forms or perhaps two degrees of emphasis on the same thesis. In early days Americans said frankly: the Negro should not be encouraged to seek cultural equality because he cannot reach it; he is not really human in the sense that other people are human. One does not encourage dogs to do the things that men do, not because one has anything against dogs, but because dogs are not men and cannot act like men. And the same way (although perhaps the analogy is overdrawn), Americans do not encourage Negroes to share modern culture because they cannot share it; we would simply make them unhappy if we let them try to reach to things which they can never reach.

Some years ago that was a logical statement and a statement difficult to answer. But in the last generation things have happened, and they have happened fast. We have had since emancipation a bounding forward of these millions of dark people in America. It does not make any difference how far you may wish to minimize what Negroes have done or what judgment you have as to its lasting value, there is no doubt about the work that has been done by these millions of emancipated slaves and their descendants in America. It is one of the wonderful accomplishments of this generation. It has few parallels in human history.

Some people might assume that this rise of the American Negro from slavery to freedom, from squalor, poverty, and ignorance to thrift and intelligence and the beginnings of wealth, would bring unstinted applause. Negroes themselves expected this. They looked eagerly forward to this day when you cannot write a history or statement of American civilization and leave the black man out, as proof of their equality and manhood and they expected their advance, incomplete or imperfect though it remains, nevertheless, to be greeted with applause.

On the contrary, all Negroes know that with all the generous praise given us there has been no phase of the advance that has not been looked on with a strong undercurrent of apprehension. America has feared the coming forward of these black men; it has looked upon it as a sort of threat—and if you should ask just why that is so, white Americans would state the thesis which they have stated before but with some modification; they would say that the coming forward of these people does not prove that they can make as great a gift to culture as the white people have made; but whether they can or not, they must not be allowed to come forward because it threatens civilization! If you ask how this can possibly be—how the advance of one-tenth of a nation can be a threat to the rest—you have various kinds of answers.

In the first place some seem to regard culture as a quantitative sort of thing; there is a certain amount of culture in the world; if you divide it up among all people you have that much less for other people. Of course everybody knows that the quantitative theory of

civilization does not hold, that the analogy is not perfect, and yet the reason we use it is because we do regard civilization today in terms of the number of our physical possessions. We are buried beneath our material wealth, and if we think, say, of motor cars, we conclude that if black people have motor cars, there are so many less for the white people to occupy. And so on. We go through the whole catalog of what a material age calls civilization, and think that if it is distributed to certain people, other people are not going to have as much.

Discarding this quantitative analogy we fall back to the other argument. After all, it is not the things which people have that makes the major part of civilization—the real civilization; real culture depends on quality and not quantity; it is not, therefore, so much a matter of distribution of goods—of distribution of quantity as of contamination of quality in goods and deeds.

And there we have brought back into the modern world the theory which the world has held and heard again and again—a few people have the chance to get unusual advancement; they have the chance to learn; they have leisure to think; they have food and shelter and encouragement; they push forward in the world, and then, after they have reached certain heights, suddenly they are overcome with admiration for themselves; suddenly it is suggested to them that they are wonderful and unusual people; that the universe was made particularly and especially for them; that never before have human beings attained such height and mastery—and finally we have the theory of the Chosen People!

The theory is as old as human culture is old, and yet today it comes back to us in the new dress of the belief that everything that has been done in modern times has been done by the Nordic people; that they are the people who are the salt of the earth; that if anything is done to change their type of civilization, then civilization fails and falls; that what we have got to be afraid of is the coming forward of a mass of black people without real gift, without real knowledge of what culture is, who are going to spoil the divine gifts of the Nordics.

To a theory of this sort, the world—the overwhelming majority of human beings who are not Nordic—have a right to two replies:

First, your theory is unproven. There is no scientific proof that modern culture is of Nordic origin or that Nordic brains and physique are of better intrinsic quality than Mediterranean, Indian, Chinese or Negro. In fact, the proofs of essential human equality of gift are overwhelming.

But, if Nordics believe in their own superiority; if they wish voluntarily to work by themselves and for the development and encouragement of their own gifts; if they prefer not to mingle their blood with other races, or contaminate their culture with foreign strains, nothing is to hinder them from carrying out this program except themselves.

Nobody is going to make Nordics marry outside of their group unless they want to marry outside. They can keep their group closed if they wish. Of course, civilization is by the definition of the term, civilization for all mankind; but nobody is going to withhold applause if you make your contribution to the world.

Of course, civilization is the rightful heritage of all and cannot be monopolized and confined to one group. A group organization to increase and forward culture is legitimate and will bring its reward in universal recognition and applause.

But this has never been the Nordic program. Their program is the subjection and rulership of the world for the benefit of the Nordics. They have overrun the earth and brought not simply modern civilization and technique, but with it exploitation, slavery and degradation to the majority of men. They have broken down native family life, desecrated homes of weaker peoples and spread their bastards over every corner of land and sea. They have been responsible for more intermixture of races than any other people, ancient or modern, and they have inflicted this miscegenation on helpless, unwilling slaves by force, fraud and insult; and this is the folk that today has the impudence to turn on the darker races when they demand a share of civilization, and cry: "You shall not marry our daughters!"

The blunt, crude reply is: Who in hell asked to marry your daughters? If this race problem must be reduced to a matter of sex, what we demand is the right to protect the decency of our own daughters.

But the insistent demand of the Darker World is far wider and deeper than this. The black and brown and yellow men demand the right to be men. They demand the right to have the artificial barriers placed in their path torn down and destroyed; they demand a voice in their own government; the organization of industry for the benefit of colored workers and not merely for white owners and masters; they demand education on the broadest and highest lines and they demand as human beings social contact with other human beings on a basis of perfect equality. . . .

9. "The Concept of Race"

Published in 1940 in *Dusk of Dawn*

. . . At Fisk, the problem of race was faced openly and essential racial equality asserted and natural inferiority strenuously denied. In some cases the teachers expressed this theory; in most cases the student opinion naturally forced it. At Harvard, on the other hand, I began to face scientific race dogma: first of all, evolution and the "Survival of the Fittest." It was continually stressed in the community and in classes that there was a vast difference in the development of the whites and the "lower" races; that this could be seen in the physical development of the Negro. I remember once in a museum, coming face to face with a demonstration: a series of skeletons arranged from a little monkey to a tall well-developed white man, with a Negro barely outranking a chimpanzee. Eventually in my classes stress was quietly transferred to brain weight and brain capacity, and at last to the "cephalic index."

In the graduate school at Harvard and again in Germany, the emphasis again was altered, and race became a matter of culture and cultural history. The history of the world was paraded before the observation of students. Which was the superior race? Manifestly that which had a history, the white race; there was some mention of Asiatic culture, but no course in Chinese or Indian history or culture was offered at Harvard, and quite unanimously in America and Germany, Africa was left without culture and without history. Even when the matter of mixed races was touched upon their evident and conscious inferiority was mentioned. I can never forget that morning in the class of the great Heinrich von Treitschke in Berlin. He was a big aggressive man, with an impediment in his speech which forced him to talk rapidly lest he stutter. His classes were the only ones always on time, and an angry scraping of feet greeted a late comer. Clothed in black, big, bushy-haired, peering sharply at the class, his words rushed out in a flood: "Mulattoes," he thundered, "are inferior." I almost felt his eyes boring into me, although probably he had not noticed me. "Sie fühlen sich niedriger!" "Their actions show it," he asserted. What contradiction could there be to that authoritative dictum?

The first thing which brought me to my senses in all this racial discussion was the continuous change in the proofs and arguments advanced. I could accept evolution and the survival of the fittest, provided the interval between advanced and backward races was not made too impossible. I balked at the usual

"thousand years." But no sooner had I settled into scientific security here, than the basis of race distinction was changed without explanation, without apology. I was skeptical about brain weight; surely much depended upon what brains were weighed. I was not sure about physical measurements and social inquiries. For instance, an insurance actuary published in 1890 incontrovertible statistics showing how quickly and certainly the Negro race was dying out in the United States through sheer physical inferiority. I lived to see every assumption of Hoffman's "Race Traits and Tendencies" contradicted; but even before that, I doubted the statistical method which he had used. When the matter of race became a question of comparative culture, I was in revolt. I began to see that the cultural equipment attributed to any people depended largely on who estimated it; and conviction came later in a rush as I realized what in my education had been suppressed concerning Asiatic and African culture.

It was not until I was long out of school and indeed after the World War that there came the hurried use of the new technique of psychological tests, which were quickly adjusted so as to put black folk absolutely beyond the possibility of civilization. By this time I was unimpressed. I had too often seen science made the slave of caste and race hate. And it was interesting to see Odum, McDougall and Brigham eventually turn somersaults from absolute scientific proof of Negro inferiority to repudiation of the limited and questionable application of any test which pretended to measure innate human intelligence.

So far I have spoken of "race" and race problems quite as a matter of course without explanation or definition. That was our method in the nineteenth century. Just as I was born a member of a colored family, so too I was born a member of the colored race. That was obvious and no definition was needed. Later I adopted the designation "Negro" for the race to which I belong. It seemed more definite and logical. At the same time I was of course aware that all members of the Negro race were not black and that the pictures of my race which were current were not authentic nor fair portraits. But all that was incidental. The world was divided into great primary groups of folk who belonged naturally together through heredity of physical traits and cultural affinity.

I do not know how I came first to form my theories of race. The process was probably largely unconscious. The differences of personal appearance between me and my fellows, I must have been conscious of when quite young. Whatever distinctions came because of that did not irritate me; they rather exalted me because, on the whole, while I was still a youth, they gave me exceptional position and a chance to excel rather than handicapping me.

Then of course, when I went South to Fisk, I became a member of a closed racial group with rites and loyalties, with a history and a corporate future, with an art and philosophy. I received these eagerly and expanded them so that when I came to Harvard the theory of race separation was quite in my blood. I did not seek contact with my white fellow students. On the whole I rather avoided them. I took it for granted that we were training ourselves for different careers in worlds largely different. There was not the slightest idea of the permanent subordination and inequality of my world. Nor again was there any idea of racial amalgamation. I resented the assumption that we desired it. I frankly refused the possibility while in Germany and even in America gave up courtship with one "colored" girl because she looked quite white, and I should resent the inference on the street that I had married outside my race.

All this theory, however, was disturbed by certain facts in America, and by my European experience. Despite everything, race lines were not fixed and fast. Within the Negro group

especially there were people of all colors. Then too, there were plenty of my colored friends who resented my ultra "race" loyalty and ridiculed it. They pointed out that I was not a "Negro," but a mulatto; that I was not a Southerner but a Northerner, and my object was to be an American and not a Negro; that race distinctions must go. I agreed with this in part and as an ideal, but I saw it leading to inner racial distinction in the colored group. I resented the defensive mechanism of avoiding too dark companions in order to escape notice and discrimination in public. As a sheer matter of taste I wanted the color of my group to be visible. I hotly championed the inclusion of two black school mates whose names were not usually on the invitation list to our social affairs. In Europe my friendships and close contact with white folk made my own ideas waver. The eternal walls between races did not seem so stern and exclusive. I began to emphasize the cultural aspects of race.

It is probably quite natural for persons of low degree, who have reached any status, to search feverishly for distinguished ancestry, as a sort of proof of their inherent desert. This is particularly true in America and has given rise to a number of organizations whose membership depends upon ancestors who have made their mark in the world. Of course, it is clear that there must be here much fable, invention and wishful thinking, facilitated by poor vital statistics and absence of written records. For the mass of Americans, and many Americans who have had the most distinguished careers, have been descended from people who were quite ordinary and even less; America indeed has meant the breaking down of class bars which imprisoned personalities and capabilities and allowing new men and new families to emerge. This is not, as some people assume, a denial of the importance of heredity and family. It is rather its confirmation. It shows us that the few in the past who have emerged are not necessarily the best; and quite certainly are not the only ones worthy of development and distinction; that, on the contrary, only a comparatively few have, under our present economic and social organization, had a chance to show their capabilities.

I early began to take a direct interest in my own family as a group and became curious as to that physical descent which I so long had taken for granted quite unquestioningly. But I did not at first think of any but my Negro ancestors. I knew little and cared less of the white forebears of my father. But this chauvinism gradually changed. There is, of course, nothing more fascinating than the question of the various types of mankind and their intermixture. . . .

Since then the concept of race has so changed and presented so much of contradiction that as I face Africa I ask myself: what is it between us that constitutes a tie which I can feel better than I can explain? Africa is, of course, my fatherland. Yet neither my father nor my father's father ever saw Africa or knew its meaning or cared overmuch for it. My mother's folk were closer and yet their direct connection, in culture and race, became tenuous; still, my tie to Africa is strong. On this vast continent were born and lived a large portion of my direct ancestors going back a thousand years or more. The mark of their heritage is upon me in color and hair. These are obvious things, but of little meaning in themselves; only important as they stand for real and more subtle differences from other men. Whether they do or not, I do not know nor does science know today.

But one thing is sure and that is the fact that since the fifteenth century these ancestors of mine and their other descendants have had a common history; have suffered a common disaster and have one long memory. The actual ties of heritage between the individuals of this group, vary with the ancestors that they have in common, and many others: Europeans and Semites, perhaps Mongolians, certainly American Indians. But the physical bond is least and the badge of color relatively unimportant save as a badge; the real essence of this kinship is its social heritage of slavery; the discrimination and insult; and this heritage binds together not simply the children of Africa, but extends through yellow Asia and into the South Seas. It is this unity that draws me to Africa. . . .

I think it was in Africa that I came more clearly to see the close connection between race and wealth. The fact that even in the minds of the most dogmatic supporters of race theories and believers in the inferiority of colored folk to white, there was a conscious or unconscious determination to increase their incomes by taking full advantage of this belief. And then gradually this thought was metamorphosed into a realization that the income-bearing value of race prejudice was the cause and not the result of theories of rare inferiority; that particularly in the United States the income of the Cotton Kingdom based on black slavery caused the passionate belief in Negro inferiority and the determination to enforce it even by arms.

I have wandered afield from miscegenation in the West Indies to race blending and segregation in America and to a glimpse of present Africa. Now to return to the American concept of race. It was in my boyhood, as I have intimated, an adventure. In my youth, it became the vision of a glorious crusade where I and my fellows were to match our mettle against white folk and show them what black folk could do. But as I grew older the matter became more serious and less capable of jaunty settlement. I not only met plenty of persons equal in ability to myself but often with greater ability and nearly always with greater opportunity. Racial identity presented itself as a matter of trammels and impediments as "tightening bonds about my feet." As I looked out into my racial world the whole thing verged on tragedy. My "way was cloudy" and the approach to its high goals by no means straight and clear. I saw the race problem was not as I conceived, a matter of clear, fair competition, for which I was ready and eager. It was rather a matter of segregation, of hindrance and inhibitions, and my struggles against this and resentment at it began to have serious repercussions upon my inner life.

It is difficult to let others see the full psychological meaning of caste segregation. It is as though one, looking out from a dark cave in a side of an impending mountain, sees the world passing and speaks to it; speaks courteously and persuasively, showing them how these entombed souls are hindered in their natural movement, expression, and development; and how their loosening from prison would be a matter not simply of courtesy, sympathy, and help to them, but aid to all the world. One talks on evenly and logically in this way, but notices that the passing throng does not even turn its head, or if it does, glances curiously and walks on. It gradually penetrates the minds of the prisoners that the people passing do not hear; that some thick sheet of invisible but horribly tangible plate glass is between them and the world. They get excited; they talk louder; they gesticulate. Some of the passing world stop in curiosity; these gesticulations seem so pointless; they laugh and pass on. They still either do not hear at all, or hear but dimly, and even what they hear, they do not understand. Then the people within may become hysterical. They may scream and hurl themselves against the barriers, hardly realizing in their bewilderment that they are screaming in a vacuum unheard and that their antics may actually seem funny to those outside looking in. They may even, here and there, break through in blood and disfigurement, and find themselves faced by a horrified, implacable, and quite overwhelming mob of people frightened for their own very existence.

It is hard under such circumstances to be philosophical and calm, and to think through

a method of approach and accommodation between castes. The entombed find themselves not simply trying to make the outer world understand their essential and common humanity but even more, as they become inured to their experience, they have to keep reminding themselves that the great and oppressing world outside is also real and human and in its essence honest. All my life I have had continually to haul my soul back and say, "All white folk are not scoundrels nor murderers. They are, even as I am, painfully human."

One development continually recurs: any person outside of this wall of glass can speak to his own fellows, can assume a facile championship of the entombed, and gain the enthusiastic and even gushing thanks of the victims. But this method is subject to two difficulties: first of all, not being possibly among the entombed or capable of sharing their inner thought and experience, this outside leadership will continually misinterpret and compromise and complicate matters, even with the best of will. And secondly, of course, no matter how successful the outside advocacy is, it remains impotent and unsuccessful until it actually succeeds in freeing and making articulate the submerged caste.

Practically, this group imprisonment within a group has various effects upon the prisoner. He becomes provincial and centered upon the problems of his particular group. He tends to neglect the wider aspects of national life and human existence. On the one hand he is unselfish so far as his inner group is concerned. He thinks of himself not as an individual but as a group man, a "race" man. His loyalty to this group idea tends to be almost unending and balks at almost no sacrifice. On the other hand, his attitude toward the environing race congeals into a matter of unreasoning resentment and even hatred, deep disbelief in them and refusal to conceive honesty and rational thought on their part. This attitude adds to the difficulties of conversation, intercourse, understanding between groups.

This was the race concept which has dominated my life, and the history of which I have attempted to make the leading theme of this book. It had as I have tried to show all sorts of illogical trends and irreconcilable tendencies. Perhaps it is wrong to speak of it at all as "a concept" rather than as a group of contradictory forces, facts and tendencies. At any rate I hope I have made its meaning to me clear. It was for me as I have written first a matter of dawning realization, then of study and science; then a matter of inquiry into the diverse strands of my own family; and finally consideration of my connection, physical and spiritual, with Africa and the Negro race in its homeland. All this led to an attempt to rationalize the racial concept and its place in the modern world.

10. *"The Negro and the Warsaw Ghetto"*

Published in 1952 in *Jewish Life*

I have been to Poland three times. The first time was fifty-nine years ago, when I was a student at the University of Berlin. I had been talking to my schoolmate, Stanislaus Ritter von Estreicher. I had been telling him of the race problem in America, which seemed to me at the time the only race problem and the greatest social problem of the world. He brushed it aside. He said, "You know nothing, really, about real race problems." Then he began to tell me about the problem of the Poles and particularly of that part of them who were included in the German empire; of their limited education; of the refusal to let them speak their own language; of the few careers that they were allowed to follow; of the continued insult to their culture and family life.

I was astonished; because race problems at the time were to me purely problems of color, and principally of slavery in the United States and near-slavery in Africa. I promised faithfully that when I went on my vacation that summer, I would stop to see him in his home at Krakow, Poland, where his father was librarian of the university.

I went down to South Germany through Switzerland to Italy, and then came back by Venice and Vienna and went out through Austria, Czechoslovakia and into German Poland and there, on the way, I had a new experience with a new race problem. I was traveling from Budapest through Hungary to a small town in Galicia, where I planned to spend the night. The cabman looked at me and asked if I wanted to stop *"unter die Juden."* I was a little puzzled, but told him "Yes." So we went to a little Jewish hotel on a small, out-of-the-way street. There I realized another problem of race or religion, I did not know which, which had to do with the treatment and segregation of large numbers of human beings. I went on to Krakow, becoming more and more aware of two problems of human groups, and then came back to the university, not a little puzzled as to my own race problem and its place in the world.

Gradually I became aware of the Jewish problem of the modern world and something of its history. In Poland I learned little because the university and its teachers and students were hardly aware themselves of what this problem was, and how it influenced them, or what its meaning was in their life. In Germany I saw it continually obtruding, but being suppressed and seldom mentioned. I remember once visiting on a social occasion in a small German town. A German student was with me and when I became uneasily aware that all was not going well, he reassured me. He whispered, "They think I may be a Jew. It's not you they object to, it's me." I was astonished. It had never occurred to me until then that any exhibition of race prejudice could be anything but color prejudice. I knew that this young man was pure German, yet his dark hair and handsome face made our friends suspicious. Then I went further to investigate this new phenomenon in my experience. . . .

Then finally, three years ago I was in Warsaw. I have seen something of human upheaval in this world: the scream and shots of a race riot in Atlanta; the marching of the Ku Klux Klan; the threat of courts and police; the neglect and destruction of human habitation; but nothing in my wildest imagination was equal to what I saw in Warsaw in 1949. I would have said before seeing it that it was impossible for a civilized nation with deep religious convictions and outstanding religious institutions; with literature and art; to treat fellow human beings as Warsaw had been treated. There had been complete, planned and utter destruction. Some streets had been so obliterated that only by using photographs of the past could they tell where the street was. And no one mentioned the total of the dead, the sum of destruction, the story of crippled and insane, the widows and orphans. . . .

The result of these three visits, and particularly of my view of the Warsaw ghetto, was not so much clearer understanding of the Jewish problem in the world as it was a real and more complete understanding of the Negro problem. In the first place, the problem of slavery, emancipation, and caste in the United States was no longer in my mind a separate and unique thing as I had so long conceived it. It was not even solely a matter of color and physical and racial characteristics, which was particularly a hard thing for me to learn, since for a lifetime the color line had been a real and efficient cause of misery. It was not merely a matter of religion. I had seen religions of many kinds—I had sat in the Shinto temples of Japan, in the Baptist churches of Georgia, in the Catholic cathedral of Cologne and in Westminster Abbey.

No, the race problem in which I was interested cut across lines of color and physique and belief and status and was a matter of cultural patterns, perverted teaching and human hate and prejudice, which reached all sorts of people and caused endless evil to all men. So that the ghetto of Warsaw helped me to emerge from a certain social provincialism into a broader conception of what the fight against race segregation, religious discrimination, and the oppression by wealth had to become if civilization was going to triumph and broaden in the world.

Chapter II

On Race Relations

"In all walks of life," wrote Du Bois in 1899, "the Negro is liable to meet some objection to his presence or some discourteous treatment." For Du Bois, the most widespread, significant, and costly fissure between human beings was that of the color line. "The problem of the twentieth century is the problem of the color-line," he declared in *The Souls of Black Folk* (1903), and he explored the consequences of that color line in nearly everything he wrote. While Du Bois acknowledged that physical differences between people are vague and inexact, and that racial groups generally reflect sociocultural designations rather than strict genetic amalgamations, he simultaneously understood that the reality of racism could not be ignored. Deconstructing race does not mean dismissing the tangible effects of racism. Innate differences between groups of people may be a myth, as Ashley Montagu would argue, but myths can be very powerful things, and the myths surrounding race have been harshly real in their consequences.

Like all the selections in this volume, those included in this chapter are but mere fragments chosen from a vast corpus of writings on race relations.

1. "Color Prejudice"

Published in 1899 in
The Philadelphia Negro

Incidentally throughout this study the prejudice against the Negro has been again and again mentioned. It is time now to reduce this somewhat indefinite term to something tangible. Everybody speaks of the matter, everybody knows that it exists, but in just what form it shows itself or how influential it is few agree. In the Negro's mind, color prejudice in Philadelphia is that widespread feeling of dislike for his blood, which keeps him and his children out of decent employment, from certain public conveniences and amusements, from hiring houses in many sections, and in general, from being recognized as a man. Negroes regard this prejudice as the chief cause of their present unfortunate condition. On the other hand most white people are quite unconscious of any such powerful and vindictive feeling; they regard color prejudice as the easily explicable feeling that intimate social intercourse with a lower race is not only undesirable but impracticable if our present standards of culture are to be maintained; and although they are aware that some people feel the aversion more intensely than others, they cannot see how such a feeling has much influence on the real situation, or alters the social condition of the mass of Negroes.

As a matter of fact, color prejudice in this city is something between these two extreme views: it is not to-day responsible for all, or perhaps the greater part of the Negro problems, or of the disabilities under which the race labors; on the other hand it is a far more powerful social force than most Philadelphians realize. The practical results of the attitude of most of the inhabitants of Philadelphia toward persons of Negro descent are as follows:

1. As to getting work:

No matter how well trained a Negro may be, or how fitted for work of any kind, he cannot in the ordinary course of competition hope to be much more than a menial servant.

He cannot get clerical or supervisory work to do save in exceptional cases.

He cannot teach save in a few of the remaining Negro schools.

He cannot become a mechanic except for small transient jobs, and cannot join a trades union.

A Negro woman has but three careers open to her in this city: domestic service, sewing, or married life.

2. As to keeping work:

The Negro suffers in competition more severely than white men.

Change in fashion is causing him to be replaced by whites in the better paid positions of domestic service.

Whim and accident will cause him to lose a hard-earned place more quickly than the same things would affect a white man.

Being few in number compared with the whites the crime or carelessness of a few of his race is easily imputed to all, and the reputation of the good, industrious and reliable suffer thereby.

Because Negro workmen may not often work side by side with white workmen, the individual black workman is rated not by his own efficiency, but by the efficiency of a whole group of black fellow workmen which may often be low.

Because of these difficulties which virtually increase competition in his case, he is forced to take lower wages for the same work than white workmen.

3. As to entering new lines of work:

Men are used to seeing Negroes in inferior positions; when, therefore, by any chance a Negro gets in a better position, most men immediately conclude that he is not fitted for it, even before he has a chance to show his fitness.

If, therefore, he set up a store, men will not patronize him.

If he is put into public position men will complain.

If he gain a position in the commercial world, men will quietly secure his dismissal or see that a white man succeeds him.

4. As to his expenditure:

The comparative smallness of the patronage of the Negro, and the dislike of other customers makes it usual to increase the charges or difficulties in certain directions in which a Negro must spend money.

He must pay more house-rent for worse houses than most white people pay.

He is sometimes liable to insult or reluctant service in some restaurants, hotels and stores, at public resorts, theatres and places of recreation; and at nearly all barbershops.

5. As to his children:

The Negro finds it extremely difficult to rear children in such an atmosphere and not have them either cringing or impudent : if he impresses upon them patience with their lot, they may grow up satisfied with their condition; if he inspires them with ambition to rise, they may grow to despise their own people, hate the whites and become embittered with the world.

His children are discriminated against, often in public schools.

They are advised when seeking employment to become waiters and maids.

They are liable to species of insult and temptation peculiarly trying to children.

6. As to social intercourse:

In all walks of life the Negro is liable to meet some objection to his presence or some discourteous treatment; and the ties of friendship or memory seldom are strong enough to hold across the color line.

If an invitation is issued to the public for any occasion, the Negro can never know whether he would be welcomed or not; if he goes he is liable to have his feelings hurt and get into unpleasant altercation; if he stays away, he is blamed for indifference.

If he meet a lifelong white friend on the street, he is in a dilemma; if he does not greet the friend he is put down as boorish and impolite; if he does greet the friend he is liable to be flatly snubbed.

If by chance he is introduced to a white woman or man, he expects to be ignored on the next meeting, and usually is.

White friends may call on him, but he is scarcely expected to call on them, save for strictly business matters.

If he gain the affections of a white woman and marry her he may invariably expect that slurs will be thrown on her reputation and on his, and that both his and her race will shun their company.

When he dies he cannot be buried beside white corpses.

7. The result:

Any one of these things happening now and then would not be remarkable or call for especial comment; but when one group of people suffer all these little differences of treatment and discriminations and insults continually, the result is either discouragement, or bitterness, or over-sensitiveness, or recklessness. And a people feeling thus cannot do their best.

Presumably the first impulse of the average Philadelphian would be emphatically to deny any such marked and blighting discrimination as the above against a group of citizens in this metropolis. Every one knows that in the past color prejudice in the city was deep and passionate; living men can remember when a Negro could not sit in a street car or walk many streets in peace. These times have passed, however, and many imagine that active discrimination against the Negro has passed with them. Careful inquiry will convince any such one of his error. To be sure a colored man to-day can walk the streets of Philadelphia without personal insult; he can go to theatres, parks and some places of amusement without meeting more than stares and discourtesy; he can be accommodated at most hotels and restaurants, although his treatment in some would not be pleasant. All this is a vast advance and augurs much for the future. And yet all that has been said of the remaining discrimination is but too true. . . .

2. "Relations of Negroes to Whites in the South"

Published in 1901 in
*Annals of the American Academy
of Political and Social Science*

I have thus far sought to make clear the physical, economic and political relations of the Negroes and whites in the South as I have conceived them, including for the reasons set forth, crime and education. But after all that has been said on these more tangible matters of human contact there still remains a part essential to a proper description of the South which it is difficult to describe or fix in terms easily understood by strangers. It is, in fine, the atmosphere of the land, the thought and feeling, the thousand and one little actions which go to make up life. In any community or nation it is these little things which are most elusive to the grasp and yet most essential to any clear conception of the group life, taken as a whole. What is thus true of all communities is peculiarly true of the South where, outside of written history and outside of printed law, there has been going on for a generation, as deep a storm and stress of human souls, as intense a ferment of feeling, as intricate a writhing of spirit as ever a people experienced. Within and without the sombre veil of color, vast social forces have been at work, efforts for human betterment, movements toward disintegration and despair, tragedies and comedies in social and economic life, and a swaying and lifting and sinking of human hearts which have made this land a land of mingled sorrow and joy, of change and excitement.

The centre of this spiritual turmoil has ever been the millions of black freedmen and their sons, whose destiny is so fatefully bound up with that of the nation. And yet the casual observer visiting the South sees at first little of this. He notes the growing frequency of dark faces as he rides on, but otherwise the days slip lazily on, the sun shines and this little world seems as happy and contented as other worlds he has visited. Indeed, on the question of questions, the Negro problem, he hears so little that there almost seems to be a conspiracy of silence; the morning papers seldom mention it, and then usually in a far-fetched academic way, and indeed almost every one seems to forget and ignore the darker half of the land, until the astonished visitor is inclined to ask if after all there *is* any problem here. But if he lingers long enough there comes the awakening: perhaps in a sudden whirl of passion which leaves him gasping at its bitter intensity; more likely in a gradually dawning sense of things he had not at first noticed. Slowly but surely his eyes begin to catch the shadows of the color line; here he meets crowds of Negroes and whites; then he is suddenly aware that he cannot discover a single dark face; or again at the close of a day's wandering he may find himself in some strange assembly, where all faces are tinged brown or black, and where he has the vague uncomfortable feeling of the stranger. He realizes at last that silently, resistlessly, the world about flows by him in two great streams. They ripple on in the same sunshine, they approach here and mingle their waters in seeming carelessness, they divide then and flow wide apart. It is done quietly, no mistakes are made, or if one occurs the swift arm of the law and public opinion swings down for a moment, as when the other day a black man and a white woman were arrested for talking together on Whitehall street, in Atlanta.

Now if one notices carefully one will see that between these two worlds, despite much physical contact and daily intermingling, there is almost no community of intellectual life or points of transferrence where the thoughts and feelings of one race can come with direct contact and sympathy with the thoughts and feelings of the other. Before and directly after the war when all the best of the Negroes were domestic servants in the best of the white families, there were bonds of intimacy, affection, and sometimes blood relationship between the races. They lived in the same home, shared in the family life, attended the same church often and talked and conversed with each other. But the increasing civilization of the Negro since has naturally meant the development of higher classes: there are increasing numbers of ministers, teachers, physicians, merchants, mechanics and independent farmers, who by nature and training are the aristocracy and leaders of the blacks. Between them, however, and the best element of the whites, there is little or no intellectual commerce. They go to separate churches, they live in separate sections, they are strictly separated in all public gatherings, they travel separately, and they are beginning to read different papers and books. To most libraries, lectures, concerts and museums Negroes are either not admitted at all or on terms peculiarly galling to the pride of the very classes who might otherwise be attracted. The daily paper chronicles the doings of the black world from afar with no great regard for accuracy; and so on throughout the category of means for intellectual communication; schools, conferences, efforts for social betterment and the like, it is usually true that the very representatives of the two races who for mutual benefit and the welfare of the land ought to be in complete understanding and sympathy are so far strangers that one side thinks all whites are narrow and prejudiced and the other thinks educated Negroes dangerous and insolent. Moreover, in a land where the tyranny of public opinion and the intolerence of criticism is for obvious historical reasons so strong as in the South, such a situation is extremely difficult to correct. The white man as well as the Negro is bound and tied by the color line and many a scheme of friendliness and philanthropy, of broad-minded sympathy, and generous fellowship between the two has dropped still-born because some busy-body has forced the color question to the front and brought the tremendous force of unwritten law against the innovators.

It is hardly necessary for me to add to this very much in regard to the social contact between the races. Nothing has come to replace that finer sympathy and love between some masters and house servants, which the radical and more uncompromising drawing of the color line in recent years has caused almost completely to disappear. In a world where it means so much to take a man by the hand and sit beside him; to look frankly into his eyes and feel his heart beating with red blood—in a world where a social cigar or a cup of tea together means more than legislative halls and magazine articles and speeches, one can imagine the consequences of the almost utter absence of such social amenities between estranged races, whose separation extends even to parks and street cars.

Here there can be none of that social going down to the people; the opening of heart and hand of the best to the worst, in generous acknowledgment of a common humanity and a common destiny. On the other hand, in matters of simple almsgiving, where there be no question of social contact, and in the succor of the aged and sick, the South, as if stirred by a feeling of its unfortunate limitations, is generous to a fault. The black beggar is never turned away without a good deal more than a crust, and a call for help for the unfortunate meets quick response. I remember, one cold winter, in Atlanta, when I refrained from contributing to a public relief fund lest Negroes should be discriminated against; I afterward inquired of a friend: "Were any black people receiving aid?" "Why," said he, "they were *all* black."

And yet this does not touch the kernel of the problem. Human advancement is not a mere question of almsgiving, but rather of sympathy and co-operation among classes who would scorn charity. And here is a land where, in the higher walks of life, in all the higher striving for the good and noble and true, the color line comes to separate natural friends and co-workers, while at the bottom of the social group in the saloon, the gambling hell and the bawdy-house that same line wavers and disappears. . . .

3. "The Negro Problem"

Published in 1911 in Papers on Inter-Racial Problems Communicated to the First Universal Race Congress Held at the University of London, July 26-29, 1911

The American Negro problem is the question of the future status of the ten million Americans of Negro descent. It must be remembered that these persons are Americans by birth and descent. They represent, for the most part, four or five American born generations, being in that respect one of the most

American groups in the land. Moreover, the Negroes are not barbarians. They are, as a mass, poor and ignorant; but they are growing rapidly in both wealth and intelligence, and larger and larger numbers of them demand the rights and privileges of American citizens as a matter of undoubted desert.

To-day these rights are largely denied. In order to realise the disabilities under which Negroes suffer regardless of education, wealth, or degree of white blood, we may divide the United States into three districts:

    a. The Southern South, containing 75 per cent. of the Negroes.

    b. The border States, containing 15 per cent. of the Negroes.

    c. The North and West, containing 10 per cent. of the Negroes.

In the Southern South by law or custom Negroes—

1. Cannot vote, or their votes are neutralised by fraud.

2. Must usually live in the least desirable districts.

3. Receive very low wages.

4. Are, in the main, restricted to menial occupations or the lower grades of skilled labour and cannot expect preferment or promotion.

5. Cannot by law intermarry with whites.

6. Cannot join white churches or attend white colleges or join white cultural organisations.

7. Cannot be accommodated at hotels and restaurants or in any place of public entertainment.

8. Receive a distinct standard of justice in the courts and are especially liable to mob violence.

9. Are segregated so far as possible in every walk of life—in railway stations, railway trains, street-cars, lifts, &c., and usually made to pay equal prices for inferior accommodations.

10. Are often unable to protect their homes from invasion, their women from insult, and their savings from exploitation.

11. Are taxed for public facilities like parks and libraries, which they may not enter.

12. Are given meagre educational facilities and sometimes none at all.

13. Are liable to personal insult unless they appear as servants or menials or show deference to white folks by yielding the road, &c.

To many of these disabilities there are personal and local exceptions. In cities, for instance, the chance to defend the home, get an education, and somewhat better wages is greater, and mob violence less frequent. Then there are always some personal exceptions— cases of help and courtesy, of justice in the courts, and of good schools. These are, however, exceptions, and, as a rule, all Negroes, no matter what their training, possessions, or desert, are subjected to the above disabilities. Within the limits of these caste restrictions there is much goodwill and kindliness between the races, and especially much personal charity and help.

The 15 per cent. of the Negro population living on the border States suffer a little less restriction. They have some right of voting, are better able to defend their homes, and are less discriminated against in the expenditure of public funds. In the cities their schools are much better and public insult is less noticeable.

In the North the remaining 10 per cent. of the Negro population is legally undiscriminated against and may attend schools and churches and vote without restriction. As a matter of fact, however, they are made in most communities to feel that they are undesirable.

They are either refused accommodation at hotels, restaurants, and theatres, or received reluctantly. Their treatment in churches and general cultural organisations is such that few join. Intermarriage with whites brings ostracism and public disfavour, and in courts Negroes often suffer undeservedly. Common labour and menial work is open to them, but avenues above this in skilled labour or the professions (save as they serve their own race), are extremely difficult to enter, and there is much discrimination in wages. Mob violence has become not infrequent in later years.

There are here also many exceptional cases; instances of preferment in the industrial and political world; and there is always some little social intercourse. On the whole, however, the Negro in the north is an ostracised person who finds it difficult to make a good living or spend his earnings with pleasure.

Under these circumstances there has grown up a Negro world in America which has its own economic and social life, its churches, schools, and newspapers; its literature, public opinion, and ideals. This life is largely unnoticed and unknown even in America, and travellers miss it almost entirely.

The average American in the past made at least pretence of excusing the discrimination against Negroes, on the ground of their ignorance and poverty and their tendencies to crime and disease. While the mass is still poor and unlettered, it is admitted by all to-day that the Negro is rapidly developing a larger and larger class of intelligent property-holding men of Negro descent; notwithstanding this more and more race lines are being drawn which involve the treatment of civilised men in an uncivilised manner. Moreover, the crux of the question to-day is not merely a matter of social eligibility. For many generations the American Negro will lack the breeding and culture which the most satisfactory human intercourse requires. But in America the discrimination against Negroes goes beyond this, to the point

of public discourtesy, civic disability, injustice in the courts, and economic restriction.

The argument of those who uphold this discrimination is based primarily on race. They claim that the inherent characteristics of the Negro race show its essential inferiority and the impossibility of incorporating its descendants into the American nation. They admit that there are exceptions to the rule of inferiority, but claim that these but prove the rule. They say that amalgamation of the races would be fatal to civilisation and they advocate therefore a strict caste system for Negroes, segregating them by occupations and privileges, and to some extent by dwelling-place, to the end that they (*a*) submit permanently to an inferior position, or (*b*) die out, or (*c*) migrate.

This philosophy the thinking Negroes and a large number of white friends vigorously combat. They claim that the racial differences between white and black in the United States offer no essential barrier to the races living together on terms of mutual respect and helpfulness. They deny, on the one hand, that the large amalgamation of the races already accomplished has produced degenerates, in spite of the unhappy character of these unions; on the other hand, they deny any desire to lose the identity of either race through intermarriage. They claim that it should be possible for a civilised black man to be treated as an American citizen without harm to the republic, and that the modern world must learn to treat coloured races as equals if it expects to advance.

They claim that the Negro race in America has more than vindicated its ability to assimilate modern culture. Negro blood has furnished thousands of soldiers to defend the flag in every war in which the United States has been engaged. They are a most important part of the economic strength of the nation, and they have furnished a number of men of ability in politics, literature, and art, as, for instance, Banneker, the mathematician; Phillis

Wheatley, the poet; Lemuel Haynes, the theologian; Ira Aldridge, the actor; Frederick Douglass, the orator; H. O. Tanner, the artist; B. T. Washington, the educator; Granville Woods, the inventor; Kelly Miller, the writer; Rosamond Johnson and Will Cook, the musical composers; Dunbar, the poet; and Chestnut, the novelist. Many other Americans, whose Negro blood has not been openly acknowledged, have reached high distinction. The Negroes claim, therefore, that a discrimination which was originally based on certain social conditions is rapidly becoming a persecution based simply on race prejudice, and that no republic built on caste can survive.

At the meeting of two such diametrically opposed arguments it was natural that councils of compromise should appear, and it was also natural that a nation, whose economic triumphs have been so noticeable as those of the United States, should seek an economic solution to the race question. More and more in the last twenty years the business men's solution of the race problem has been the development of the resources of the South. Coincident with the rise of this policy came the prominence of Mr. B. T. Washington. Mr. Washington was convinced that race prejudice in America was so strong and the economic position of the freedmen's sons so weak that the Negro must give up or postpone his ambitions for full citizenship and bend all his energies to industrial efficiency and the accumulation of wealth. Mr. Washington's idea was that eventually when the dark man was thoroughly established in the industries and had accumulated wealth, he could demand further rights and privileges. This philosophy has become very popular in the United States, both among whites and blacks.

The white South hastened to welcome this philosophy. They thought it would take the Negro out of politics, tend to stop agitation, make the Negro a satisfied labourer, and eventually convince him that he could never be

recognised as the equal of the white man. The North began to give large sums for industrial training, and hoped in this way to get rid of a serious social problem.

From the beginning of this campaign, however, a large class of Negroes and many whites feared this programme. They not only regarded it as a programme which was a dangerous compromise, but they insisted that to stop fighting the essential wrong of race prejudice just at the time, was to encourage it.

This was precisely what happened. Mr. Washington's programme was announced at the Atlanta Exposition in 1896. Since that time four States have disfranchised Negroes, dozens of cities and towns have separated the races on street cars, 1,250 Negroes have been publicly lynched without trial, and serious race riots have taken place in nearly every Southern State and several Northern States, Negro public school education has suffered a set back, and many private schools have been forced to retrench severely or to close. On the whole, race prejudice has, during the last fifteen years, enormously increased.

This has been coincident with the rapid and substantial advance of Negroes in wealth, education, and morality, and the two movements of race prejudice and Negro advance have led to an anomalous and unfortunate situation. Some, white and black, seek to minimise and ignore the flaming prejudice in the land, and emphasise many acts of friendliness on the part of the white South, and the advance of the Negro. Others, on the other hand, point out that silence and sweet temper are not going to settle this dangerous social problem, and that manly protest and the publication of the whole truth is alone adequate to arouse the nation to its great danger.

Moreover, many careful thinkers insist that, under the circumstances, the "business men's" solution of the race problem is bound to make trouble: if the Negroes become good cheap labourers, warranted not to strike or complain, they will arouse all the latent prejudice of the white working men whose wages they bring down. If, on the other hand, they are to be really educated as men, and not as "hands," then they need, as a race, not only industrial training, but also a supply of well-educated, intellectual leaders and professional men for a group so largely deprived of contact with the cultural leaders of the whites. Moreover, the best thought of the nation is slowly recognising the fact that to try to educate a working man, and not to educate the man, is impossible. If the United States wants intelligent Negro labourers, it must be prepared to treat them as intelligent men.

This counter movement of intelligent men, white and black, against the purely economic solution of the race problem, has been opposed by powerful influences both North and South. The South represents it as malicious sectionalism, and the North misunderstands it as personal dislike and envy of Mr. Washington. Political pressure has been brought to bear, and this insured a body of coloured political leaders who do not agitate for Negro rights. At the same time, a chain of Negro newspapers were established to advocate the dominant philosophy.

Despite this well-intentioned effort to keep down the agitation of the Negro question and mollify the coloured people, the problem has increased in gravity. The result is the present widespread unrest and dissatisfaction. Honest Americans know that present conditions are wrong and cannot last; but they face, on the one hand, the seemingly implacable prejudice of the South, and, on the other hand, the undoubted rise of the Negro challenging that prejudice. The attempt to reconcile these two forces is becoming increasingly futile, and the nation simply faces the question: Are we willing to do justice to a dark race despite our prejudices? Radical suggestions of wholesale segregation or deportation of the race have now and then been suggested; but the cost in

time, effort, money, and economic disturbance is too staggering to allow serious consideration. The South, with all its race prejudice, would rather fight than lose its great black labouring force, and in every walk of life throughout the nation the Negro is slowly forcing his way. There are some signs that the prejudice in the South is not immovable, and now and then voices of protest and signs of liberal thought appear there. Whether at last the Negro will gain full recognition as a man, or be utterly crushed by prejudice and superior numbers, is the present Negro problem of America.

4. "Bleeding Ireland"

Published in 1921 in *The Crisis*

No people can more exactly interpret the inmost meaning of the present situation in Ireland than the American Negro. The scheme is simple. You knock a man down and then have him arrested for assault. You kill a man and then hang the corpse for murder. We black folk are only too familiar with this procedure. In a given city, a mob attacks us unprepared, unsuspecting, and kills innocent and harmless black workingmen in cold blood. The bewildered Negroes rush together and begin to defend themselves. Immediately by swift legerdemain the mob becomes the militia or a gang of "deputy sheriffs". They search, harry and kill the Negroes. They disarm them and loot their homes, and when the city awakes after the "race riot", the jail is filled with Negroes charged with rioting and fomenting crime!

So in Ireland! The Irish resist, as they have resisted for hundreds of years, various and exasperating forms of English oppression. Their resistance is called crime and under ordinary conditions would be crime; in retaliation not only the "guilty" but the innocent among them are murdered and robbed and public property is burned by English guardians of the Peace!

All this must bring mingled feelings of dismay to Irishmen. No people in the world have in the past gone with blither spirit to "kill niggers" from Kingston to Delhi and from Kumassi to Fiji. In the United States, Irish influence not only stood behind the mob in Cincinnati, Philadelphia and New York, but still stands in the American Federation of Labor to keep out Negro workingmen. All this contains no word of argument against the ultimate freedom of Ireland—which God speedily grant!—but it does make us remember how in this world it is the Oppressed who have continually been used to cow and kill the Oppressed in the interest of the Universal Oppressor.

5. *"The Shape of Fear"*

Published in 1926 in
North American Review

Faced by the fact of the Ku Klux Klan, the United States has tried to get rid of it by laughing it off. We have talked of masquerading "in sheets and pillow cases"; we have caricatured the Klan upon the stage; we have exposed its silly methods, the dishonesty of some of its leaders, and the like. But we have not succeeded in scaring it away by ridicule. It is there. . . .

In the East, New England and New Jersey, the Klan has been mobilized; and need one mention the South?

What is the cause of all this? There can be little doubt but that the Klan in its present form is a legacy of the World War. Whatever there was of it before that great catastrophe was negligible and of little moment. The wages of War is Hate; and the End, and indeed the

Beginning, of Hate is Fear. The civilized world today and the world half-civilized and uncivilized are desperately afraid. The Shape of Fear looms over them. Germany fears the Jew, England fears the Indian; America fears the Negro, the Christian fears the Moslem, Europe fears Asia, Protestant fears Catholic, Religion fears Science. Above all, Wealth fears Democracy. These fears and others are ancient or at least long-standing fears. But they are renewed and revivified today because the world has at present a severe case of nerves; it feels it necessary to be nervous because the Unexpected has happened. . . .

The . . . method of Force which hides itself in secrecy. . . is the method of the Ku Klux Klan. It is a method as old as humanity. The kind of thing which men are afraid or ashamed to do openly and by day, they accomplish secretly, masked and at night. The method has certain advantages. It uses Fear to cast out Fear; it dares things at which open methods hesitate; it may with a certain impunity attack the high and the low; it need hesitate at no outrage of maiming or murder; it shields itself in the mob mind and then throws over all a veil of darkness which becomes glamor. It attracts people who otherwise could not be reached. It harnesses the mob.

How is it that men who want certain things done by brute force can so often depend upon the mob? Total depravity, human hate and *shadenfreude*, do not explain fully the mob spirit in this land. Before the wide eyes of the mob is ever the Shape of Fear. Back of the writhing, yelling, cruel-eyed demons who break, destroy, maim and lynch and burn at the stake is a knot, large or small, of normal human beings and these human beings at heart are desperately afraid of something. Of what? of many things but usually of losing their jobs, of being declassed, degraded or actually disgraced; of losing their hopes, their savings, their plans for their children; of the actual pangs of hunger; of dirt, of crime. And of all this, most ubiquitous in modern industrial society is that fear of unemployment.

It is this nucleus of ordinary men that continually gives the mob its initial and awful impetus. Around this nucleus, to be sure, gather snowball-wise all manner of flotsam, filth and human garbage and every inhibition of alcohol and current fashion. But all this is the horrible covering of this inner nucleus of Fear.

How then is the mob to be met and quelled? If it represents public opinion, even passing, passionate public opinion, it cannot permanently be put down by the police which public opinion appoints and pays. Three methods of quelling the mob are at hand, analogous to the three attitudes noted above: the first, by proving to its human, honest nucleus that the Fear is false, ill-grounded, unnecessary; or secondly, if its Fear is true or apparently or partially true, by attacking the fearful thing openly either by the organized police power or by frank civil war as did Mussolini and George Washington; or thirdly, by secret, hidden and underground ways, the method of the Ku Klux Klan.

Why do we not take the first way? Because this is a world that believes in War and Ignorance and has no hope in our day of realizing an intelligent majority of men and Peace on Earth. There are many, many exceptions but in general it is true that there is scarcely a Bishop in Christiandom, a priest in New York, a President, Governor, mayor or legislator in the United States, a college professor or public school teacher who does not in the end stand by War and Ignorance as the main method for the settlement of our pressing human problems. And this despite the fact that they may deny it with their mouths every day.

But here again open civil war like Italy's is difficult, costly and hard to guide. The Right toward which it aims must be made obvious even if it is Wrong. In 1918 in order to win the war we *had* to make Germans into Huns and rapists. Today we *have* to make Negroes into rapists and idiots. Tomorrow we *must* make

Latins, South-Eastern Europeans, Turks and other Asiatics into actual "lesser breeds without the law". Some seem to see today anti-Christ in Catholicism, and in Jews, international plotters of the Protocol. Even if these things be true it is difficult to bring the truth clearly before the ignorant mob and guide it toward the overthrow of evil. But if these be half true or wholly false, the mob can only be stirred by wholesale lying, and this is costly; or by secret underground whispering, the methods of night and mask, the psychology of vague and unknown ill, the innuendo that cannot be answered.

Now there are two things that stand out in this explanation of the mob and the Klan. First, the double tongues of our leaders in religion and social uplift; and secondly, this fear of losing jobs. Dayton, Tennessee brought the first vividly to our minds. We heard of a sudden, people talking a religious *patois* which educated folk had well nigh forgotten: Biblical Truth; the Plan of Salvation; the Blood of Christ. And suddenly we began to see what results widespread ignorance of modern science not only had brought but could bring under the leadership of the demagogue. It sent a thrill of amazement through us.

But whom had we to blame? Manifestly, not the farmers and shopkeepers of Tennessee, but those intellectual leaders of the United States who have been willing to subscribe to a religious dogma that they did not honestly believe and yet which they were willing that the mass of people should think they were believing. Was there any surer way of destroying the ability of the Man of the Street to think straight and argue logically? And to stop even his endeavor to think, comes the Fundamentalist; and his answer to Science is Dogma; and his reason for bringing it forward is again, not perverse hatred of the Truth, but the Shape of Fear. The religionist of today sees the sanctions of moral conduct being swept and battered away, laughed at and caricatured.

How shall he meet this wicked thing? He can do it by intelligence and argument and persuasion or he can do it by dogma which is spiritual mob-violence; today he is choosing the mob.

Or again; why is it that in a rich country like the United States, in many respects the richest and most prosperous organization of men in the world, we continually have mobs fighting and doing unutterable things because at bottom men are afraid of being unable to earn a respectable living? The answer is that our postwar prosperity is built more on gambling than on honest productive industry. Gambling was the result of war, born in war time and coming from the sudden demand for technique machinery and goods, which paid those who happened to hold them enormous marginal rents. The chance to the gambler, the promoter and the manipulator of industry has come during the reconstruction since the war, in the monopoly of land and homes, in the manipulation of industrial power, in the use of new inventions and discoveries, in the reorganization of corporate ownership.

We have today in the United States, cheek by jowl, Prosperity and Depression. Depression among those who are selling their services, raising raw material and manufacturing goods; prosperity among those who are manipulating prices, monopolizing land and mortgaging ability and output.

How shall we meet this situation? Again we revert to the three paths: first and foremost by the spread of wider and deeper understanding among the masses of men of the modern industrial process and the method of distributing income, so that intelligently we may attack Production and Distribution and re-make industrial society. Or, a second method, by hue and cry and propaganda to stop all criticism and desire for change by dubbing every reformer "Bolshevik" and by frightening the wage earner with loss of the very foundation of his wage. And this is the kind of attack that

again easily sinks to the whispering courses underground and attempts to save modern industry through mobs engineered by the secret Ku Klux Klan.

I can no better illustrate my meaning than by an actual case. The world has forgotten Mer Rouge—the Red Sea of Louisiana where a few years ago a terrible series of murders was laid at the doors of the Ku Klux Klan. It was so horrible a tale that we hastened to forget it before we really understood it. But it deserved thought and intelligent comprehension.

The cotton and sugar soil of the Mississippi and Red River valleys form a junction in Louisiana. It is a section bounded on the south by the scene of Uncle Tom's Cabin, on the north by the Helena riots, and on the east by that bit of hell which is sometimes called the Mississippi Delta. In the center of this district, in northeastern Louisiana, is Morehouse Parish and in the midst of Morehouse Parish is Mer Rouge. Mer Rouge has the peculiar problems of a little town in the Black Belt. It is ruled by the whites, and since the whites must stand united as rulers there is among them a rather extreme sense of social equality which even wealth and education cannot wholly break down. They go to the same churches and there their social life centers. They send their children to the same schools except the few that go away to boarding school. All this works out fairly well as long as the character of the ruling class of whites is essentially homologous. But today a change is taking place in Morehouse Parish. There are about 20,000 inhabitants there. The white population has increased from five to six thousand in the last ten years while the Negro population has decreased from fourteen to thirteen thousand. This is because of the migration of Negro laborers to the city and north; so that instead of being a county three-fourths black it is today about two-thirds black. To replace these migrating Negroes the poor whites from the neighborhood have been pressing in. They stream in especially from one poor county directly toward the east where there is a majority of poor whites and these new comers bring problems, problems of unrest, of drink, of gambling, of wayward women.

Now Mer Rouge has traditions of the time when its white folk were great landowners protecting their women in elaborate homes and having a pretentious social code. These newer and poorer whites coming in not only brought a lower moral tone but a new economic condition. They have become tenant farmers, so that between 1900 and 1920 there was an increase of nearly one-third in the number of tenants. But the great landowners are still in the ascendancy, two hundred and fifty of them with farms of one hundred to more than a thousand acres, with crops valued at two and one half million dollars a year, chiefly cotton, corn and sugar cane. In addition to this the value of the land is rapidly increasing. It has doubled every ten years since 1900. Then too, to complicate the situation further there are a number of small Negro farmers who own their own land, some two hundred and thirty-one in all as compared with the two hundred and fifty large white landowners and one hundred and nineteen small white owners. One can easily scent here tremendous and bitter rivalry between the rich and poor white owners, between the owners and tenants, between the white and black owners, and crushed under all of it lie the mass of black tenants. These tenants are ignorant, forty per cent. of them acknowledge that they cannot read or write, and in truth this number should probably be sixty or seventy per cent. There is no modern wage system, but nearly all is barter and debt peonage. The county reported only one hundred dollars a year in wages for each worker, and this included the white workers as well as the colored.

Here then we have the setting. Here is the little town of Mer Rouge, which proposes to stop the growing lawlessness among the whites and the breaking down of social conventions. Shall it openly appeal to the ballot? Certainly not. There are 6,524 Negroes of voting age and only 3,000 whites; but of course there is no question in Mer Rouge of the black man's voting. A thousand or more Negroes are landowners able to read and write, but they cannot vote. The white women, too, are disfranchised despite the law, so that the voting population consists of about 1,500 white men, and among these the new white tenants, shopkeepers, artisans and small landowners, or in other words the lawless and easy-going new comers, could outvote the whole aristocracy.

Mer Rouge, therefore, turned to the Ku Klux Klan, and when afterward the matter came out it defended itself and claimed with undoubted truth that the Ku Klux Klan was an organization of the best elements in the community and that they were trying to put down the worst, believing that they could do by secrecy and force what they could not do openly at the polls. It was natural for them to come to this conclusion. Secrecy, force and murder have been part of the Black Belt social economy for fifty years. The landlords lived with their hands on the trigger. Formerly this was because of the fear of servile revolt or the hint of it. That fear is still there; but in addition to that there is another fear and these men did not hesitate. They were used to taking the law in their hands. They face baffling social problems. A white face is no longer a badge of aristocracy. A white woman may be rival to a black concubine. Formerly the relations of white men and colored women were open and complacent. The sheriff's son recently was killed in a colored woman's cabin. Then too the sex distribution is illuminating: More colored women than colored men and eleven per cent. more white men than white women. To this are added the bootleggers and the loose white women. There is no place, no treatment for them. Colored women, however decent, can always be treated like prostitutes; but unless white prostitutes are treated like ladies the whole scheme of white supremacy fails.

All this led logically, as Mer Rouge thought, to one solution: bootleggers, gamblers and bad women were to be driven out by the Ku Klux Klan. But they miscalculated. The new whites fought back. They were not scared by hoods and nightgowns. The result was appalling. Kidnapping, whipping, murder almost whole-sale, torture that would shame the Middle Ages, an atmosphere of terror, hatred and feud that attracted the attention of the world. And in the midst of it all the black, driven cattle who form sixty-eight per cent. of the popula-tion were dumb.

Here were white men afraid of degradation; here were white men afraid of hunger; here were black men afraid of hunger and black men afraid of death. And here were secret mid-night oath and murder seeking to right it all.

Such were the elements that make for secret mob law: economic rivalry, race hatred, class hatred, sex rivalry, religious dogmatism and before all the Shape of Fear. For years and centuries this method of organized secrecy, sworn to unlimited and ruthless action, has been used to accomplish certain things. Strong arguments have been brought to defend it and it may be admitted that one can easily see cir-cumstances when the only way to make the survival of certain ideas and ideals certain, would be to force them through by secrecy and stealth.

But are we ready to say that this is the case in the first half of the twentieth century? Can we for a moment admit this? Is not the very thought a monstrous attack upon all that civilization and religion have accomplished?

What is there after all, of truth back of what the Klan attacks? And perhaps first, what does the Klan attack? I will not stop to argue this. I simply quote from their own blank application for membership seven of their twenty questions: "7.—Were your parents born in the United States of America?" "8.—Are you a Gentile or Jew?" "9.—Are you of the white race or of a colored race?" "13.—Do you believe in White Supremacy?" "15.—What is your religious faith?" "17.—Of what religious faith are your parents?" "20.—Do you owe ANY KIND of allegiance to any foreign nation, government, institution, sect, people, ruler or person?"

Here then is clearly the groundwork for opposition to the foreign-born, the Jew, the colored races and the Catholic Church. I am not the one to defend Catholic or Jew. The Catholic Church and modern European civi-lization are largely synonymous and to attack the one is to accuse the other. For the alleged followers of Jesus Christ and worshipers of the Old Testament to revile Hebrew culture is too impudent for words. But in this crazy combi-nation of hates fathered by the Ku Klux Klan (and so illogical that in any intelligent country it would be laughed out of court), is included the American Negro. What is the indictment against him? He was a slave. He is ignorant. He is poor. He has the stigmata of poverty and ignorance—that is crime. He laughs and sings and dances. He is black. He isn't all black. The very statement of such a bill of indictment is like accusing ashes of fire. The real arraign-ment of the Negro is the fear that white America with its present machinery is not going to be able to keep black folk down. They are achieving equality with startling swiftness. Neither caricature nor contempt, rape of women or insult of children, murder or burning at the stake, have succeeded in daunt-ing this extraordinary group.

Against it open reasoning and argument has been employed but it has failed to convince even those who employed it. This was followed by propaganda; and the propaganda of empha-sizing "race", "racial" characteristics, "racial" inferiority, is a propaganda which according to all modern scientific dicta is unreliable and untrue. Yet these terms flourish and these things are taught in school and college; they appear in books and lectures and they are used because of what men want them to accomplish, namely, the continual fear and hate of black folk instead of that natural rebound of sympathy and admiration which their work in a half century deserves.

But as I have said, even this propaganda has not been successful. What next then? Next comes the Ku Klux Klan. Next comes the leadership of mob and perpetration of outrage by forces, secret, hidden and underground. And the danger and shame are not in the movement itself, so much as in the wide tolerance and sympathy which its methods evoke among educated and decent Americans. These people see in the Ku Klux Klan a way of doing and saying that which they themselves are ashamed to do and say. Go into any western town from Pittsburgh to Kansas City: "The Klan? Silly— *but!*—You see these Catholics, rich, powerful, silent, organized. Got all the foreigners corraled—I don't *know*. And Jews—the Jews own the country. They are trying to rule the world. They are too smart, pushing, impudent. And *niggers!* And that isn't all. Dagoes, Japs; and then *Russia!* I tell you we gotta *do* something. The Klan?—silly, of course— *but—*."

Thus the Ku Klux Klan is doing a job which the American people, or certainly a considerable portion of them, want done; and they want it done because as a nation they have fear of the Jew, the immigrant, the Negro. They realize that the American of English descent is not holding his own physically or spiritually in this country; that America survives and flourishes because of the alien immigrant with his strong arm, his simple life, his faith and hope, his song, his art, his religion. They realize that no group in the United States is working harder to push themselves forward and upward than the Negroes; and over all this rises the Shape of Fear.

The worst aspect of all this is that when we resort to the underground method it involves a conscious surrender of Truth. It must base itself upon lies. One of the greatest difficulties in estimating the power and spread of the Ku Klux Klan is that its members are evidently sworn to lie. They are ordered to deny their membership in the Klan; they are ordered to deny their participation in certain of its deeds; they are ordered above all to keep at least partially secret its real objects and desires. Now the lie has often been used to advance human culture, but it is an extremely dangerous weapon, and surely we have lived beyond the need of it today.

Consequently the greatest thing that we have to fear in any such underground movement as the Ku Klux Klan, a thing that makes it much more fearful than anything that has been alleged of Bolshevism or Fascism, is the danger and ease of its being used for exactly the opposite of the things for which it is established or which the thoughts or ideals which its leaders profess. If it is possible to establish a widespread underground movement against Jews, Negroes and Catholics, why isn't it just as easy to establish similar movements against millionaires, machinery and foreign commerce, or against "Anglo-Saxons", Protestants and Germans, or against any set of people or set of ideas which any particular group of people dislike, hate or fear? It may be said that at present it is possible to mobilize larger numbers of people in a common hatred against the Hebrew race, the black race, and the Catholic Church than against any similar things; but this is not necessarily true and it certainly is not true in all places and will not be true at all times.

Without doubt, of all the dangerous weapons that civilized man has attempted to use in order to advance human culture the secret mass lie is the most dangerous and the most apt to prove a boomerang. This is the real thing that we are to fear in the Ku Klux Klan. We need not fear its logic. It has no logic. Whatever there is of truth in its hatred of three groups of Americans can be discussed openly and fearlessly by civilized men. If Negroes are ignorant underbidders of labor, unhealthy and lazy aspirants to undeserved equality there are plain and well-known social restraints and remedies. First, to improve the condition of Negroes so far as it is improvable; secondly, to teach them the reason behind the objections to their rise so far as there are reasons; and above all to examine thoroughly and honestly what the real questions at issue are. If the hierarchy of the Catholic Church is in any way threatening democracy in America there is a chance for perfectly open and honest investigation and conference between this young democracy and that old and honorable government of the spirit of men. If the Jew in self-defense against age-long persecution has closed his fist against the world there is more than a chance to clasp that human hand. In fine, unless we are willing to give up human civilization in order to preserve civilization we cannot for a moment contemplate turning to secret, underground methods as a cure for anything; and the appearance of such a movement is not a case where we stop to ask whether the movement in itself has at present laudable objects or not. It does not make any difference what the Ku Klux Klan is fighting for or against. Its method is wrong and dangerous and uncivilized, and those who oppose it, whether they be its victims like the Jews, Catholics and Negroes, or those who are lauded as its moral sponsors like the white Southerners, the American Legion and the "Anglo-Saxons", it is the duty of all these people to join together in solemn phalanx against the method which is an eternal menace to human culture.

6. "Segregation"

Published in 1924 in *The Crisis*

The thinking colored people of the United States must stop being stampeded by the word segregation. The opposition to racial segregation is not or should not be any distaste or unwillingness of colored people to work with each other, to co-operate with each other, to live with each other. The opposition to segregation is an opposition to discrimination. The experience in the United States has been that usually when there is racial segregation, there is also racial discrimination.

But the two things do not necessarily go together, and there should never be an opposition to segregation pure and simple unless that segregation does involve discrimination. Not only is there no objection to colored people living beside colored people if the surroundings and treatment involve no discrimination, if streets are well lighted, if there is water, sewerage and police protection, and if anybody of any color who wishes, can live in that neighborhood. The same way in schools, there is no objection to schools attended by colored pupils and taught by colored teachers. On the contrary, colored pupils can by our own contention be as fine human beings as any other sort of children, and we certainly know that there are no teachers better than trained colored teachers. But if the existence of such a school is made reason and cause for giving it worse housing, poorer facilities, poorer equipment and poorer teachers, then we do object, and the objection is not against the color of the pupils' or teachers' skins, but against the discrimination.

In the recent endeavor of the United States government to redistribute capital so that some of the disadvantaged groups may get a chance for development, the American Negro should voluntarily and insistently demand his share. Groups of communities and farms inhabited by colored folk should be voluntarily formed. In no case should there be any discrimination against white and blacks. But, at the same time, colored people should come forward, should organize and conduct enterprises, and their only insistence should be that the same provisions be made for the success of their enterprise that is being made for the success of any other enterprises. It must be remembered that in the last quarter of a century, the advance of the colored people has been mainly in the lines where they themselves working by and for themselves, have accomplished the greatest advance.

There is no doubt that numbers of white people, perhaps the majority of Americans, stand ready to take the most distinct advantage of voluntary segregation and cooperation among colored people. Just as soon as they get a group of black folk segregated, they use it as a point of attack and discrimination. Our counter attack should be, therefore, against this discrimination; against the refusal of the South to spend the same amount of money on the black child as on the white child for its education; against the inability of black groups to use public capital; against the monopoly of credit by white groups. But never in the world should our fight be against association with ourselves because by that very token we give up the whole argument that we are worth associating with.

Doubtless, and in the long run, the greatest human development is going to take place under experiences of widest individual contact. Nevertheless, today such individual contact is made difficult and almost impossible by petty prejudice, deliberate and almost criminal propaganda and various survivals from prehistoric heathenism. It is impossible, therefore, to wait for the millennium of free and normal intercourse before we unite, to cooperate among themselves in groups of like-minded people and in groups of people suffering from the same disadvantages and the same hatreds.

It is the class-conscious working man uniting together who will eventually emancipate labor throughout the world. It is the race-conscious black man cooperating together in his own institutions and movements who will eventually emancipate the colored race, and the great step ahead today is for the American Negro to accomplish his economic emancipation through voluntary determined cooperative effort.

7. *"Anti-Semitism"*

Published in 1940 in *Amsterdam News*

There is no question but that the wave of anti-Semitic prejudice and persecution which is sweeping the world is being shared and imitated by large numbers of American Negroes. It is no uncommon thing to hear intelligent Negroes assert with some evidence of satisfaction that they "do not like" Jews. There is perhaps no more discouraging evidence of our failure to grasp the fundamental truth of present civilization. The source of anti-Semitism for American Negroes is not far to seek. It is simply slavish imitation of the whites. It is the feeling that if we agree with powerful white groups in their prejudice and hatreds we shall in that way be brought closer to them and in wider sympathy. This cowardly and shortsighted attitude is then rationalized and strengthened by the knowledge which Negroes think they have of Jews. In truth the knowledge which one persecuted minority has of the other is seldom truth. They see each other through the eyes and hear of each other with the ears of the persecuting majority. What most Negroes know of Jews is simply what most Nordics say about them and they receive that at one hundred per cent of its alleged value never stopping to consider that other people's accepting that same sort of testimony with regard to Negroes explains a large part of anti-Negro hatred. Even the direct contacts between Jews and Negroes; between the proprietor of the corner store and the Negro laborer; between the Jewish capitalist and the Negro consumer; all that is distorted by ignorance concerning the pressure which is put upon Jews and the terrible history of their efforts at emancipation. We have got to realize that the forces in the world back of anti-Semitism are exactly the same facts that are back of color prejudice.

8. "My Evolving Program for Negro Freedom"

Published in 1944 in *What the Negro Wants*

Beyond all this, and when legal inequalities pass from the statute books, a rock wall of social discrimination between human beings will long persist in human intercourse. So far as such discrimination is a method of social selection, by means of which the worst is slowly weeded and the best protected and encouraged, such discrimination has justification. But the danger has always been and still persists, that what is weeded out is the Different and not the Dangerous; and what is preserved is the Powerful and not the Best. The only defense against this is the widest human contacts and acquaintanceships compatible with social safety.

So far as human friendship and intermingling are based on broad and catholic reasoning and ignore petty and inconsequential prejudices, the happier will be the individual and the richer the general social life. In this realm lies the real freedom, toward which the soul of man has always striven: the right to be different, to be individual and pursue personal aims and ideals. Here lies the real answer to the leveling compulsions and equalitarianisms of that democracy which first provides food, shelter and organized security for man.

Once the problem of subsistence is met and order is secured, there comes the great moment of civilization: the development of individual personality; the right of variation; the richness

of a culture that lies in differentiation. In the activities of such a world, men are not compelled to be white in order to be free: they can be black, yellow or red; they can mingle or stay separate. The free mind, the untrammelled taste can revel. In only a section and a small section of total life is discrimination inadmissible and that is where my freedom stops yours or your taste hurts me. Gradually such a free world will learn that not in exclusiveness and isolation lie inspiration and joy, but that the very variety is the reservoir of invaluable experience and emotion. This crowning of equalitarian democracy in artistic freedom of difference is the real next step of culture.

The hope of civilization lies not in exclusion, but in inclusion of all human elements; we find the richness of humanity not in the Social Register, but in the City Directory; not in great aristocracies, chosen people and superior races, but in the throngs of disinherited and underfed men. Not the lifting of the lowly, but the unchaining of the unawakened mighty, will reveal the possibilities of genius, gift and miracle, in mountainous treasure-trove, which hitherto civilization has scarcely touched; and yet boasted blatantly and even glorified in its poverty. In world-wide equality of human development is the answer to every meticulous taste and each rare personality.

9. "Bound by the Color Line"

Published in 1946 in *New Masses*

Many friends of American Negroes would say that we tend to emphasize our problem of race above that of the more basic problems of labor, poverty and ignorance. But to this we would reply that our problems are so fundamentally human that they often underlie the broader but more abstract social problems. Nothing illustrates this better than the history of America where development of work, income and education have had the greatest field for expansion the world has ever known; and yet continually have been hindered from the progress they might have made by problems of race and color which have been, and still form, the central thread of our history.

Despite desperate efforts to rewrite and distort this history, a few of us must recall that in 1776, when three million white Americans proclaimed the equality of all men, they were at that very moment holding five hundred thousand black folk in slavery and classifying them not even as animals but as real estate. Their prosperity had been built on two centuries of this slavery and the independence which they demanded was mainly freedom to pursue this exploitation of men in raw material and in trade.

When in the War for Independence these slaves threatened to revolt to the English, the American army not only used five thousand of them to win the war but welcomed volunteers from that Haiti which for a half century afterward they refused to recognize as a nation. The emancipation which was implicit in this use of the slave was thereupon begun in the United States, but it was halted in 1820 when the Cotton Kingdom, based on slave labor, together with plans for vaster empires centered in the Caribbean and South America, became backbone and vision of the American economy.

For the next half century the meaning of America was not the winning of the West, nor the development of democracy, as history insists, but a bitter fight as to whether American labor was to be slave or free. It flamed into bloody Civil War: a war caused by Negro slavery and in singular paradox stopped, as Abraham Lincoln himself testified, when two hundred thousand black soldiers reinforced the North and brought emancipation of both white labor and black to a nation that had never wanted it.

Thereupon the nation was faced by the logical contradiction that unless they used slaves as voters they could not control the former slaveholders or hold the United States in permanent union. Black votes and black labor, as well as white, reconstructed the union and attempted to reconstruct democracy, but northern capital and southern land monopoly bound southern labor to the chariot wheels of new free enterprise, which became powerful enough to disfranchise labor. This disfranchised labor was immediately thrown into two antagonistic competing groups by a legal caste of black folk reminiscent of the Middle Ages established by consent of the nation in the center of the twentieth century.

How in such a case could real democracy develop in this land? Remember that tonight in nine states of the Union a meeting like this would be illegal; and that in at least eight other states it would not be advisable because of the danger of mob law. Remember that today you cannot in the United States either attack this basic caste or carry out social reform by legal methods because in your way there stands a bloc of 134 electoral votes based on color caste, which makes a third-party movement impossible and prevents any clear-cut voting on education, economic security or health. It takes 126,000 of your votes to send a representative to Congress but it needs only 44,000 to send such a representative from the South. In Bilbo's Mississippi, 150,000 votes have the same power in the Senate as 6,000,000 votes in New York. These figures are so fantastic that most people do not know them and cannot believe them when they are stated. Yet it remains true that New York's 6,024,597 votes in 1944 elected the same number of Senators that Mississippi elected with 152,712. President Truman, backed by a majority of the voters of the nation, can implement no program of reform as long as the South, with political power based on disfranchisement and caste, can outcount the majority in the presidential election and in Congress.

Thus we Negroes insist that there can be no attack upon social problems by free democratic methods because we have neither freedom nor democracy. We have bound our own hands by the color line entrenched in the rotten boroughs of the South. By the same token the significance of America in the world is not freedom, democracy, education and economic security but rather alliance with colonial imperialism and class dictatorship in order to enforce the denial of freedom to the colored peoples of the world. Whatever may be the sentiment in this room and in this state or even in this section, we cannot tonight for a moment forget that there are millions of Americans of wealth, education and power who believe that the necessity of keeping black men from ever becoming free citizens is more important than the triumph of democracy in the world. Under such circumstances you cannot blame us if we stress, sometimes perhaps unduly, the importance of the Negro problem, not simply for ourselves but for you.

Chapter III

On International Relations

The wealthiest nations in the world today are predominantly European or of European lineage and are nations that benefited from colonial exploitation and/or slavery. The poorest nations today are predominantly African or Southeast Asian and are nations that suffered enormously under colonial occupation and/or forced enslavement. Colonialism and slavery were systems predicated upon severe racism, but they were also systems of international capitalism. The point here—a point emphasized by Du Bois for decades—is that the color line is not something limited to an early twentieth-century lunch counter in Mississippi; it runs across the globe and has been present for centuries.

Du Bois was one of the earliest social theorists to study the history and consequences of slavery as well as to passionately critique colonialism. Both of these endeavors were carried out by illustrating and emphasizing their international scope. From the West Indies to China, from Central America to Africa, from Europe to India, Du Bois was persistently global in his scholarship.

1. "The Hands of Ethiopia"

Published in 1920 in *Darkwater*

. . . Always Africa is giving us something new or some metempsychosis of a world-old thing. On its black bosom arose one of the earliest, if not the earliest, of self-protecting civilizations, which grew so mightily that it still furnishes superlatives to thinking and speaking men. Out of its darker and more remote forest fastnesses, came, if we may credit many recent scientists, the first welding of iron, and we know that agriculture and trade flourished there when Europe was a wilderness.

Nearly every human empire that has arisen in the world, material and spiritual, has found some of its greatest crises on this continent of Africa, from Greece to Great Britain. As Mommsen says: "It was through Africa that Christianity became the religion of the world." In Africa the last flood of Germanic invasions spent itself within hearing of the last gasp of Byzantium, and it was through Africa that Islam came to play its great rôle of conqueror and civilizer. . . .

The present problem of problems is nothing more than democracy beating itself helplessly against the color bar,—purling, seeping, seething, foaming to burst through, ever and again overwhelming the emerging masses of white men in its rolling backwaters and held back by those who dream of future kingdoms of greed built on black and brown and yellow slavery.

The indictment of Africa against Europe is grave. For four hundred years white Europe was the chief support of that trade in human beings which first and last robbed black Africa of a hundred million human beings, transformed the face of her social life, overthrew organized government, distorted ancient industry, and snuffed out the lights of cultural development. Today instead of removing laborers from Africa to distant slavery, industry built on a new slavery approaches Africa to deprive the natives of their land, to force them to toil, and to reap all the profit for the white world.

It is scarcely necessary to remind the reader of the essential facts underlying these broad assertions. A recent law of the Union of South Africa assigns nearly two hundred and fifty million acres of the best of natives' land to a million and a half whites and leaves thirty-six million acres of swamp and marsh for four and a half-million blacks. In Rhodesia over ninety million acres have been practically confiscated. In the Belgian Congo all the land was declared the property of the state.

Slavery in all but name has been the foundation of the cocoa industry in St. Thome and St. Principe and in the mines of the Rand. Gin has been one of the greatest of European imports, having increased fifty per cent. In ten years and reaching a total of at least twenty-five million dollars a year today. Negroes of ability have been carefully gotten rid of, deposed from authority, kept out of positions of influence, and discredited in their people's eyes, while a caste of white overseers and governing officials has appeared everywhere.

Naturally, the picture is not all lurid. David Livingstone has had his successors and Europe has given Africa something of value in the beginning of education and industry. Yet the balance of iniquity is desperately large; but worse than that, it has aroused no world protest. A great Englishman, familiar with African problems for a generation, says frankly today: "There does

not exist any real international conscience to which you can appeal."

Moreover, that treatment shows no certain signs of abatement. Today in England the Empire Resources Development Committee proposes to treat African colonies as "crown estates" and by intensive scientific exploitation of both land and labor to make these colonies pay the English national debt after the war! German thinkers, knowing the tremendous demand for raw material which would follow the war, had similar plans of exploitation. "It is the clear, common sense of the African situation," says H. G. Wells, "that while these precious regions of raw material remain divided up between a number of competitive European imperialisms, each resolutely set upon the exploitation of its 'possessions' to its own advantage and the disadvantage of the others, there can be no permanent peace in the world. It is impossible."

We, then, who fought the war against war; who in a hell of blood and suffering held hardly our souls in leash by the vision of a world organized for peace; who are looking for industrial democracy and for the organization of Europe so as to avoid incentives to war,—we, least of all, should be willing to leave the backward world as the greatest temptation, not only to wars based on international jealousies, but to the most horrible of wars,—which arise from the revolt of the maddened against those who hold them in common contempt.

Consider, my reader,—if you were today a man of some education and knowledge, but born a Japanese or a Chinaman, an East Indian or a Negro, what would you do and think? What would be in the present chaos your outlook and plan for the future? Manifestly, you would want freedom for your people,— freedom from insult, from segregation, from poverty, from physical slavery. If the attitude of the European and American worlds is in the future going to be based essentially upon the same policies as in the past, then there is but one thing for the trained man of darker blood to do and that is definitely and as openly as possible to organize his world for war against Europe. He may have to do it by secret, underground propaganda, as in Egypt and India and eventually in the United States; or by open increase of armament, as in Japan; or by desperate efforts at modernization, as in China; but he must do it. He represents the vast majority of mankind. To surrender would be far worse than physical death. There is no way out unless the white world opens the door. Either the white world gives up such insult as its modern use of the adjective "yellow" indicates, or its connotation of "chink" and "nigger" implies; either it gives up the plan of color serfdom which its use of the other adjective "white" implies, as indicating everything decent and every part of the world worth living in,—or trouble is written in the stars!

It is, therefore, of singular importance after disquieting delay to see the real Pacifist appear. Both England and Germany have recently been basing their claims to parts of black Africa on the wishes and interests of the black inhabitants. Lloyd George has declared "the general principle of national self-determination application at least to German Africa," while Chancellor Hertling once welcomed a discussion "on the reconstruction of the world's colonial possessions."

The demand that an Africa for Africans shall replace the present barbarous scramble for exploitation by individual states comes from singularly different sources. Colored America demands that "the conquered German colonies should not be returned to Germany, neither should they be held by the Allies. Here is the opportunity for the establishment of a nation that may never recur. Thousands of colored men, sick of white arrogance and hypocrisy, see in this their race's only salvation."

Sir Harry H. Johnston recently said: "If we are to talk, as we do, sentimentally but justly about restoring the nationhood of Poland, about giving satisfaction to the separatist feeling in Ireland, and about what is to be done for European nations who are oppressed, then we can hardly exclude from this feeling the countries of Africa."

Laborers, black laborers, on the Canal Zone write: "Out of this chaos may be the great awakening of our race. There is cause for rejoicing. If we fail to embrace this opportunity now, we fail to see how we will be ever able to solve the race question. It is for the British Negro, the French Negro, and the American Negro to rise to the occasion and start a national campaign, jointly and collectively, with this aim in view."

From British West Africa comes the bitter complaint "that the West Africans should have the right or opportunity to settle their future for themselves is a thing which hardly enters the mind of the European politician. That the Balkan States should be admitted to the Council of Peace and decide the government under which they are to live is taken as a matter of course because they are Europeans, but no extra-European is credited, even by the extremest advocates of human equality, with any right except to humbly accept the fate which Europe shall decide for him."

Here, then, is the danger and the demand; and the real Pacifist will seek to organize, not simply the masses in white nations, guarding against exploitation and profiteering, but will remember that no permanent relief can come but by including in this organization the lowest and the most exploited races in the world. World philanthropy, like national philanthropy, must come as uplift and prevention and not merely as alleviation and religious conversion. Reverence for humanity, as such, must be installed in the world, and Africa should be the talisman.

Black Africa, including British, French, Belgian, Portuguese, Italian, and Spanish possessions and the independent states of Abyssinia and Liberia and leaving out of account Egypt and North Africa, on the one hand, and South Africa, on the other, has an area of 8,200,000 square miles on a population well over one hundred millions of black men, with less than one hundred thousand whites.

Commercial exploitation in Africa has already larger results to show than most people realize. Annually $200,000,000 worth of goods was coming out of black Africa before the World War, including a third of the world's supply of rubber, a quarter of all of the world's cocoa, and practically all of the world's cloves, gum-arabic, and palm-oil. In exchange there was being returned to Africa one hundred millions in cotton cloth, twenty-five millions in iron and steel, and as much in foods, and probably twenty-five millions in liquors.

Here are the beginnings of a modern industrial system: iron and steel for permanent investment, bound to yield large dividends, cloth as the cheapest exchange for invaluable raw material; liquor to tickle the appetites of the natives and render the alienation of land and the break-down of customary law easier; eventually forced and contract labor under white drivers to increase and systematize the production of raw materials. These materials are capable of indefinite expansion: cotton may yet challenge the southern United States, fruits and vegetables, hides and skins, lumber and dye-stuffs, coffee and tea, grain and tobacco, and fibers of all sorts can easily follow organized and systematic toil.

Is it a paradise of industry we thus contemplate? It is much more likely to be a hell. Under present plans there will be no voice or law or custom to protect labor, no trades unions, no eight-hour laws, no factory legislation,—nothing of that great body of legislation built up in modern days to protect mankind from sinking to the level of beasts of burden. All the industrial deviltry, which civilization has been driving to the slums and the backwaters, will have a voiceless continent to conceal it. If

the slave cannot be taken from Africa, slavery can be taken to Africa.

Who are the folk who live here? They are brown and black, curly and crisp-haired, short and tall, and longheaded. Out of them in days without date flowed the beginnings of Egypt; among them rose, later, centers of culture at Ghana, Melle, and Timbuktu. Kingdoms and empires flourished in Songhay and Zymbabwe, and art and industry in Yoruba and Benin. They have fought every human calamity in its most hideous form and yet today they hold some similar vestiges of a mighty past,—their work in iron, their weaving and carving, their music and singing, their tribal government, their town-meeting and marketplace, their desperate valor in war.

Missionaries and commerce have left some good with all their evil. In black Africa today there are more than a thousand government schools and some thirty thousand mission schools, with a more or less regular attendance of three-quarters of a million school children. In a few cases training of a higher order is given chiefs' sons and selected pupils. These beginnings of education are not much for so vast a land and there is no general standard or set plan of development, but, after all, the children of Africa are beginning to learn.

In black Africa today only one-seventeenth of the land and a ninth of the people in Liberia and Abyssinia are approximately independent, although menaced and policed by European capitalism. Half the land and the people are in domains under Portugal, France, and Belgium, held with the avowed idea of exploitation for the benefit of Europe under a system of caste and color serfdom. Out of this dangerous nadir of development stretch two paths: one is indicated by the condition of about three per cent of the people who in Sierra Leone, the Gold Coast, and French Senegal, are tending toward the path of modern development; the other path, followed by a fourth of the land and people, has local self-government and native customs and might evolve, if undisturbed, a native culture along their own peculiar lines. A tenth of the land, sparsely settled, is being monopolized and held for whites to make an African Australia. To these later folk must be added the four and one-half millions of the South African Union, who by every modern device are being forced into landless serfdom.

Before the World War tendencies were strongly toward the destruction of independent Africa, the industrial slavery of the mass of the blacks and the encouragement of white immigration, where possible, to hold the blacks in subjection.

Against this idea let us set the conception of a new African World State, a Black Africa, applying to these peoples the splendid pronouncements which have of late been so broadly and perhaps carelessly given the world: recognizing in Africa the declaration of the American Federation of Labor, that "no people must be forced under sovereignty under which it does not wish to live"; recognizing in President Wilson's message to the Russians, the "principle of the undictated development of all peoples"; recognizing the resolution of the recent conference of the Aborigines Protection Society of England, "that in any reconstruction of Africa, which may result from this war, the interests of the native inhabitants and also their wishes, in so far as those wishes can be clearly ascertained, should be recognized as among the principal factors upon which the decision of their destiny should be based." In other words, recognizing for the first time in the history of the modern world that black men are human.

It may not be possible to build this state at once. With the victory of the Entente Allies, the German colonies, with their million of square miles and one-half million black inhabitants, should form such a nucleus. It would give Black Africa its physical beginnings. Beginning with the German colonies two other sets of colonies could be added, for obvious reasons.

Neither Portugal nor Belgium has shown any particular capacity for governing colonial peoples. Valid excuses may in both cases be advanced, but it would certainly be fair to Belgium to have her start her great task of reorganization after the World War with neither the burden nor the temptation of colonies; and in the same way Portugal has, in reality, the alternative of either giving up her colonies to an African State or to some other European State in the near future. These two sets of colonies would add 1,700,000 square miles and eighteen million inhabitants. It would not, however, be fair to despoil Germany, Belgium, and Portugal of their colonies unless, as Count Hertling once demanded, the whole question of colonies be opened.

How far shall the modern world recognize nations which are not nations, but combinations of a dominant caste and a suppressed horde of serfs? Will it not be possible to rebuild a world with compact nations, empires of self-governing elements, and colonies of backward peoples under benevolent international control?

The great test would be easy. Does England propose to erect in India and Nigeria nations brown and black which shall be eventually independent, self-governing entities, with a full voice in the British Imperial Government? If not, let these states either have independence at once or, if unfitted for that, be put under international tutelage and guardianship. It is possible that France, with her great heart, may welcome a Black France,—an enlarged Senegal in Africa; but it would seem that eventually all Africa south of twenty degrees north latitude and north of the Union of South Africa should be included in a new African State. Somaliland and Eritrea should be given to Abyssinia, and then with Liberia we would start with two small, independent African states and one large state under international control.

Does this sound like an impossible dream? No one could be blamed for so regarding it before 1914. I, myself, would have agreed with them. But since the nightmare of 1914–1918, since we have seen the impossible happen and the unspeakable become so common as to cease to stir us; in a day when Russia has dethroned her Czar, England has granted the suffrage to women and is in the act of giving Home Rule to Ireland; when Germany has adopted parliamentary government; when Jerusalem has been delivered from the Turks; and the United States has taken control of its railroads,—is it really so far-fetched to think of an Africa for the Africans, guided by organized civilization?

No one would expect this new state to be independent and self-governing from the start. Contrary, however, to present schemes for Africa the world would expect independence and self-government as the only possible end of the experiment. At first we can conceive of no better way of governing this state than through that same international control by which we hope to govern the world for peace. A curious and instructive parallel has been drawn by Simeon Strunsky: "Just as the common ownership of the northwest territory helped to weld the colonies into the United States, so could not joint and benevolent domination of Africa and of other backward parts of the world be a cornerstone upon which the future federation of the world could be built?"

...The real effort to modernize Africa should be through schools rather than churches. Within ten years, twenty million black children ought to be in school. Within a generation young Africa should know the essential outlines of modern culture and groups of bright African students could be going to the world's great universities. From the beginning the actual general government should use both colored and white officials and later natives should be worked in. Taxation and industry could follow the newer ideals of industrial democracy, avoiding private land monopoly and poverty, and promoting co-operation in production and the socialization of income. Difficulties as to capital and revenue would be far less than many imagine. If a capable English administrator of British Nigeria could with $1,500 build up a cocoa industry of twenty million dollars annually, what might not be done in all Africa, without gin, thieves, and hypocrisy?

Capital could not only be accumulated in Africa, but attracted from the white world, with one great difference from present usage: no return so fabulous would be offered that civilized lands would be tempted to divert to colonial trade and invest materials and labor needed by the masses at home, but rather would receive the same modest profits as legitimate home industry offers.

There is no sense in asserting that the ideal of an African State, thus governed and directed toward independence and self-government, is impossible of realization. The first great essential is that the civilized world believe in its possibility. By reason of a crime (perhaps the greatest crime in human history) the modern world has been systematically taught to despise colored peoples. Men of education and decency ask, and ask seriously, if it is really possible to uplift Africa. Are Negroes human, or, if human, developed far enough to absorb, even under benevolent tutelage, any appreciable part of modern culture? Has not the experiment been tried in Haiti and Liberia, and failed?

One cannot ignore the extraordinary fact that a world campaign beginning with the slave-trade and ending with the refusal to capitalize the word "Negro," leading through a passionate defense of slavery by attributing every bestiality to blacks and finally culminating in the evident modern profit which lies in degrading blacks,—all this has unconsciously trained millions of honest, modern men into the belief that black folk are sub-human. This belief is not based on science, else it would be held as a postulate of the most tentative kind, ready at any time to be withdrawn in the face of facts; the belief is not based on history, for it is absolutely contradicted by Egyptian, Greek, Roman, Byzantine, and Arabian experience; nor is the belief based on any careful survey of the social development of men of Negro blood to-day in Africa and America. It is simply passionate, deep-seated heritage, and as such can be moved by neither argument nor fact. Only faith in humanity will lead the world to rise above its present color prejudice.

Those who do believe in men, who know what black men have done in human history, who have taken pains to follow even superficially the story of the rise of the Negro in Africa, the West Indies, and the Americas of our day know that our modern contempt of Negroes rests upon no scientific foundation worth a moment's attention. It is nothing more than a vicious habit of mind. It could as easily be over-thrown as our belief in war, as our international hatreds, as our old conception of the status of women, as our fear of educating the masses, and as our belief in the necessity of poverty. We can, if we will, inaugurate on the Dark Continent a last great crusade for humanity. . . .

2. Colonies

Published in 1936
in the *Pittsburgh Courier*

The theory of colonial imperialism succeeded the African slave trade. The slave trade transported labor to rich land to raise raw material. The raw material was manufactured to the great profit of the leading commercial nations of the world. This trade and labor was so manipulated that the slaves themselves did not actually land in any but the areas where slavery was established. The goods to buy them, on the other hand, went out from Boston and Liverpool; and the raw materials which they

raised went to New York and London. The slaves went to South America, the West Indies, and the Southern United States. But both the cruelty and the cost of this procedure aroused on the one hand the philanthropy of men like Wilberforce, and on the other, the attention of statesmen like Palmerston.

Very gradually during the nineteenth century a new policy came into being. Under this policy, colonies were no longer regarded as places where white men settled and lived, but rather as areas where colored men lived under the domination of white men; and that domination was not primarily political, but economic. Instead of transporting labor, capital was transported. The raw material was raised not in new foreign lands, but in these old areas. This material was transported to the manufacturing and commercial countries and there transmuted into gold.

The result was a double saving: First, in human sentiment and sympathy. There was no open and bloody slave trade. The serfs could be whipped and cowed and murdered at home; and secondly, the cost of transporting labor was saved and there was only the cost of transporting the raw material. Thus empire which had been political rule, became empire which was investment, and the philanthropic plan of carrying civilization to the natives became one and the same as the commercial plan of making native labor pay.

Elaborate propaganda showed the perfect fitness of this arrangement. Lazy and inferior races were made thrifty workers, increasing their own well-being and the income of the whites; and if the increase of well-being among the natives was not always clear and certain, what would you? Was it not better to die working for imperial industry than die sleeping in the shade? To understand the present enterprise of Italy, one must remember that this colonial theory of dominance of the colored races is the thing in the minds of Italians today.

The first breakdown of the theory of colonial enterprise came in the revelations of astonishing and terrible oppression and degradation under colonial rule. One remembers the indictment against the Belgian Congo.

3. " The Trade in Men"

Published in 1939 in *Black Folk: Then and Now*

The new thing in the Renaissance was not simply freedom of spirit and body, but a new freedom to destroy freedom; freedom for eager merchants to exploit labor; freedom for white men to make black slaves. The ancient world knew slaves and knew them well; but they were slaves who worked in private and personal service, or in public service like the building of pyramids and making of roads. When such slaves made goods, the goods made them free because men knew the worker and the value of his work and treated him accordingly. But when, in the later fifteenth century, there came slaves, and mainly black slaves, they performed an indirect service. That service became for the most part not personal but labor which made crops, and crops which sold widely in unknown places and in the end promised vaster personal services than previous laborers could directly give.

This then was not mere labor but capitalized labor; labor transmitted to goods and back to services; and the slaves were not laborers of the older sort but a kind of capital goods; and capital, whether in labor or in goods, in men or in crops, was impersonal, inhuman, and a dumb means to mighty ends.

Immediately black slaves became not men but things; and were valued as things are valued, by the demand and supply of their labor force as represented by their bodies. They belonged, it happened, to a race apart, unknown, unfamiliar, because the available supply of people of that race was for the moment cheaper; because religious feuds and political conquest in Africa

rendered masses of men homeless and defenseless, while state-building in feudal Europe conserved and protected the peasants. Hence arose a doctrine of race based really on economic gain but frantically rationalized in every possible direction. The ancient world knew no races; only families, clans, nations; and degrees and contrasts of culture. The medieval world evolved an ideal of personal worth and freedom for wide groups of men and a dawning belief in humanity as such. Suddenly comes America; the sale of men as goods in Africa; the crops these goodsmen grew; the revolution in industry and commerce, in manufacture and transport; in trade and transformation of goods for magnificent service and power. "The Commercial Revolution of the sixteenth century through the opening of new trade routes to India and America, the development of world markets, and the increased output of silver from the German, Austrian and Mexican mines, made possible the productive use of capital which had heretofore been employed chiefly in military operations, and which resulted in its rapid increase. Great companies flourished and a new class of wealthy merchants arose to vie in luxury not only with the great landed proprietors but even with princes and kings. Many parallels are to be found between this and the Industrial Revolution three centuries later."

It was not a mere case of parallelism but of cause and effect: the African slave trade of the sixteenth and seventeenth centuries gave birth to the Industrial Revolution of the eighteenth and nineteenth. The cry for the freedom of man's spirit became a shriek for freedom in trade and profit. The rise and expansion of the liberal spirit were arrested and diverted by the theory of race, so that black men became black devils or imbeciles to be consumed like cotton and sugar and tobacco, so as to make whiter and nobler men happier.

There are two reasons why the history of Africa is peculiar. Color of skin is not one that was regarded as important before the eighteenth century. "I am black but comely, O ye daughters of Jerusalem," cries the old Hebrew love song. Cultural backwardness was no reason—Africa, as compared with Europe, Asia, and America, was not backward before the seventeenth century. It was different, because its problems were different. At times Africa was in advance of the world. But *climate:* hot sun and flooding rains made Africa a land of desert, jungle, and disease, where culture could indeed start even earlier than in ice-bound Europe, but where, unaided by recent discoveries of science, its survival and advance was a hard fight. And finally, and above all, beginning with the fifteenth century and culminating in the eighteenth and nineteenth, *mankind in Africa became goods*— became merchandise, became even real estate. Men were bought and sold for private profit and on that profit Europe, by the use of every device of modern science and technique, began to dominate the world.

How did Africans become goods? Why did they submit? Why did the white world fight and scheme and steal to own them? Negroes were physically no weaker than others, if as weak; they were no more submissive. Slavery as an institution is as old as humanity; but never before the Renaissance was the wealth and well-being of so many powerful and intelligent men made squarely dependent not on labor itself but on the buying of labor power. And never before nor since have so many million workers been so helpless before the mass might and concentrated power of greed, helped on by that Industrial Revolution which black slavery began in the sixteenth century and helped to culmination in the nineteenth.

A new and masterful control of the forces of nature evoked a Frankenstein, which Christianity could not guide. But the Renaissance also gave birth to an idea of individual freedom in Europe and emphasized the Christian ideal of the worth of the common man. The new industry, therefore, which was as eager to buy and sell white labor as black, was canalized off toward the slavery of blacks, because the beginnings of the democratic ideal acted so as to protect the white workers. To dam this philanthropy and keep it from flooding into black slavery, the theory of the innate and eternal inferiority of black folk was invented and diffused. It was not until the nineteenth century that the floods of human sympathy began to burst through this artificial protection of slavery and in the abolition movement start to free the black worker.

Fortunately, as Gobineau rationalized this subjection of men, Marx saw the virus of labor exploitation, of labor regarded and treated as goods, poisoning Europe. He saw the social revolution; revolution in ideas which traffic in labor force for power and personal enjoyment brought; and he saw this becoming the object of that very industrial revolution to which black slavery gave birth. Freedom then became freedom to enslave all working classes and soon the emancipation of the new wage slaves, arising out of the hell of the Industrial Revolution, was hindered by chattel slavery and then men began dimly to see slavery as it really was.

Then chattel slavery of black folk fell, but immediately and in its very falling it was rebuilt on African soil, in the image and pattern of European wage slavery of the eighteenth and nineteenth centuries, which at the time was yielding before a new labor movement. The abolitionists, however, did not realize where the real difference between white and black workers had entered. Initially the goods which the white workers made had made them free; because they began to get their share; but the goods which black slaves made did not make them free. It long kept them slaves with a minimum share, because these workers were isolated in far and wild America. The eaters and wearers and smokers of their crops, even the owners of their crops and bodies, did not see them working or know their misery or realize the injustice of their economic situation. They were workers isolated from the consumer and consumers bargained only with those who owned the fruit of their stolen toil, often fine, honest, educated men.

Those then who in the dying nineteenth century and dawning twentieth saw the gleam of the new freedom were too busy to realize how land monopoly and wage slavery and forced labor in present Africa were threatening Europe of the twentieth century, re-establishing the worst aspects of the factory system and dehumanizing capital in the world, at the time when the system was diligently attacked in cultured lands. They did not see that here was the cause of that new blossoming of world wars which instead of being wars of personal enmity, of dynastic ambition, or of national defense, became wars for income and income on so vast a scale that its realization meant the enslavement of the majority of men. They therefore did not finish the task, and today in the twentieth century, as the white worker struggles toward a democratization of industry, there is the same damming and curtailment of human sympathy to keep the movement from touching workers of the darker races. On their exploitation is being built a new fascist capitalism. Hence the significance of that slave trade which we now study.

Greece and Rome had their chief supplies of slaves from Europe and Asia. Egypt enslaved races of all colors, and if there were more blacks than others among her slaves, there were also more blacks among her nobles and Pharaohs, and both facts are explained by her racial origin and geographical position. The fall of Rome led to a cessation of the slave trade, but after a long interval came the white slave trade of the Saracens and Moors, and finally the modern trade in Negroes.

Slavery as it exists universally among primitive people is a system whereby captives in war are put to tasks about the homes and in the fields, thus releasing the warriors for systematic fighting and the women for leisure. Such slavery has been common among all people and was widespread in Africa. The relative number of African slaves under these conditions varied according to tribe and locality, but usually the labor was not hard; and slaves were recognized members of the family and might and did often rise to high position in the tribe.

Remembering that in the fifteenth century there was no great disparity between the civilization of Negroland and that of Europe, what made the striking difference in subsequent development? European civilization, cut off by physical barriers from further incursions of barbaric races, settled more and more to systematic industry and to the domination of one religion; African culture and industry were not only threatened by powerful African barbarians from the west and central regions of the continent, but also by invading Arabs with a new religion precipitating from the eleventh to the sixteenth centuries a devastating duel of cultures and faiths.

When, therefore, a demand for workmen arose in America, European exportation was limited by unity of religious ties and economic stability. African exportation was encouraged not simply by the Christian attitude toward heathen, but also by the Moslem enmity toward the unconverted. Two great modern religions, therefore, agreed at least in the policy of enslaving heathen blacks; while the conquest of Egypt, the overthrow of the black Askias by the Moors at Tondibi, brought economic chaos among the advanced Negro peoples. Finally the duel between Islam and Fetish left West Africa naked to the slave-trader.

The modern slave trade began with the Mohammedan conquests in Africa, when heathen Negroes were seized to supply the harems, and as soldiers and servants. They were bought from the masters and seized in war, until the growing wealth and luxury of the conquerors demanded larger numbers. Then Negroes from the Egyptian Sudan, Abyssinia, and Zanzibar began to pass into Arabia, Persia, and India in increased numbers. As Negro kingdoms and tribes rose to power they found the slave trade lucrative and natural, since the raids in which slaves were captured were ordinary inter-tribal wars. It was not until the eighteenth and nineteenth centuries that the demand for slaves made slaves the object, and not the incident, of African wars.

There was, however, between the Mohammedan and American slave trade one fundamental difference which has not heretofore been stressed. The demand for slaves in Mohammedan countries was to a large extent a luxury demand. Black slaves were imported as soldiers and servants or as porters of gold and ivory rather than industrial workers. The demand, therefore, was limited by the wealth of a leisure class or the ambitions of conquest and not by the prospect of gain on the part of a commercial class. Even where the idle rich did not support slavery in Africa, other conditions favored its continuance, as Cooley points out, when he speaks of the desert as a cause of the African slave trade.

"It is impossible to deny the advancement of civilization in that zone of the African continent which has formed the field of our inquiry. Yet barbarism is there supported by natural circumstances with which it is vain to think of coping. It may be doubted whether, if mankind had inhabited the earth only in populous and adjoining communities, slavery would have ever existed. The Desert, if it be not absolutely the root of the evil, has, at least, been from the earliest times the great nursery of slave hunters. The demoralization of the towns on the southern borders of the desert has been pointed out, and if the vast extent be considered of the region in which man has no riches but slaves, no enjoyment but slaves, no article of trade but slaves, and where the hearts of wandering thousands are closed against pity by the falling misery of life, it will be difficult to resist the conviction that the solid buttress on which slavery rests in Africa, is—The Desert."

In Mohammedan countries there were gleams of hope in slavery. In fiction and in truth the black slave had a chance. Once converted to Islam, he became a brother to the best, and the brotherhood of the faith was not the sort of idle lie that Christian slave masters made it. In Arabia black leaders arose like Antar; in India black slaves carved out principalities where their descendants still rule.

Some Negro slaves were brought to Europe by the Spaniards in the fourteenth century, and a small trade was continued by the Portuguese, who conquered territory from the "tawny" Moors of North Africa in the early fifteenth century. Later, after their severe repulse at Al Kasr Al Kebir, the Portuguese swept farther down the West Coast in quest of trade with Negroland, a new route to India and the realm of Prester John. As early as 1441, they reached the River of Gold, and their story is that their leader seized certain free Moors and the next year exchanged them for ten black slaves, a target of hide, ostrich eggs, and some gold dust. The trade was easily justified on the ground that the Moors were Mohammedans and refused to be converted to Christianity, while heathen Negroes would be better subjects for conversion and stronger laborers.

In the next few years a small number of Negroes continued to be imported into Spain and Portugal as servants. We find, for instance, in 1474, that Negro slaves were common in Seville. There is a letter from Ferdinand and Isabella in the year 1474 to a celebrated Negro, Juan de Valladolid, commonly called the "Negro Count" (El Conde Negro), nominating him to the office of "mayoral of the Negroes" in Seville. The slaves were apparently treated kindly, allowed to keep their own dances and festivals, and to have their own chief, who represented them in the courts, as against their own masters, and settled their private quarrels.

In Portugal, "the decline of the population, in general, and the labor supply, in particular, was especially felt in the southern provinces, which were largely stripped of population. This resulted in the establishment there of a new industrial system. The rural lands were converted into extensive estates held by absentee landlords, and worked by large armies of black bondmen recently brought from Africa. Soon the population of Algarve was almost completely Negro; and by the middle of the Sixteenth century, blacks outnumbered whites in Lisbon itself. As intermarriage between the two races went on from the beginning, within a few generations Ethiopian blood was generally diffused throughout the nation, but it was notably pronounced in the south and among the lower classes."

Between 1455 and 1492 little mention is made of slaves in the trade with Africa. Columbus is said to have suggested Negroes for America, but Ferdinand and Isabella refused. Nevertheless, by 1501, we have the first incidental mention of Negroes going to America in a declaration that Negro slaves "born in the power of Christians were to be allowed to pass to the Indies, and the officers of the royal revenue were to receive the money to be paid for their permits."

About 1504 Ovando, Governor of Spanish America, was objecting to Negro slaves and "solicited that no Negro slaves should be sent to Hispaniola, for they fled amongst the Indians and taught them bad customs, and never could be captured." Nevertheless a letter from the king to Ovando, dated Segovia, in September, 1505, says, "I will send more Negro slaves as you request; I think there may be a hundred. At each time a trustworthy person will go with them who may have some share in the gold they may collect and may promise them ease if they work well." There is a record of a hundred slaves being sent out this very year, and Diego Columbus was notified of fifty to be sent from Seville for the mines in 1510.

After this time frequent notices show that Negroes were common in the New World. When Pizarro, for instance, had been slain in Peru, his body was dragged to the cathedral by two Negroes. After the battle of Anaquito, the head of the viceroy was cut off by a Negro; and during the great earthquake in Guatemala a most remarkable figure was a gigantic Negro seen in various parts of the city. Núñez had thirty Negroes with him on the top of the Sierras, and there was rumor of an aboriginal tribe of Negroes in South America. One of the last acts of King Ferdinand was to urge that no more Negroes be sent to the West Indies, but, under Charles V, Bishop Las Casas drew up a plan of assisted migration to America and asked in 1517 the right for immigrants to import twelve Negro slaves each, in return for which the Indians were to be freed.

Las Casas, writing in his old age, owns his error: "This advice that license should be given to bring Negro slaves to these lands, the Clerigo Casas first gave, not considering the injustice with which the Portuguese take them and make them slaves; which advice, after he had apprehended the nature of the thing, he would not have given for all he had in the world. For he always held that they had been made slaves unjustly and tyrannically; for the same reason holds good of them as of the Indians."

As soon as the plan was broached, a Savoyard, Lorens de Gomenot, Governor of Bresa, obtained a monopoly of this proposed trade and shrewdly sold it to the Genoese for twenty-five thousand ducats. Other monopolies were granted in 1523, 1527, and 1528. Thus the American trade became established and gradually grew, passing successively into the hands of the Portuguese, the Dutch, the French, and the English.

At first the slave trade was of the same kind and volume as that already passing northward over the desert routes. Soon, however, the American trade developed. A strong, unchecked demand for brute labor in the West Indies and on the continent of America grew, until it culminated in the eighteenth century, when Negro slaves were crossing the Atlantic at the rate of fifty to one hundred thousand a year. This called for slave raiding on a scale that drew slaves from most parts of Africa, although centering on the West Coast, from the Senegal to St. Paul de Loanda. The Mohammedan trade continued along the East Coast and the Nile Valley.

Carleton Beals says: "This vast labor army, conscripted for developing the Americas, represented a force of many millions of man power. It was taken from all parts of Africa; from Angola and from the deep Congo, from Bonny River and the central Niger and Hausaland, from Lagos, Dahomey, Old Calabar; from Madagascar and Ethiopia and Gabun. The Portuguese, Spanish, Flemish, Dutch, English, French recruiting agents with their platoons of soldiers reached far above Stanley Pool to the Mozambique, clear south of Kunene River. Portuguese Guinea and the Gold Coast poured forth their contingents. Not only the Yoruba, Egba, Jebu, Sokoto, the Mandingo, but the Hottentots and Bushmen gave up forced levies.

"Mohammedan Negro settlements are found in Brazil, the Guianas and elsewhere. Some of them still speak and use Arabic."

Herskovits believes: "From contemporary documentary evidence that the region from which the slaves brought to the New World were derived, has limits that are less vast than stereotyped belief would have them. . . . That some, perhaps in the aggregate, even impressive numbers of slaves, came from the deep interior, or from East or South Africa, does not make less valid the historical evidence that by far the major portion of the slaves brought to the New World came from a region that comprises only a fraction of the vast bulk of the African continent."

There was thus begun in modern days a new slavery and slave trade. It was different from that of the past, because more and more

it came in time to be founded on racial caste, and this caste was made the foundation of a new industrial system. For four hundred years, from 1450 to 1850, European civilization carried on a systematic trade in human beings of such tremendous proportions that the physical, economic, and moral effects are still plainly to be remarked throughout the world. To this must be added the large slave trade of Mussulman lands, which began with the seventh century and raged almost unchecked until the end of the nineteenth century.

These were not days of decadence, but a period that gave the world Shakespeare, Martin Luther, Raphael, Haroun-al-Raschid and Abraham Lincoln. It was the day of the greatest expansion of two of the world's most pretentious religious, and of the beginnings of modern organization of industry. In the midst of this advance and uplift, this slave trade and slavery spread more human misery, inculcated more disrespect for and neglect of humanity, a greater callousness to suffering, and more petty, cruel, human hatred than can well be calculated. We may excuse and palliate it, and write history so as to let men forget it; it remains a most inexcusable and despicable blot on modern history.

The Portuguese built the first slave-trading fort at Elmina, on the Gold Coast, in 1482, and extended their trade down the West Coast and up the East Coast. Under them the abominable traffic grew larger and larger, until it became far the most important in money value of all the commerce of the Zambesi basin. There could be no extension of agriculture, no mining, no progress of any kind where it was so extensively carried on.

It was the Dutch, however, who launched the overseas slave trade as a regular institution. They began their fight for freedom from Spain in 1579; in 1595, as a war measure against Spain, which at that time was dominating Portugal, they made their fight for slaves in their first vogage to Guinea. By 1621 they had captured Portugal's various slave forts on the West Coast and they proceeded to open sixteen forts along the coast of the Gulf of Guinea. Ships sailed from Holland to Africa, got slaves in exchange for their goods, carried the slaves to the West Indies or Brazil, and returned home laden with New World produce. In 1621 the private companies trading in the west were all merged into the Dutch West India Company, which sent in four years fifteen thousand four hundred and thirty Negroes to Brazil, carried on war with Spain, supplied even the English plantations, and gradually became the great slave carrier of the day.

The commercial supremacy of the Dutch early excited the envy and emulation of the English. The Navigation Ordinance of 1651 was aimed at them, and two wars were necessary to wrest the slave trade from the Dutch and place it in the hands of the English. The final terms of peace, among other things, surrendered New Netherlands to England and opened the way for England to become henceforth the world's greatest slave trader.

The English trade began with Sir John Hawkins' voyages in 1562 and later, in which "the Jesus, our chiefe shippe," played a leading part. Desultory trade was kept up by the English until the middle of the seventeenth century, when English chartered slave-trading companies began to appear. In 1662 the "Royal Adventurers," including the king, the queen dowager, and the Duke of York, invested in the trade, and finally the Royal African Company, which became the world's chief slave trader, was formed in 1672 and carried on a growing trade for a quarter of a century. Jamaica had finally been captured and held by Oliver Cromwell in 1655 and formed the West Indian base for the trade in men.

The chief contract for trade in Negroes was the celebrated "Asiento" or agreement of the King of Spain to the importation of slaves into Spanish domains. The Pope's Bull of Demarcation, 1493, debarred Spain from African possessions, and compelled her to contract with other nations for slaves. This contract was in the hands of the Portuguese in 1600; in 1640 the Dutch received it, and in 1701, the French. The War of the Spanish Succession was motivated not so much by royal rivalries as to bring this slave trade monopoly to England.

This Asiento of 1713 was an agreement between England and Spain by which the latter granted the former a monopoly of the Spanish colonial slave trade for thirty years; and England engaged to supply the colonies within that time with at least one hundred and forty-four thousand slaves at the rate of forty-eight hundred per year. The English counted this prize as the greatest result of the Treaty of Utrecht (1713), which ended the mighty struggle against the power of Louis XIV. The English held the monopoly for thirty-five years until the Treaty of Aix-la-Chapelle, although they had to go to war over it in 1739.

It has been shown by a recent study made at Howard University that the development of England as a great capitalist power was based directly and mainly upon the slave trade. English industry and commerce underwent a vast expansion in the early seventeenth century, based on the shipment of English goods to Africa, of African slaves to the West Indies, and of West Indian products back to England. About 1700 Bristol became an important center of the slave trade, followed by London and Liverpool. Liverpool soon overtook both Bristol and London. In 1709 it sent out one slaver of thirty tons burden; encouraged by Parliamentary subsidies which amounted to nearly a half million dollars between 1729 and 1750, the trade increased to fifty-three ships in 1751; eighty-six in 1765, and at the beginning of the nineteenth century, one hundred and eighty-five, which carried forty-nine thousand two hundred and thirteen slaves in one year. In 1764 a quarter of the shipping of Liverpool was in the African trade and Liverpool merchants conducted one half of England's trade with Africa. The value of all English goods sent to Africa was 464,000 pounds sterling of which three-fourths was of English manufactures.

This growth of Liverpool indicated the evolution of the capitalist economy in England. Liverpool did not grow because it was near the Lancaster manufacturing district, but, on the contrary, Lancaster manufacturers grew because they were near the Liverpool slave trade and largely invested in it. Thus Liverpool made Manchester.

Karl Marx emphasized the importance of slavery as the foundation of the capitalist order. He said, "Slavery is an economic category just as any other. Direct slavery is the pivot of bourgeois industry, just as are machinery and credit, etc. Without slavery there is no cotton; without cotton, there is no modern industry. It is slavery that has given value to universal commerce, and it is world trade which is the condition of large scale industry. Thus, slavery is an economic category of the first importance."

The tremendous economic stake of Great Britain in the African and West Indian trade is shown by these figures, after Bryan Edwards: from 1701 to 1787 British ships took to Africa goods to the value of twenty-three million pounds sterling. Of these, fourteen million pounds sterling were of British manufacture. Slaves, gold and other products were purchased with these goods. The slaves were transported to the West Indies. From the West Indies in the century from 1698 to 1798 Great Britain imported goods to the value of over two hundred million pounds.

The basis of the English trade, on which capitalism was erected, was Negro labor. This labor was cheap and was treated as capital goods and not as human beings. The purchase of slaves furnished a large market for British manufacture, especially textiles. African gold became the medium of exchange which rising capitalism and the profits of African trade demanded. The large fortunes which were turned to industrial investment, and especially to the African trade, stimulated industries like ship building, which helped make England mistress of the seas. The West Indies too as a seat of slavery furnished an outlet for British manufacture and a source of raw materials. From this again large fortunes arose which were transferred to the mother country and invested.

All this spelled revolution: world-wide revolution starting in Europe; sinister and fatal revolution in West Africa. The city-state represented by Yoruban civilization had fought with the empire builders of the Sudan and retreated toward the Gulf of Guinea. Here they came in contact with the new western slave trade. It stimulated trade and industry; but the trade was not only in gold and oil and ivory, it was in men; and those nations that could furnish slaves were encouraged and prospered. The ruder culture of Ashanti and Dahomey outstripped Yoruba. Benin was changed. Blood lust was encouraged and the human culture which the slave trade helped build up for Europe, tore down and debauched West Africa.

The culture of Yoruba, Benin, Mossiland and Nupe had exhausted itself in a desperate attempt to stem the on-coming flood of Sudanese expansion. It had succeeded in maintaining its small, loosely federated city-states suited to trade, industry, and art. It had developed strong resistance toward the Sudan state builders toward the north, as in the case of the fighting Mossi; but behind this warlike resistance lay the peaceful city life which gave industrial ideas to Byzantium and shared something of Ethiopian and Mediterranean culture.

The first advent of the slave traders increased and encouraged native industry, as is evidenced by the bronze work of Benin; but soon this was pushed into the background, for it was not bronze metal but bronze flesh that

Europe wanted. A new state-building tyranny, ingenious, well organized but cruel, and built on war, forced itself forward in the Niger Delta. The powerful state of Dahomey arose early in the eighteenth century. Ashanti, a similar kingdom, began its conquests in 1719 and grew with the slave trade because the profits of the trade and the insatiable demands of the Europeans disrupted and changed the older native economy.

Thus state building in West Africa began to replace the city economy; but it was a state built on war and on war supported and encouraged largely for the sake of trade in human flesh. The native industries were changed and disorganized. Family ties and government were weakened. Far into the heart of Africa this devilish disintegration, coupled with Christian rum and Mohammedan raiding, penetrated.

Few detailed studies have been made of the Mohammedan slave trade. Slave raiding was known in the Nile Valley from the time of the Egyptians and with the advent of Islam it continued, but it was incidental to conquest and proselytism. Later, however, it began to be commercialized; it was systematically organized with raiders, factories, markets, and contractors. By the nineteenth century African slaves were regularly supplied to Egypt, Turkey, Arabia, and Persia; and also to Morocco there came from the Western Sudan and Timbuktu about four thousand annually.

Egyptians in the nineteenth century tried to stop this slave trade, but they encountered vested interests making large profits. The trade continued to exist as late as 1890. The English charge that under the Madhi in the Egyptian Sudan, slavery and slave raiding were widespread; but this was the result of the very misrule and chaos which caused the Madhist movement and for which it was not responsible. Doubtless many of the Madhist followers were enslaved and robbed under cover of religious frenzy; but the Madhi could not in the midst of war curb an evil which forced recognition even from Chinese Gordon. From the East African coast and especially the lake districts a stream of slaves went to the coast cities, whence they were sent to Madagascar, Arabia and Persia. In 1862, nineteen thousand slaves a year were passing from the regions about Lake Nysasa to Zanzibar. Minor trade in slaves took place in and about Abyssinia and Somaliland. Turkey began to check the slave traffic between 1860 and 1890. In Morocco it continued longer.

The face of Africa was turned south and west toward these slave traders instead of northward toward the Mediterranean, where for two thousand years and more Europe and Africa had met in legitimate trade and mutual respect. The full significance of the battle at Tondibi, which overthrew the Askias, was now clear. Hereafter Africa for centuries was to appear before the world, not as the land of gold and ivory, of Gongo Mussa and Meroe, but as a bound and captive slave, dumb and degraded.

The natural desire to avoid a painful subject has led historians to gloss over the details of the slave trade and leave the impression that it was a local African West Coast phenomenon and confined to a few years. It was, on the contrary, continent wide and centuries long; an economic, social, and political catastrophe probably unparalleled in human history.

Usually the slave trade has been thought of from its sentimental and moral point of view; but it is its economic significance that is of greatest moment. Whenever the human element in industry is degraded, society must suffer accordingly. In the case of the African slave trade the human element reached its nadir of degradation. Great and significant as was the contribution of black labor to the seventeenth, eighteenth, and nineteenth centuries, its compensation approached zero, falling distinctly and designedly below the cost of human reproduction; and yet on this system was built the wealth and power of modern civilization. One can conceive no more dangerous foundation; because even when the worst aspects were changed and the slave trade limited and the slave given certain legal rights of freedom, nevertheless the possibilities of low wages for the sake of high profits remained an ideal in industry, which made the African slave trade the father of industrial imperialism, and of the persistence of poverty in the richest lands.

As Marx declared: "Under the influence of the colonial system, commerce and navigation ripened like hot-house fruit. Chartered companies were powerful instruments in promoting the concentration of capital. The colonies provided a market for the rising manufactures, and the monopoly of this market intensified accumulation. The treasures obtained outside Europe by direct looting, enslavement, and murder, flowed to the motherland in streams, and were there turned into capital."

The exact proportions of the slave trade can be estimated only approximately. From 1680 to 1688 we know that the English African Company alone sent two hundred forty-nine ships to Africa, shipped there sixty thousand, seven hundred eighty-three Negro slaves, and after losing fourteen thousand, three hundred eighty-seven on the middle passage, delivered forty-six thousand, three hundred ninety-six in America.

It seems probable that 25,000 Negroes a year arrived in America between 1698 and 1707. After the Asiento of 1713 this number rose to 30,000 annually, and before the Revolutionary War it had reached at least 40,000 and perhaps 100,000 slaves a year.

The total number of slaves imported is not known. Dunbar estimates that nearly 900,000 came to America in the sixteenth century, 2,750,000 in the seventeenth, 7,000,000 in the eighteenth, and over 4,000,000 in the nineteenth, perhaps 15,000,000 in all. Certainly it seems that at least 10,000,000 Negroes were expatriated. The Mohammedan slave trade meant the expatriation or forcible migration in Africa of millions more. (Many other millions were left dead in the wake of the raiders.) It would be conservative, then, to say that the slave trade cost Negro Africa from a fourth to a third of its population. And yet people ask today the cause of the stagnation of culture in that land since 1600! Such a large number of slaves could be supplied only by organized slave raiding. The African continent gradually became revolutionized. Whole regions were depopulated, whole tribes disappeared; the character of people developed excesses of cruelty instead of the flourishing arts of peace. The dark, irresistible grasp of fetish took firmer hold on men's minds. Advances toward higher civilization became more difficult. It was a rape of a continent to an extent seldom if ever paralleled in ancient or modern times.

In the American trade, there were not only the horrors of the slave raid, which lined the winding paths of the African jungles with bleached bones, but there were also the horrors of what was called the "middle passage," that is the voyage across the Atlantic. As Sir William Dolben said, "The Negroes were chained to each other hand and foot, and stowed so close that they were not allowed above a foot and a half for each in breadth. Thus crammed together like herrings in a barrel, they contracted putrid and fatal disorders; so that they who came to inspect them in a morning had occasionally to pick dead slaves out of their rows, and to unchain their carcases from the bodies of their wretched fellow-sufferers to whom they had been fastened."

It was estimated that out of every one hundred lot shipped from Africa only about fifty lived to be effective laborers across the sea; and among the whites more seamen died in that trade in one year than in the whole remaining trade of England in two. The full realization of the horrors of the slave trade was slow in reaching the ears and conscience of the modern world, just as today the treatment of natives in European colonies is brought to publicity with the greatest difficulty. The first move against the slave trade in England came in Parliament in 1776, but it was not until thirty-one years later, in 1807, that the trade was banned through the arduous labors of Clarkson, Wilberforce, Sharpe, and others.

Denmark had already abolished the trade, and the United States attempted to do so the following year. Portugal and Spain were induced to abolish the trade between 1815 and 1830. Not withstanding these laws, the contraband trade went on until the beginning of the Civil War in America. The reasons for this were the enormous profit of the trade and the continued demand of the American slave barons, who had no sympathy with the efforts to stop their source of cheap labor supply.

However, philanthropy was not working alone to overthrow Negro slavery and the slave trade. It was seen, first in England and later in other countries, that slavery as an industrial system could not be made to work satisfactorily in modern times. Its cost tended to become too great, as the sources of supply of slaves dried up, on the other hand, the slave insurrections from the very beginning threatened the system, as modern labor strikes have threatened capitalism, from the time when the slaves rose on the plantation of Diego Columbus down to the Civil War in America. Actual and potential slave insurrections in the West Indies, in North and South America, kept the slave owners in apprehension and turmoil, or called for a police system difficult to maintain.

The red revolt of Haiti struck the knell of the slave trade. In North America revolt finally took the form of organized running away to the North. All this with the growing scarcity of suitable land led to the abolition of the slave trade, the American Civil War and the disappearance of the American slave system. Further effort stopped the Mohammedan slave raider, but slowly because its philanthropic objects were clouded and hindered by the new Colonial Imperialism of Christian lands, which sought not wholly to abolish slavery but rather to reestablish it under new names, with a restricted slave trade.

Such is the story of the Rape of Ethiopia— a sordid, pitiful, cruel tale. Raphael painted, Luther preached, Corneille wrote, and Milton sang; and through it all, for four hundred years, the dark captives wound to the sea amid the bleaching bones of the dead; for four hundred years the sharks followed the scurrying ships; for four hundred years America was strewn with the living and dying millions of a transplanted race; for four hundred years Ethiopia stretched forth her hands unto God.

4. "Mexico and Us"

Published in 1940 in *The Amsterdam News*

It came quite suddenly at my dinner table: "I hope Mexico gets a good revolution and stops picking on us." I gasped. Mexico "picking" and on "Us!" My God, we stole Mexico's land and made it into Texas, Arizona, New Mexico and California, in order to make more territory for stealing and working Negro slaves. We stole her soil, paying her traitors like Diaz at the rate of less than a cent an acre. We filched her oil and minerals at an enormous profit, and when the stricken peons struggled up from their mud and pain and said: "This land is ours and for us!" we sent our troops and our liars to threaten and browbeat the new Mexico. When the bluff failed and Mexico started to reclaim her soil and her heritage from predatory English and Americans; started to educate her peons and give them land; started to compel capital to pay a living wage—then with unparalleled impudence, we demanded pay and immediate pay for "our losses" We ought to be made to disgorge some of the millions we highjacked from Mexico in the last hundred years.

But, insisted my dinner table neighbor, "Mexicans do not like Negroes; you would have difficulty getting a visa even for a visit." Mexicans do not want in their country, any more penniless, ignorant workers than they already have. And all that Mexico hears of Negroes comes from the same source which furnishes us news of them; namely, the average American news agencies. Indeed, consider this: all disadvantaged minority peoples, know each other and each other's problems, not by direct contact, but by indirect and systematic misinformation from those who hate and despite both.

5. "The Future of Europe in Africa"

Given as a speech in 1942 at Yale University

Two great world movements in modern times have had to do with the relation of Africa to the rest of the world; the first was the African slave trade which established capitalism in England and the Sugar Empire and the Cotton Kingdom in America. The second was the partitioning of Africa which was foreshadowed in the Congress of Berlin in 1878 and planned in detail in the Berlin Conference of 1884.

Since this partitioning there has been invested in Africa a sum estimated at six thousand five hundred million dollars which is a sum larger than the total gold reserves of the British Empire and France in 1939. As a result of this investment, there were exported from Africa in 1935, seven hundred million dollars worth of exports consisting of gold, diamonds, copper, wool, corn, cotton, palm products, cocoa, rubber and ground nuts. Since 1900, the total capital owned by the United States in Africa has increased from five hundred millions

to fifteen hundred millions and is nearly equal to British investment.

One would think that a continent which was so integral a part of the world trade and world industrial organization, inhabited as it is by at least one hundred fifty million of people, would be carefully considered in any plans for post-war reconstruction. This is not the case. If we consider the proposed peace plans we find that Africa is practically unmentioned or referred to only vaguely in general phrases which have the same intent and connotation. In President Roosevelt's four freedoms, May 1941, he manifestly was not thinking of Africa when he mentioned freedom of speech, freedom from want and freedom from terror. When Pope Pius XII spoke in June 1941, on peace and the changing social order, his only reference which could have been to Africa was "The more favorable distribution of men on the earth's surface."

The British Christian leaders in May 1941, made ten proposals for a lasting peace. The tenth reference was to the resources of the earth which "should be used as God's gifts to the whole human race." The American Friends Services Committee in June 1941 asked that all nations be assured "equitable access to markets." The eight points of the Atlantic Charter were so obviously aimed at European and North American conditions, that Churchill frankly affirmed this to be the case although he was afterward contradicted by President Roosevelt. Later have come the proposals of Streit and Luce which propose a domination of the world by English-speaking peoples, that is, by the peoples who have led in fostering the slave trade and color caste.

One can see in all these proposals the persistence of old patterns; the need of raw materials from Africa and the assumption that this raw material must be made cheap by land monopoly and low wage; and that the object of the whole organization of Africa must remain primarily the economic advantage of

Europe. Yet it is clear that these old patterns of thought and action will be changed if not entirely swept away by the two world wars.

Looking toward such a result, it would be well for thinkers of the modern world to realize much more clearly than they do, just what Africa means. In the first place there is no one Africa. There is in Africa no such unity of physical characteristics; of cultural development; of historical experiences; or of racial identity, that can possibly allow us to look upon the continent as a unity. We may distinguish today at least ten Africas: North Africa with Tunis and Algeria which are in reality a part of Europe; there is French West Africa, a vast and loosely integrated region, where in one small part a splendid educational and cultural development of the natives has gone on together with some economic progress. There is Egypt whose history is well-known and which is still a satellite in the British Empire. From this has been arbitrarily cut off the Anglo-Egyptian Sudan, forming a different problem, a different economy and facing a different destiny. There is Ethiopia only recently discovered by the United States.

Turning westward again we have French Equatorial Africa, an economic echo of the Belgian Congo, the seat in the past of terrible exploitation and in the present of a curious military movement. There is British West Africa consisting of four colonies representing the most advanced possibilities of the Negro race in Africa but held in check by a denial of all real democracy and by carefully organized exploitation. There is the Belgian Congo whose astonishing history is known to all.

British East Africa, consisting of Uganda, Kenya and Tanganyika, combines an advanced native state with the European land-aggression in Kenya and the spoil of German Africa in Tanganyika. There is Portuguese Africa torn in two by the British and dependent upon British economic organization and yet individual and different. And finally, there is South Africa

and the Rhodesias where three million white people are holding ten million natives in economic slavery while they rape the land of its priceless gold, jewels, and metals.

There is an extraordinary amount of misinformation and contradiction current concerning this continent, despite the scientific study recently carried on. First of all and most fundamental, is perhaps this singular paradox that African colonies, and indeed all colonies, are never profitable to the mother country and thus represent a sort of philanthropic enterprise, which is to be commended for whatever education and social service it has given, and not to be blamed if these services are miserably inadequate as compared to the need. Directly contradictory to this kind of assertion is the well-known fact that modern colonial imperialism has been a source of immense profit and power to Great Britain, France, Germany and other countries.

The truth of the matter is, that so far as government investment is concerned the money which Great Britain and France and Germany have invested in Africa has yielded small direct returns in taxes and revenue. But on the other hand this governmental investment has been the basis upon which private investors have builded being thus furnished free capital by home taxation; and while the mass of people in the mother country have been taxed heavily for this governmental gift abroad, the private capitalist investors in the colonies have reaped not only interest from their own investment but returns from investments which they did not make protected by armies and navies which they do not support. And in addition, immense sums from raw material and labor whose price is kept at a minimum and sold in the mother country as processed goods at the highest monopoly prices. The net return, therefore, of the white races, for their investment in colored labor and material in Africa has been immense and this, with similar returns from Asia and other parts of the world, has been the cause of the high standard of living, the luxury expenditure and the consumption for show which characterizes modern civilization. This is the basis of the indictment which Africa has against the modern world and this indictment must be answered by the present war or by wars which are bound to come.

The question as to what we want the future of the African people to be; and what they themselves want, must be clearly envisaged. . . .

Looking forward to the World Peace which must eventually follow World War, certain basic principles governing our thought and action in regard to the people of Africa, seem clear. . . .

1. We have no warrant for assuming that there are a few large groups of mankind, called Races, whose hereditary differences, as shown by color, hair and measurements of the bony skeleton, fix forever their relations to each other, and indicate their possibilities. There is no proof that persons and groups in Africa are not as capable of useful lives and effective progress, as peoples in Europe and America.

2. The great problem facing the World, is to achieve such wide contact of human cultures and mutually beneficent intercourse of human beings as will gradually by inspiration, comparison and wise selection, evolve the best civilization for the largest number of human beings.

3. To accomplish this, there is need of a great crusade, a religious mission, guided by the proven conclusions of science, the object of which shall be the continuous progress of mankind, regardless of race and color.

4. It must be clearly recognized that the main hindrance to such a movement, is today the more or less conscious feeling, wide-spread among the white peoples of the world, that

other folk exist not for themselves, but for their uses to Europe; that white Europe and America have the right to invade the territory of colored peoples, to force them to work and to interfere at will with their cultural patterns, while demanding for whites themselves a preferred status. On the other hand, colored folk have their contacts with other and higher cultures seriously and arbitrarily restricted.

5. The most dangerous excuse for this situation is the relation between European capital and colored labor involving high profit, low wages and cheap raw material. The strong motive of private profit is thus placed in the foreground of our interracial relations, while the greater objects of cultural understanding and moral uplift lurk in the background.

6. So long as broad scientific philanthropy is thus hobbled by greed, the results will be and have been slavery, cultural disintegration, disease, death and war.

7. We are slowly but surely recognizing facts analogous to these within the confines of the advanced countries themselves. Here we are curbing and guiding the activities of industry and limiting the profits of private enterprise in the interest of the laboring masses. Not so in colonies and in quasi-colonial areas. There, for the most part, we are tending to repeat and perpetuate the errors of the worst days of capitalistic exploitation in Europe. This hurts not only the backward peoples by restricting their initiative, by ruining their best culture and substituting no adequate cultural patterns; but also this colonial economy frustrates and nullifies much of the reform effort within the more progressive lands which own and control colonies.

8. It seems clear, therefore, that our future attitude toward Africa should be based upon principles something like these:

A. The land and natural resources of Africa should be regarded as belonging primarily to the native inhabitants, to be administered for their advancement and well being. Where land has already been alienated, it should be eventually restored. Industry in Africa should be directed primarily toward the consumption needs of the inhabitants and only secondarily to the European demand for raw material. The necessary capital, instead of being imported quickly and at high cost, should be gradually and increasingly raised from the savings of the Natives.

B. In ascertaining the legitimate wants of the native African, his own wishes must be taken into account and allowed the broadest possible sway under the guidance of carefully ascertained scientific principles and well-tried cultural standards; and without the interference of religious dogma or the brute force of modern wage slavery. Especially must an educated class among the natives be systematically and increasingly trained according to modern standards and its opinion given due voice and weight, instead of being, as at present, largely excluded by careless misrepresentation and deliberate design.

C. Political control must be taken from commercial and business interests owned and conducted in the foreign nations dominating the colonies and vested provisionally in an international Mandates Commission. This commission must be controlled by recognized statesmen and philanthropists of the highest character, with the collaboration of unprejudiced and rigorously tested science. Its rule should be carried out with the increasing participation of such educated persons as share the blood and culture of the persons affected; to the end that gradually the systematic increase of democratic methods will transfer political power to the mass of the native people as that people gains in intelligence and civilization.

D. There need be no minimizing of the extreme difficulties, frustrations and mistakes that will inevitably accompany the attempt to understand, change and improve the cultural status of any people through contact with people of higher culture and through educational effort and moral teaching. But these difficulties instead of being regarded either as negligible or as insurmountable must be faced as the real kernel of the problem of human uplift and humanitarian effort.

E. Within such [a] vast framework, the real work of civilizing the world can proceed, and a new crusade of real religion and a new modern abolition of slavery will begin to build a world-wide system of culture on the trained knowledge and free will of all men regardless of race and color.

As I look upon the world in revolution today, I can well believe that the Democracy which will crown the twentieth century will, in contrast to the nineteenth, involve the social control of the masses of men over the methods of producing goods and of distributing wealth and services. And the freedom which this abolition of poverty will involve, will be freedom of thought and not freedom for private profit-making. For this reason, the colonial and quasi-colonial peoples will be more ready to achieve and accept this Democracy of industry, than the misled people of Europe whose conception of democracy has been industrial anarchy with the spirit of man in chains. Anarchy of the Spirit alone is the true Freedom.

6. "Colonialism, Democracy, and Peace After the War"

Given as a speech in 1944 in Haiti

In the lectures which I am planning to deliver in Haiti, I want to examine with you the prospective status of the colonial groups in the world after the conclusion of this war and in the organization of peace for the future. You will I am sure bear with my imperfect French in this intricate and difficult task.

First of all I am deliberately using the word "colonial" in a much broader sense than is usually given it. A colony, strictly speaking, is a country which belongs to another country, forms a part of the mother country's industrial organization, and exercises such powers of government, and such civic and cultural freedom, as the dominant country allows. But beyond this narrower definition, there are manifestly groups of people, countries and nations, which while not colonies in the strict sense of the word, yet so approach the colonial status as to merit the designation semicolonial. The classic example of this status has long been China. There are other groups, like the Negroes of the United States, who do not form a separate nation and yet who resemble in their economic and political condition a distinctly colonial status. It was a governor of the state of Georgia [Ellis G. Arnall] who said in the recent Democratic nominating convention in Chicago: "We cannot continue as a nation to treat thirteen millions of our citizens as semi-colonials." Then, too, there are a number of nations whose political independence is undisputed and who have a certain cultural unity; and yet by reason of their economic ties with the great industrial and capital-exporting countries, find themselves severely limited in their freedom of action and opportunity for cultural development. They are in a sense the economic colonies of the owners of a closely knit world of global industry. The Balkan countries and those of South and Central America, and the Caribbean area occupy in varying degrees this sort of semicolonial status.

Looking therefore upon this colonial and semicolonial world, I wish first to ask what common characteristics we may discern; how these characteristics exhibit themselves in the different groups, and how these groups suffer common disabilities and hindrances with social classes in the more advanced lands of the world; and finally, what place these colonies should and will occupy in the democracy which we hope will gradually inherit the earth.

There are in the first place certain characteristics of colonial peoples, which are so common and obvious that we seldom discuss them and often actually forget them; colonial and quasi-colonial peoples are as a mass, poverty-stricken, with the lowest standards of living; they are for the most part illiterate and unacquainted with the systematized knowledge of modern science; and they have little or no voice in their own government, with a consequent lack of freedom of development. Naturally these characteristics vary widely among different groups and nations; so that before we generalize, make comparisons and seek remedies, we must stop to examine certain specific types of colonial countries. This examination, I shall make in very general terms in this lecture. Later I hope to treat in more detail various selected lands.

Let us first consider the colonies proper: the countries of America, Africa and Asia which we usually designate as colonies. In America, we have the British West Indies, the French islands, the American acquisitions. All of these conform to a well-known type: at the top, a group of varying size, consisting mainly of whites and mulattoes; they are in income, often well-to-do and sometimes rich; they are literate and in some cases highly cultured, and they have some voice in government. Below this group, and composing from seventy-five to ninety percent, are a mass of people, predominantly of direct African descent, illiterate largely, and making a decent living with difficulty; subject to disease, with high infant mortality, and having for the most part no voice in government, and with restricted personal freedom.

Discussion of this situation in the past and largely today, confines itself to the persisting disabilities of the elite, to questions of their political power and cultural recognition. There can be no question but that these matters are of grave concern and call for remedy. But our preoccupation with these problems which in so many cases are peculiarly personal, must no longer blind us to the much vaster problem: as to how far it is necessary that in the most beautiful part of the New World, the overwhelming mass of the inhabitants be precluded by poverty, ignorance, disease and disfranchisement from taking any effective part in modern civilization. White citizens of the United States and most Englishmen find nothing unusual or alarming in this situation. They have argued from the days of the slave trade that not more than a tenth of the Caribbean peoples are capable of modern civilization or conceivable participants in political and cultural democracy. Without any profound dissent, many of the colored folk themselves have accepted this dictum without question and confined their protest against social conditions to the situation of the élite, which certainly and justly demands betterment.

But how has it been decided, and who has decided, that the social distribution of the Caribbean is normal and inevitable? We are led to question the conclusion all the more, when we remember that it is not long since when the overwhelming proportion of the populations of most European countries was as poor and ignorant as modern colonial peoples. In answer to this reflection, the nineteenth century posed the question of "Race," of the existence of such inborn and ineradicable difference between stocks of human beings as made the proportion of civilizable people vastly different in Europe and America, and between the lighter and darker folk. I need not remind you how fierce a controversy arose over this theory of race, and how that pseudo-science long hindered not

simply remedy for the degradation of colonials, but even conception of the possibility of remedy. Today as we stand near halfway through a century which has proven the biological theories of unchangeable race differences manifestly false, what difference of action does this call for on our part?

First of all it calls our attention to the fact that so far as science is concerned, there is no earthly reason why the elite of Haiti, Jamaica, Martinique and Cuba should not comprise nine-tenths instead of one-tenth of the population. If this be true, what hinders steps toward its realization? Such steps must begin with knowledge; with concerted effort such as I am indicating in this lecture, to study colonial and quasi-colonial status in various parts of the world. Turning to the colonies of Africa, we find certain differences and contrasts with the West Indies. In the colonies of West Africa and East Africa, the emerging group of the elite as a recognizable class is largely missing. There are outstanding personalities, and social movements, but instead of conforming to the European class pattern, they link themselves to another and a different social heritage. The tradition of a strong and ancient organization persists—an organization that linked the mass of the people directly to the chief through an intricate nobility; in this society the tribe became an integral state in which the interests of no individual were neglected.

There has recently been published a most thoroughgoing study of the Kingdom of Nupe in Nigeria. Any person, white or black, who has a lingering conception that Africa evolved no political state, should read this book. But in this case as in most African colonies, there has cut across this ancient pattern, changing, spoiling and even partially obliterating it, the modern colonial system, born in the West Indies and transferred to the source of the developed slave trade. This system substitutes for the local, home-born and home-developed elite, foreign control, represented by a mere handful of more or less temporary representatives, who govern the tribe or state. The objects of this government determine the character of the colony. The earlier African colonies were for purposes of trade, and all government was directed toward facilitating trade. Outside that, the colony conducted its own affairs in its own way.

Then certain valuable articles of trade came into greater demand and pressure was brought to bear to increase the supply. Slave trade and slavery resulted overseas, but on the African mainland, gold, vegetable oils, copper and diamonds, became more valuable than slaves in the West Indies, and the tribal organization was partially or wholly disrupted to supply regular labor. The value of these new products undermined the foundations of slavery in the new world. Slavery, therefore, disappeared from the New World especially when Toussaint and others used force to accelerate this development. On the other hand, the African colony became therefore a vast business organization to reap profit for European investors out of the invested capital and forced labor of Africa. Across this cut the efforts of missionaries and philanthropists and West Indian and American Free Negroes. The result today is a series of African colonies, conducted for profits, and yet with their policy modified so as to recognize in varying degree the development and progress of the native. With all the advance made, it is fair to say that the investment motive is still supreme in West and East Africa. It is less powerful in French Senegal, but in the Belgian Congo, while changed materially from the disgraces of Leopold, it is still an investment far more than a philanthropy. In South Africa, strong tribal organization met modern industrial exploitation and finance capital, head-on. The result is the most complicated race problem on earth, with retrogression and reaction fighting against almost every forward movement of the native proletariat and opposed by a small but growing philanthropy on the part of the whites.

Turning now to Asia, we face the problem of India, the largest colony in the world and the one that poses the greatest colonial problem. In India we have an ancient culture, an intricate political history, and a long economic development. On this fell the power of the West and East: the East with organized military power; the West, first with the religious might of organized Mohammedanism, meeting the spiritual seeds of indigenous Buddhism. On this was thrown in the century before the widest growth of the African slave trade, the newly organized power of the new capitalism, which American slavery had given birth to in England. The loot of India by European political adventurers and merchants established modern capitalism in Europe and with the accompanying technical and scientific inventions, gave Europe mastery of the world. Capitalism was a great and beneficent method of satisfying human wants, without which the world would have lingered on the edge of starvation. But like all invention, the results depend upon how it is used and for whose benefit. Capitalism has benefited mankind, but not in equal proportions. It has enormously raised the standard of living in Europe and even more in North America. But in the parts of the world where human toil and natural resources have made the greatest contribution to the accumulation of wealth, such parts of the earth, curiously enough, have benefited least from the new commerce and industry. This is shown by the plight of Africa and India today. To be sure Africans and Indians have benefited by modern capital. In education, limited though it be; in curbing of disease, slow and incomplete as it is; in the beginning of the use of machines and labor technique; and in the spread of law and order, both Negroes and Hindus have greatly benefited; but as compared with what might have been done; and what in justice and right should have been accomplished, the result is not only pitiful, but so wrong and dangerous as already to have helped cause two of the most destructive wars in human history, and is today threatening further human death and disaster.

To realize this, look at India today. No one has ever tried to prove that its vast horde of three hundred and fifty million people are not normal human beings and as gifted as the Europeans. No one denies that Indians have worked hard and long, have been cunning in technique, profound in thought and lofty in religious ideal. Yet this land after three hundred years' subjection to European political control and industrial domination, is poverty-stricken to an inconceivable degree, is ninety percent illiterate, is diseased and famine-cursed, and has limited voice in its own government. It is for instance in this war not by its own consent but by declaration of Great Britain. Thousands of its leaders who have dared peacefully to protest against this situation are today in jail.

Dutch and French India approach, with some modifications and variations, the British Indian pattern; in other words, India, while a partner in the development of modern capitalistic civilization, and while sharing some of its benefits, has received so small and inadequate a share as compared with Europe that its present plight is a disgrace to the world. And this is because the modern world under the guidance of Europe and North America has become used to thinking that the plight of the human millions of Asia and Africa is normal, essentially right and unchangeable except after long periods of evolution if even then.

Let us now turn to certain states which are not colonies but which for various reasons approximate the colonial status. Some of these are China, many of the countries of South America and groups like the Negroes in the United States and the Indians of the Americas. To these may be added the majority of the Balkan states, the states of the Near East, and the independent Negro countries, Liberia, Haiti and Ethiopia. In these cases there is recognized political independence, and a cultural heritage of varying strength and persistence. But on the other hand in all these cases, the economic dependence of the country on European and North American industrial organization, in commerce, in sale of raw materials and especially in obtaining the use of capital in the shape of machinery and manufactured material—this dependence on world industry makes the country largely dependent on financial interests and cultural ideals quite outside the land itself. There have been many cases where this partnership between a land of labor and material, and a land of wealth, technical efficiency and accumulated capital goods, has worked advantageously for both. But in most modern instances, the wealthy country is thinking in terms of profit, and is obsessed with the long-ingrained conviction that the needs of the weaker country are few and its capacity for development narrow or nonexistent. In that case, this economic partnership works to the distinct disadvantage of the weaker country. The terms of sale for raw materials, the prices of goods and rent of capital; even the wages of labor are dictated by the stronger partner, backed by economic pressure and military power.

The case of China is well known. The seat of the oldest civilization surviving in the world, China was compelled at gunpoint to trade with Europe. This procedure was justified as leading to the Christianization and economic uplift of this great land. The results justified this method only in part. For the most part the colonial pattern prevailed: a mass of poverty-stricken people, illiterate and diseased, with their political autonomy partially nullified; until when native resentment revolted in the late nineteenth century, Europe planned to divide the country into colonies. This was delayed by the rise of Japan as a major power and her insistence on sharing the spoils. From this point the path to World War was straight and clear.

The Indian and Negro group in America have paused on a threshold, leading by one door to complete integration with the countries where they reside; and by another door leading to the organization of a sort of nation within a nation, which approaches colonial status on the one hand and eventual incorporation on the other. The Indians have taken one path, and the Negroes of the United States the other. The eventual result is not clear, and depends to a degree on the development of the colonial status among other peoples of the world. In the case of the Balkans and the Near East, a strong cultural tradition, urges them toward independent nationhood, while the elite of their own people, especially the great landlords, the new manufacturers and home capitalists, stand in such close alliance with and dependence on the European industrial and financial organization, that most of these countries remain bound hand and foot by a web of their own weaving. This is peculiarly true of Poland, Hungary, Bulgaria and Rumania. In South America, the pattern changes, because the cultural heritage and bond is weaker, and the social conditions in Europe become guide and ideal for the independent American colony. The normal situation, with poverty, ignorance, disease and disfranchisement seems in the eternal nature of things and nearly all effective effort is expended on raising an elite which shall be recognized by Europe and share the privileges of Europeans. Only in comparatively recent days, has an ideal arisen in lands like Chile, Peru and Brazil, of a spiritually independent South America, with a people of white, red and black blood intermingled, and with a laboring class as high in standards of living and political rights as the best of European lands.

The independent Negro nations, Haiti, Liberia and Ethiopa, suffer first from the widespread assumption of the nineteenth century, that Africa and the black race were not an integral part of the human picture and consequently could not and must not be allowed to try to develop like other nations along the lines of economic uplift, social development and political independence. We Negroes who in the last half century have convinced ourselves of our equality with mankind and our ability to share modern culture, scarcely realize how high a wall of prejudice based on color we have still to surmount today. This makes us all the more eager to force recognition of our worth, and too often forgetful of how the burden rests on us as on all peoples, to increase and increase rapidly and widely among the masses of people within our group who are still depressed in poverty, ignorance, and disease, and incapable of adding to the total of the emerged classes, the ability, physical strength and spiritual wealth, of which they are possessed. The studied and bitter attack on Liberia because of alleged slave raiding was of minor importance so far as the facts were concerned. Britain, France, Spain, Belgium and other countries had been pursuing and still were pursuing in some cases in Africa identical methods of labor recruitment as Liberia.

But beyond the bare facts was the allegation that Liberia was using against her own people the methods which she protested when used by whites. Even this was not really true, but it had enough semblance of truth, to hurt Liberia deeply. The same tactics used against Ethiopia almost fixed the charge of slavery upon this land at the very time she was making hard effort to abolish the slave status. I need not remind you how often and persistently the charge of voodooism brought against you has so twisted the clear truth as to emphasize the denial of cultural equality to a land which has in so many instances led America in cultural development. Yet here the truth is that your cultural elite, with all its fine accomplishment, is not anywhere near as large as wealth, education and health might raise up from your peasantry.

Now let me sum up this preliminary survey of the colonial problem: the depressed peoples and classes of the world form the vast majority of mankind today in the era of the highest civilization the world has known. The majority of human beings do not today have enough to eat and wear or sufficient shelter for decent existence; the majority of the world's peoples do not understand what the world is, what it has been and what the laws of its growth and development are; and they are unable to read the record of this history. Most human beings suffer and die years before this is necessary and most babies die before they ever really live. And the human mind with all its visions and possibilities is today deliberately distorted and denied freedom of development by people who actually imagine that such freedom would endanger civilization. Most of these disinherited folk are colored, not because there is any essential significance in skin color, but because most people in the world are colored.

What now can be done about this, in this day of crisis, when with the end of a horrible and disgraceful war in sight, we contemplate Peace and Democracy? What has Democracy to do with Colonies and what has skin-color to do with Peace?

7. "Haiti"

Unpublished essay written sometime in 1944

People, naturally, see in strange places and lands what they expect to see; what they have been taught that they will see. To most lands we thus carry in our thoughts and memories as much or even more than we receive from the new impressions of the visit—the more so if our visit is brief. Americans especially have definite expectations in Haiti: a land of "Negroes" with all that the name connotes; with poverty and disease and exploitation by a small group of mulattoes aping whites; especially Voodoo: weird, decadent African rites,

hidden in the mountains, vigorously denied but evidenced clearly by the drums that echo of Saturday nights; and by twice-told tales; on the whole a "funny" land seeking the impossible, the abnormal. This is what most white visitors to Haiti expect to see and naturally this is about what they do see, although here and there and lately a visitor may have a word of appreciation for the well-educated and cultivated persons with whom he comes in contact; or he may conceive some revision of his older idea of "Voodoo" rites.

But if one visits Haiti with the minimum of pre-judgment and with open ears and eyes capable of new and fresh impressions, he is struck first by the singular physical beauty of the "land of mountains" as the name means. Port-au-Prince lies like a white pearl between the enfolding arms of the mountain ranges which jut into the sea; clean, simple, quaint and lovely, with its white public buildings, its villas, its rows of narrow homes. Above and behind, range on range of mountains roll upward and eastward leaving high valleys here and there where the great plantations of old used to stand; with little towns and cities which seem quiet and peaceful, with palms, cottonwood and oaks shading them. Especially, always passing in stream of silent, dark humanity, are the busy straight-backed, hard-working peasants. Their thatched huts nestle, almost hidden from the casual eye, on mountain side and in secret valley—each one its own tiny homestead of land. Compared with Europe and North America, the standard of living for the peasants and for the middle classes is low. Compared with Spain, Italy and eastern Europe, extreme poverty is not conspicuous. There is sickness, malaria and tuberculosis. Wages are meager but crime is low. But above all there is a singularly urbane elite, handsome, well-mannered; men and women with culture and traditions who know how to live graciously on comparatively low income. There are lovely homes, with flowers and foliage beneath great palms; there are clubs and restaurants; and the ceremonials of marriage and death are absorbing; early marriage and many children are widely the rule. Five lively daily papers feed Port-au-Prince alone.

There is a national crop, coffee, and coffee of high grade which formerly only France bought and used; but now America is learning its rich flavor. There is cacao, logwood, cotton, sugar, rum, hard woods and new crops like sisal. There are some small industries like wood-carving and weaving.

There is effort at education, not only with the new university just set up by combining the older schools of medicine and law with new efforts in engineering and liberal arts; but the city high schools and the few country schools that can be reached by road and foot path. There is effort to encourage agriculture through the new school at Damien and its branches whose young trained teachers come from Cornell, Ames and other American schools. All this is but a drop in the bucket but it is effort based on older and long-standing institutions.

In government there is law and order. The cabinet of the president is composed of quite young men, men in their forties, many of them America-trained, some of them trained in France and Germany. The civil service is large and poorly paid, and the economic outlook is curiously inhibited and strained. Here lies the meat of the cocoanut. This is because there is in Haiti a cultural tradition coming straight down from eighteenth century France and now with twentieth century American influence. Life is suave, kindly, conventional. There is still prejudice and church influence against educating girls; development of theatre and dance is hindered by ideas of the role of "jeunes filles."Almost unconsciously, however, Haitian life is built upon a preexisting African cultural pattern. It is this cultural pattern, loosely described in some of its superficial phases as "voodoo," which vicious and ignorant white criticism of the nineteenth century caricatured and led Haiti to try in vain to suppress and repudiate. It survives today not only as an ethical basis for standards of peasant living but as a growing incentive to art and literature.

Here then is the curious situation: a cultivated conventional leading class founded on French eighteenth century culture, a peasantry of three millions whose culture harks back to seventeenth century West Africa with its intricately organized cultural patterns. The slow imperfect interaction of these two cultures; French peasant land-holding, building and education from Christophe and Petion; religion, family life and government from Africa; language from both; now at last, technique and public schools from America; music, literature and art from Africa. But the crux and center of all is technique, industry; work and wage, earning a living.

One-fourth of the wealth made by hard-working Haitians is going today to pay debts to North America. Haiti must operate and extend its government with all the multitudinous things which need to be done on 5 ½ million dollars a year. On the other hand, the legitimacy of these debts is a matter of treaty obligation and not of justice. Haiti rescued her country from pawn after the American Occupation by acceding to practically all the claims set up by various exploiting persons and corporation, just as in previous years under Boyer, Haiti consented to pay France for recognition of her independence, a sum out of all proportion to her ability to pay. But it seemed the only way to regain political independence from American Marines; and on the other hand it led in the past to internal stress and dissension.

Haiti, like so many undeveloped regions of the world, is a land of potential wealth; of water power that might be developed; of soil denuded but capable of fairly quick restoration; of forests of precious woods prematurely cut and yet yielding some woods now and capable of responding quickly to reforestation;

and above all a peasantry, stubborn and independent but capable of efficient work if they can see results of that work. They differ from the usual peasantry, because the great and wise Christophe in his eager panting effort to build a nation in a moment, distributed lands to the Haitian peasants and thus gave them a unique position among the peasantry of the world. The peasant is able to live and sustain a family on three acres of land and thus has enough of economic independence to drive a real bargain with his would-be employer and to save from his toil leisure for enjoyment, festival and happiness. Thus with labor tied to the land, with a climate suited to rapid vegetable growth, with mineral wealth and water power, with simple needs in food and clothing and with guiding traditions from Europe, America and Africa, there are wide possibilities in Haiti.

So what! we may say. What is the significance of all this? What can one propose for Haiti's future? In the past, Haiti has been of deep meaning to the modern world: a meaning which the world does not acknowledge, chiefly because it does not realize it. Mercer Cook, the historical expert on Haiti, who guided me up to the greatest human monument of the New World, the Citadel of Christophe, said paradoxically, "Revolution did not come to Haiti from France; Revolution came to France from Haiti." He meant by this that repeated slave revolts in Haiti, the first and richest of modern colonies, the father of the colonial idea, influenced France in matters of income, liberal thought and labor revolt in the seventeenth and early eighteenth centuries. He reminded us how the Haitians had helped the American Revolution with money and troops. Millions of dollars were given to Washington and the American army by the Haitian planters and the money came through the hands not only of white but mulatto planters; and by whosoever's hands it came, it was wealth piled up by black slaves. Actually, Haiti landed troops on

American soil and once saved the American army from annihilation at Savannah. Christophe was among them, and Petion. The Americans that lived and died that day did not sneer at these blacks and mulattoes.

When revolution came in France, Haiti sought to make it include all free people of the island, whether white or of Negro descent and this precipitated civil war in 1971, which was soon going against the mulattoes; then suddenly and to the world's astonishment, four hundred thousand black slaves rose, joined the revolt and seized the island and its property, under the great Toussaint. The world stood aghast. Europe and America were so frightened that even today their bitter resentment at successful slave revolt tinges and colors their whole thought of Haiti and Haitians. Reaction against revolution and class struggle came in Europe, led by Napoleon; and if he had succeeded in putting behind this reaction the might of an American empire, a different Europe might have emerged from the Napoleonic era.

The struggle of empire centered in Haiti: England sought to seize the island and use it against her most feared enemy, France; Spain sought to seize Haiti and rebuild her fallen empire; and France sent a great army to overthrow the impudent black rebel and build a new French empire in America. But Toussaint and his lieutenants and the fever beat them all and Haiti became autonomous. Then France tried treachery where she had failed by arms and killed Toussaint but the Haitian revolt was not a matter of one single leader: it was a people determined to be free; so that Dessalines made Haiti independent and Christophe and Petion organized the North and South. Napoleon in bitter chagrin tossed Louisiana as a gift to England's revolting colonies, turned his continental might on England and failed in 1815. Christophe defended Haiti with his mighty Citadel, its peasant land-ownership, its beginnings of education. Petion defended Haiti by education and by helping to free

South America from Spain. Only yesterday Venezuela paid singular homage to the present president of Haiti as representative of Petion, the friend and savior of Bolivar.

Meantime the American slave power bolstered its falling fortunes by using the horrible example of Haitian slave revolt to retard the emancipation movement and bolster a new biological doctrine of race differences, which became the foundation of colonial aggression throughout the nineteenth and twentieth centuries. The result was the debt slavery of Haiti which made her a quasi-colony, bound in economic chains first to France and then to America, despite her political independence. Enforced and bitter poverty was at the bottom of the continued internal dissension and occasional anarchy which finally resulted in the American Occupation. The political power of the North American Negro coupled with peasant proprietorship and the stubborn refusal to cooperate on the part of Haiti's educated elite rescued Haiti from open political control by the United States but left subordination to American capital with such help from American technique which would insure Haiti's ability to pay her debt quite as much as willingness to develop a new and stable culture.

Now what? What can be done with this land? First, there is the primary need of getting rid of that fatalistic attitude toward Haiti which says that nothing can become of this entrancingly beautiful island rich in material resources and culture because its people are predominantly of Negro descent. This attitude of mind, more than any other fact, is Haiti's world handicap today. It has distorted her history; separated her deliberately from normal cultural contracts in America and Europe. If we ignore this attitude and refuse to let it divert us we can easily discern in this island, an extraordinary opportunity for human culture; for culture in microcosm rather than on world imperial scale. There is no reason why there should not arise in Haiti a new Afro-French-American

culture which could in many respects set new ideals for the world. First of all the peasant land-ownership should be strengthened, confirmed and broadened. More land should be given each family and boundaries and records confirmed. Haiti and the world should learn that this settling of the land question can place Haiti in the van of economic progress, particularly if this individualism and security in ownership went hand in hand with socialized methods of cultivation, state aid in agricultural science and consumers' cooperation in marketing and buying. With this should go industrialization in town and city. This is beginning in small ways which are the chief remaining results of the American Occupation and of the guidance of European refugees: there are a sugar refinery, sisal plantations, attempts to raise rubber, wood carving and other corporate and individual efforts. There has not come to this land any considerable realization of the possibilities of socialized capital and consumers' cooperation; yet here is a peculiar chance successfully to introduce both and to build up internal and carefully grounded opposition to large industry, private profit for absentee investors, and local class exploitation.

To lead such a movement there is an established cultural class. North America does not have in any of its other territories, a group of people better fitted for social leadership on a broad and gracious scale; who knows as well how to live and enjoy life, who have more engaging manners and keener intellects. They have, however, been long culturally isolated, which has at once enriched and individualized their patterns and yet deepened them. They, therefore, today stand between the world-old temptation of becoming a ruling class existing for itself and its own enjoyment and set over against an exploited working peasantry [and], on the other hand, [the chance] of becoming as a class, masters of modern industrial technique and attacking the problem of a class joined to them by ties of blood and cultural history.

The peasants inherit an ancient cultural pattern coming down directly from Africa and of singular dignity and efficiency. Most modern countries have been built by smashing their cultural past, detaching themselves from it, despising it through ignorance, and seeking to build anew. Haiti far more than most modern lands has not yet accomplished this, in spite of contempt for "voodoo" and its rites, which sprung from white ignorance and was widely shared by the Haitian elite itself. This ancient cultural pattern has preserved the family life, guided work, set standards of right and wrong and of living and is today a most potent force in Haiti. It is beginning to be recognized by the elite as an art impulse, and if it can now be combined with scientific technique and economic progress a miracle might be accomplished.

Why could not America vary its blatant but sterile religious missionary effort with new missions not only of health but of economic reconstruction who would work in Haiti and other lands, not for the private profit of foreign investors but primarily and determinedly for the economic uplift of a small, self-contained, beautiful and historic land?

8. "Prospect of a World Without Racial Conflict"

Published in 1944 in the
American Journal of Sociology

It is with great regret that I do not see after this war, or within any reasonable time, the possibility of a world without race conflict; and this is true despite the fact that race conflict is playing a fatal role in the modern world. The supertragedy of this war is the treatment of the Jews in Germany. There has been nothing comparable to this in modern history. Yet its technique and its reasoning have been based upon a race philosophy similar to that which has dominated both Great Britain and the United States in relation to colored people.

This philosophy postulates a fundamental difference among the greater groups of people in the world, which makes it necessary that the superior peoples hold the inferior in check and rule them in accordance with the best interest of these superiors. Of course, many of the usual characteristics were missing in this outbreak of race hate in Germany. There was in reality little of physical difference between German and Jew. No one has been able to accuse the Jews of inferiority; rather it was the superiority of the Jews in certain respects which was the real cause of conflict. Nevertheless, the ideological basis of this attack was that of fundamental biological difference showing itself in spiritual and cultural incompatibility. Another difference distinguishes this race war. Usually the cure for race persecution and subordination has been thought to be segregation, but in this case the chance to segregate the Jews, at least partially, in Palestine, has practically been vetoed by the British government.

In other parts of the world the results of race conflict are clear. The representative of Prime Minister Churchill presiding over the British war cabinet has been the prime minister of the Union of South Africa. Yet South Africa has without doubt the worst race problem of the modern world. The natives have been systematically deprived of their land, reduced to the status of a laboring class with the lowest of wages, disfranchised, living and working under caste conditions with only a modicum of education, and exposed to systematic public and private insult. There is a large population of mixed-bloods, and the poverty, disease, and crime throughout the Union of South Africa are appalling. Here in a land which furnishes gold and diamonds and copper, the insignia of the luxury and technique of modern civilization, this race hate has flourished and is flourishing. Smuts himself, as political leader of the Union of South Africa, has carried out much of the legislation upon which this race conflict is based; and, although from time to time he has expressed liberal ideas, he has not tried or succeeded in basically ameliorating the fundamental race war in that part of the world.

The situation in India is another case of racial conflict. The mass of people there are in the bondage of poverty, disfranchisement, and social caste. Despite eminent and widely known leadership, there has not come on the part of the British any effective attempt fundamentally to change the attitude of the governing country toward the subject peoples. The basic reason for this, openly or by inference, is the physical difference of race which makes it, according to British thought, impossible that these peoples should within any reasonable space of time become autonomous or self-governing. There have been promises, to be sure, from time to time, and promises are pending; but no one can doubt that if these people were white and of English descent, a way out of the present impasse would have long since been found.

There is no doubt but that India is a congery of ignorant, poverty-stricken, antagonistic groups who are destined to go through all the hell of internal strife before they emancipate themselves. But it is just as true that Europe of the sixteenth century was no more ready for freedom and autonomy than India. But Europe was not faced and coerced by a powerful overlord who did not believe Europeans were men and was determined to treat them as serfs to minister to his own comfort and luxury.

In India we have the first thoroughgoing case of modern colonial imperialism. With the capitalism built on the African slave trade and on the sugar, tobacco, and cotton crops of America, investment in India grew and spread for three hundred years, until there exists the greatest modern case of the exploitation of one people by another. This exploitation has been modified in various ways: some education has been furnished the Indians, a great system of railroads has been installed, and industrialism has been begun. But nothing has been done to loosen to any appreciable degree the stranglehold of the British Empire on the destinies of four hundred million human beings. The prestige and profit of the control of India have made it impossible for the British to conceive of India as an autonomous land.

The greatest and most dangerous race problem today is the problem of relations between Asia and Europe: the question as to how far "East is East and West is West" and of how long they are going to retain the relation of master and serf. There is in reality no difference between the reaction to this European idea on the parts of Japan and China. It is a question simply of the method of eliminating it. The idea of Japan was to invoke war and force—to drive Europe out of Asia and substitute the domination of a weak Asia by a strong Japan. The answer of China was cooperation and gradual understanding between Great Britain, France, America, and China.

Chinese leaders are under no illusions whatever as to the past attitude of Europe toward Chinese. The impudence, browbeating, robbery, rape, and insult is one long trail of blood and tears, from the Opium War to the kowtowing before the emperor in Berlin. Even in this present war and alliance, there has occurred little to reassure China: certain courtesies from the British and belated and meager justice on the part of the United States, after the Soong sister had swept in on us with her retinue, jade, and jewels. There has not only been silence concerning Hong Kong, Burma, and Singapore, but there is the continued assumption that the subjugation of Japan is in the interest of Europe and America and not of Asia. American military leaders have insisted that we must have in the Pacific after this war American bases for armed force. But why? If Asia is going to develop as a self-governing, autonomous part of the world, equal to other parts, why is policing by foreigners necessary? Why cannot Asia police itself? Only because of the deep-seated belief among Europeans and Americans that yellow people are the biological inferiors to the whites and not fit for self-government.

Not only does Western Europe believe that most of the rest of the world is biologically different, but it believes that in this difference lies congenital inferiority; that the black and brown and yellow people are not simply untrained in certain ways of doing and methods of civilization; that they are naturally inferior and inefficient; that they are a danger to civilization, as civilization is understood in Europe. This belief is so fundamental that it enters into the very reforms that we have in mind for the postwar world.

In the United States, the race problem is peculiarly important just now. We see today a combination of northern investors and southern Bourbons desiring not simply to overthrow the New Deal but to plunge the United States into a fatal reaction. The power of the southerners arises from the suppression of the Negro and poor-white vote, which gives the rotten borough of Mississippi four times the political power of Massachusetts and enables the South through the rule of seniority to pack the committees of Congress and to dominate it. Nothing can be done about this situation until we face fairly the question of color discrimination in the South; until the social, political, and economic equality of civilized men is recognized, despite race, color, and poverty.

In the Caribbean area, in Central and South America, there has been for four hundred years wide intermixture of European, African, and Red Indian races. The result in one respect is widely different from that of Europe and North America; the social equality of Negroes, Indians, and mulattoes who were civilized was recognized without question. But the full results of this cultural liberalism were largely nullified by the economic control which Western Europe and North America held over these lands. The exploitation of cheap colored labor through poverty and low prices for materials was connived at as usual in the civilized world and the spoils shared with local white politicians. Economic and social prestige favored the whites and hindered the colored. A legend that the alleged backwardness of the South Americans was due to race mixture was so far stressed in the world that South America feared it and catered to it; it became the habit to send only white Brazilians, Bolivians, and Mexicans abroad to represent their countries; to encourage white immigration at all costs, even to loss of autonomy; to draw color lines in the management of industry dominated by Europe and in society where foreigners were entertained. In short, to pretend that South America hated and distrusted dark blood as much as the rest of the world, often even when the leaders of this policy were known themselves to be of Negro and Indian descent.

Thus the race problem of South and Central America, and especially of the islands of the Caribbean, became closely allied with European and North American practice. Only in the past few decades are there signs of an insurgent native culture, striking across the color line toward economic freedom, political self-rule, and more complete social equality between races. . . .

Our attitude toward poverty represents the constant lesion of race thinking. We have with difficulty reached a place in the modern white world where we can contemplate the abolition of poverty; where we can think of an industrial organization with no part of its essential co-operators deprived of income which will give them sufficient food and shelter, along with necessary education and some of the comforts of life. But this conception is confined almost entirely to the white race. Not only do we refuse to think of similar possibilities for the colored races but we are convinced that, even though it were possible, it would be a bad thing for the world. We must keep the Negroes, West Indians, and Indonesians poor. Otherwise they will get ambitious: they will seek strength and organization; they will demand to be treated as men, despite the fact that we know they are not men; and they will ask social equality for civilized human beings the world over.

There is a similar attitude with regard to health: we want white people to be well and strong, to "multiply and replenish the earth"; but we are interested in the health of colored people only insofar as it may threaten the health and wealth of whites. Thus in colonies where white men reside as masters, they segregate themselves in the most healthful parts of the country, provided with modern conveniences, and let the natives fester and die in the swamps and lowlands. It is for this reason that Englishmen and South Africans have seized the high land of Kenya and driven the most splendid of races of East Africa into the worst parts of the lowland, to the parts which are infested by the tsetse fly, where their cattle die, and they are forced laborers on white farms. . . .

What now can be done by intelligent men who are aware of the continuing danger of present racial attitudes in the world? We may appeal to two groups of men: first, to those leaders of white culture who are willing to take action, and second, to the leaders of races which are victims of present conditions. White leaders and thinkers have a duty to perform in making known the conclusions of science on the subject of biological race. It takes science long to percolate to the mass unless definite effort is made. Public health is still handicapped by superstitions long disproved by science; and race fiction is still taught in schools, in newspapers, and in novels. This careless ignorance of the facts of race is precisely the refuge where antisocial economic reaction flourishes.

We must then, first, have wide dissemination of truth. But this is not all: we need

deliberate and organized action on the front where race fiction is being used to prolong economic inequality and injustice in the world. Here is a chance for a modern missionary movement, not in the interest of religious dogma, but to dissipate the economic illiteracy which clouds modern thought. Organized industry has today made the teaching of the elementary principles of economic thought almost impossible in our schools and rare in our colleges; by outlawing "communistic" propaganda, it has effectually in press and on platform almost stopped efforts at clear thinking on economic reform. Protest and revelation fall on deaf ears, because the public does not know the basic facts. We need a concerted and determined effort to make common knowledge of the facts of the distribution of property and income today among individuals; accurate details of the sources of income and conditions of production and distribution of goods and use of human services, in order that we may know who profits by investment in Asia and Africa as well as in America and Europe, and why and how they profit.

Next we need organized effort to release the colored laborer from the domination of the investor. This can best be accomplished by the organization of the labor of the world as consumers, replacing the producer attitude by knowledge of consumer needs. Here the victims of race prejudice can play their great role. They need no longer be confined to two paths: appeal to a white world ruled by investors in colored degradation, or war and revolt. There is a third path: the extrication of the poverty-striken, ignorant laborer and consumer from his bondage by his own efforts as a worker and consumer, united to increase the price of his toil and reduce the cost of the necessities of life. This is being done here and there, but the news of it is suppressed, the difficulties of united action deliberately increased, and law and government united in colonial areas to prevent organization, manipulate prices, and stifle thought by force. Here colored leaders must act; but, before they act, they must know. Today, naturally, they are for the most part as economically illiterate as their masters. Thus Indian money-lenders are the willing instruments of European economic oppression in India; and many American and West Indian Negroes regard as economic progress the chance to share in the exploitation of their race by whites:

A union of economic liberals across the race line, with the object of driving exploiting investors from their hideout behind race discrimination, by freeing thought and action in colonial areas is the only realistic path to permanent peace today.

A great step toward this would be an international mandates commission with native representation, with power to investigate and report, and with jurisdiction over all areas where the natives have no effective voice in government.

9. "The Disfranchised Colonies"

Published in 1945 in
Color and Democracy

Colonies are the slums of the world. They are today the places of greatest concentration of poverty, disease, and ignorance of what the human mind has come to know. They are centers of helplessness, of discouragement of initiative, of forced labor, and of legal suppression of all activities or thoughts which the master country fears or dislikes.

They resemble in some ways the municipal slums of the nineteenth century in culture lands. In those days men thought of slums as inevitable, as being caused in a sense by the wretched people who inhabited them, as yielding to no remedial action in any conceivable time. If abolished, the dregs of humanity

would re-create them. Then we were jerked back to our senses by the realization that slums were investments where housing, sanitation, education, and spiritual freedom were lacking, and where for this reason the profits of the landlords, the merchants, and the exploiters were enormous.

To most people this characterization of colonies will seem overdrawn, and of course in one major respect colonies differ radically from slums. Municipal slums are mainly festering sores drawing their substance from the surrounding city and sharing the blood and the culture of that city. Colonies, on the other hand, are for the most part quite separate in race and culture from the peoples who control them. Their culture is often ancient and historically fine and valuable, spoiled too often by misfortune and conquest and misunderstanding. This sense of separation, therefore, makes colonies usually an integral entity beyond the sympathy and the comprehension of the ruling world. But in both city and colony, labor is forced by poverty, and crime is largely disease.

What, then, are colonies? Leaving analogies, in this case none too good, we look to facts, and find them also elusive. It is difficult to define a colony precisely. There are the dry bones of statistics; but the essential facts are neither well measured nor logically articulated. After all, an imperial power is not interested primarily in censuses, health surveys, or historical research. Consequently we know only approximately, and with wide margins of error, the colonial population, the number of the sick and the dead, and just what happened before the colony was conquered.

For the most part, today the colonial peoples are colored of skin; this was not true of colonies in other days, but it is mainly true today. And to most minds, this is of fatal significance; coupled with Negro slavery, Chinese coolies, and doctrines of race inferiority, it proves to most white folk the logic of the modern colonial system: Colonies are filled with peoples who never were abreast with civilization and never can be.

This rationalization is very satisfactory to empire-builders and investors, but it does not satisfy science today, no matter how much it did yesterday. Skin color is a matter of climate, and colonies today are mainly in the hot, moist tropics and semitropics. Naturally, here skins are colored. But historically these lands also were seats of ancient cultures among normal men. Here human civilization began, in Africa, Asia, and Central America. What has happened to these folk across the ages? They have been conquered, enslaved, oppressed, and exploited by stronger invaders. But was this invading force invariably stronger in body, keener in mind, and higher in culture? Not necessarily, but always stronger in offensive technique, even though often lower in culture and only average in mind.

Offensive technique drew the conquerors down upon the conquered, because the conquered had the fertile lands, the needed materials, the arts of processing goods for human needs. With the conquerors concentrating time and thought on these aspects of culture, usually the conquered could not oppose the barbarians with muscle, clubs, spears, gunpowder, and capital. In time, the invaders actually surpassed, and far surpassed, the weaker peoples in wealth, technique, and variety of culture patterns, and made them slaves to industry and servants to white men's ease.

But what of the future? Have the present masters of the world such an eternal lien on civilization as to ensure unending control? By no means; their very absorption in war and wealth has so weakened their moral fiber that the end of their rule is in sight. Also, the day of the colonial conquered peoples dawns, obscurely but surely.

Today, then, the colonial areas lie inert or sullenly resentful or seething with hate and unrest. With unlimited possibilities, they have but scraps of understanding of modern accumulations of knowledge; but they are pressing toward education with bitter determination. The conquerors, on the other hand, are giving them only the passing attention which preoccupation with problems of wealth and power at home leaves for colonial "problems."

What, then, do modern colonies look like, feel like? It is difficult to draw any universal picture. Superficial impressions are common: black boys diving for pennies; human horses hitched to rickshaws; menial service in plethora for a wage near nothing; absolute rule over slaves, even to life and death; fawning, crawling obeisance; high salaries, palaces, and luxury coupled with abject, nauseating, diseased poverty—this in a vague, imperfect way paints the present colonial world.

It is not nearly so easy as it would appear to fill in this outline and make it precise and scientific. Empires do not want nosy busybodies snooping into their territories and business. Visitors to colonies are, to be sure, allowed and even encouraged; but their tours are arranged, officials guide them in space and in thought, and they see usually what the colonial power wants them to see and little more. Dangerous "radicals" are rigorously excluded. My own visits to colonies have been rare and unsatisfactory. Several times I have tried in vain to visit South Africa. No visas were obtainable. I have been in British and French West Africa and in Jamaica.

In Sierra Leone I landed at Freetown in 1923. I was passed through the customs without difficulty, as my papers were in order. Then for some reason the authorities became suspicious. With scant courtesy, I was summoned peremptorily down to headquarters, to a room off the common jail, with pictures of escaped criminals decorating the walls. What did I want in Sierra Leone? I handed in my passport, showing that I was United States Minister Plenipotentiary to Liberia, stopping simply to visit on my way home. The commissioner unbent and dismissed me. That afternoon I was invited to a tea party at the governor's mansion! What would have happened to me if I had not had a diplomatic passport, or if I had been merely a colored man seeking to study a British colony?

The same year I visited Senegal and Conakry. I was received with great courtesy, but into the ruling caste; I had no contact with the mass of the colonial people. I lodged with the American consul; the French consul had me at dinner and the English consul at tea in his palatial mansion. But little did I see or learn of the millions of Negroes who formed the overwhelming mass of the colonial population.

In 1915, I visited Jamaica. I landed at Kingston and then, being tired and on vacation, did the unconventional thing of walking across the island to Mantego Bay. I immediately became an object of suspicion. It was wartime. I was in a sense, albeit unconsciously, intruding into Jamaica's backyard. I had proper visas, but I was not following the beaten path of the tourist. I was soon warned by a furtive black man that the police were on my track. My only recourse was to look up a long-time friend, principal of the local school. He ostentatiously drove me downtown, seated with him high in his surrey behind prancing horses. Thus was I properly introduced and vouched for. The point is that in all these cases one saw the possibility of arbitrary power without appeal and of a race and class situation unknown in free countries.

In the main, colonial peoples are living abnormally, save those of the untouched or inert mass of natives. Where the whites form a small ruling group, they are most abnormal and are not, as is assumed, replicas of the home group. They consist chiefly of representatives of commercial concerns whose first object is to make money for themselves and the corporations they represent. They are in the main hard-boiled, often ruthless businessmen, unrestrained by the inhibitions of home

in either law or custom. Next come the colonial officials, either identical with the commercial men or more or less under their domination, especially through home influence. Colonials and businessmen clash, but business usually wins. Sometimes philanthropic career officials get the upper hand; but they are in danger of being replaced or losing promotion. The official class—heads, assistants, clerks, wives, and children—are apt to be arrogant, raised above their natural position and feeling their brief authority; they lord it over despised natives and demand swift and exemplary punishment for any affront to their dignity. The courts presided over by whites are usually even-handed in native quarrels, but through fear are strict, harsh, and even cruel in cases between natives and whites. White prestige must be maintained at any cost. There is usually a considerable group of white derelicts, hangers-on, sadistic representatives of the "superior race," banished to colonies by relatives who are ashamed to keep them at home.

This whole group of whites forms a caste apart, lives in segregated, salubrious, and protected areas, seldom speaks the vernacular or knows the masses except officially. Their regular income from colonial services is liberal according to home standards and often fantastic according to the standard of living in colonies. Conceive of an income of $10,000 a year for a colonial governor over people whose average income is $25 a year! The officials get frequent vacations with pay, and are pensioned after comparatively short service. The pensions are paid for life by colonial taxation, and the pensioners are regarded as experts on colonial matters the rest of their lives.

Where the white resident contingent is relatively large, as in South Africa and Kenya, the caste conditions are aggravated and the whites become the colony while the natives are ignored and neglected except as low-paid labor largely without rights that the colonists need respect.

Below this group of white overlords are the millions of natives. Their normal and traditional life has been more or less disrupted and changed in work, property, family life, recreation, health habits, food, religion, and other cultural matters. Their initiative, education, freedom of action, have been interfered with to a greater or less extent. Authority has been almost entirely withdrawn from their control and the white man's word is law in most cases. Their native standards of life have been destroyed and the new standards cannot be met by a poverty that is the worst in the world. The mass of natives sink into careless, inert, or sullen indifference, making their contact with whites as rare as possible, and incurring repeated punishment for laziness and infraction of arbitrary or inexplicable rules.

Up from these rise two groups: the toadies or "white folks niggers," who use flattery and talebearing to curry favor; and the resentful, bitter, and ambitious who seek by opposition or education to achieve the emancipation of their land and people. The educated and the half-educated, in particular, are the object of attack and dislike by the whites and are endlessly slandered in all testimony given visitors and scientists.

The missionaries form another class. They have been of all sorts of persons: unworldly visionaries, former pastors out of a job, social workers with and without social science, theologians, crackpots, and humanitarians. Their vocation is so unconventional that it is almost without standards of training or set norms of effort. Yet missionaries have spent tens of millions of dollars and influenced hundreds of millions of men with results that literally vary from heaven to hell. Missionaries represent the oldest invasion of whites, and incur at first the enmity of business and the friendship of natives. Colonial officials, on pressure from home, compromise differences, and the keener natives thereupon come to suspect missionary motives and the native toadies rush to get converted and cash in on benefits. The total result varies tremendously according to the pressure of these elements.

Despite a vast literature on colonial peoples, there is today no sound scientific basis for comprehensive study. What we have are reports of officials who set out to make a case for the imperial power in control; reports of missionaries, of all degrees of reliability and object; reports of travelers swayed by every conceivable motive and fitted or unfitted for testimony by widely varying education, ideals, and reliability. When science tries to study colonial systems in Africa and Asia, it meets all sorts of hindrances and incomplete statements of fact. In few cases is there testimony from the colonial peoples themselves, or impartial scientific surveys conducted by persons free of compulsion from imperial control and dictation.

The studies we have of colonial peoples and conditions are therefore unsatisfactory. Even the great *African Survey* edited by Lord Hailey is mainly based on the testimony and the figures of colonial officials; that is, of men who represent the colonial organization, who are appointed on recommendation of persons whose fortunes are tied up with colonial profits, and who are naturally desirous of making the best-possible picture of colonial conditions. This does not mean that there is in this report, or in many others, deliberate and conscious deception; but there is the desire to make a case for the vested interests of a large and powerful part of the world's property-owners.

Other studies are made by visitors and outsiders who can get at the facts only as the government officials give them opportunity. Many opportunities have been afforded such students in the past, but the opportunities fall far short of what complete and scientific knowledge demands. Moreover, such visitors arrive more or less unconsciously biased by their previous education and contacts, which lead them to regard the natives as on the whole a low order of humanity, and especially to distrust more or less completely the efforts of educated and aspiring Natives. The native elite, when through education and contact they get opportunity to study and tell of conditions, often, and naturally, defeat their own cause before a prejudiced audience by their bitterness and frustration and their inability to speak with recognized authority.

Thus, unfortunately, it is not possible to present or refer to any complete and documented body of knowledge which can give an undisputed picture of colonies today. This does not mean that we have no knowledge of colonial conditions; on the contrary, we have a vast amount of testimony and study; but practically every word of it can be and is disputed by interested parties, so that the truth can be reached only by the laborious interpretation of careful students. Nearly every assertion of students of colonial peoples is disputed today by colonial officials, many travelers, and a host of theorists. Despite this, greater unanimity of opinion is growing, but it is far from complete.

If, for instance, we complain of the conquest of harmless, isolated, and independent groups by great powers, it is answered that this is manifest destiny; that the leaders of world civilization must control and guide the backward peoples for the good of all. Otherwise these peoples relapse into revolting barbarism. If under this control colonial peoples are unhappy, it is answered that they are happier than they were formerly without control; and that they make greater progress when guided than when left alone.

If slavery and forced labor are complained of, the answer is that the natives are congenitally lazy and must be made to work for the good of mankind. Indeed, if they were not enslaved by Europeans, they would enslave each other. Low wages are justified by the fact that these peoples are simple, with low standards of living, while their industrialization is a boon to the world, and the world's welfare is paramount. Lack of broad educational plans is

justified by their cost. Can England be asked to undertake the education of British Africa when she has not yet fully planned the education of British children at home? Moreover, why educate these simple folk into unhappiness and discontent? If they are trained at all, it should be to produce wealth for the benefit of themselves in part and of the empire in general. The seizing of the land and dividing it is looked upon not only as a policy which puts unused acreage into remunerative use, but also as one that compels folk to work who otherwise would sing and dance and sit in the sun. And in general, it is not clear from the testimony of history that the mass of colonial peoples can progress only under the guidance of the civilized white people, and is not the welfare of the whites in reality the welfare of the world?

Practically every one of these assertions has a certain validity and truth, and at the same time is just false and misleading enough to give an entirely unfair picture of the colonial world. The recent advance of anthropology, psychology, and other social sciences is beginning to show this, and beginning to prove on how false a premise these assertions are based and how fatal a body of folklore has been built upon it. These beliefs have been influenced by propaganda, by caricature, and by ignorance of the human soul. Today these attitudes must be challenged, and without trying to approach anything like completeness of scientific statement we may allude here to certain general matters concerning colonial peoples the truth of which cannot be disputed. . . .

10. "Peace is Dangerous"

Published in 1951 as a
pamphlet by *National Guardian*

Peace is dangerous; not to all folk, but certainly to those whose power and standard of living depend on war. The danger of war to the majority of men is all too obvious: The killing and maiming of the young; the destruction of property and interference with normal reproduction; the distortion of culture patterns and discouragement of creative effort. When we realize that at least thirty million of the best specimens of the world's youth have been killed in wars since 1914, and many more millions crippled in body and soul, we can get some partial idea of the loss to modern civilization through war.

Why then does war persist? What decisive interests promote and continue it against irretrievable loss on the part of the majority of men? Those who gain from war and suffer from peace are easily discernible at cursory glance: The munition makers and those who furnish war materials and machines. Not so readily seen are those who profit by the financial changes which war inevitably brings about. Still further in the background are investors and workers whose income is raised by war industries.

Even these large and important groups do not explain the popularity of war or at least the weak resistance to war hysteria. For explanation of this phenomenon we must look further to that vast number of Americans to whom present conditions bring comfort and satisfaction. This mass of intelligent persons either know or fear that if the present system of social and industrial organization prevalent in Western Europe and North America undergoes any essential change, they may not be able to enjoy what they consider the "American way of life". This standard of living does not necessarily call for luxury or conspicuous expenditure. It asks for a comfortable home, enough suitable clothing and sufficient nourishing food; not necessarily an automobile, but convenient transportation facilities, a telephone, medical care, vacations, education for children and provision for a decent old age.

That is what the average American expects from the "American way of life," or wants to be able to expect. It is not, to be sure, what the average American gets. Probably two-thirds of American families do not get it and half of these do not dare hope for it, although it remains their ideal. But a large and influential part of the American middle class do get these things. They believe they deserve them and they are willing to fight to keep them.

The basic question now is: Must this way of life, actual or believed possible for a large minority or even a majority of Americans, be defended by war or is it seriously endangered by peace? Our fear today undoubtedly is that peace is dangerous for this way of life for a large number of Americans and for the hope of it by the majority of our citizens.

This furnishes the reason behind the huge majority of the nation now rushing toward a third and final world war. The time of all times, then, to examine this thesis and disclose its truth or falsity is now.

Causes of Poverty: The Forbidden Subject

First of all, some Americans are convinced that our industrial system is so good that the mere existence of any other system is a threat. Most intelligent persons do not go this far. They acknowledge the shortcomings of our economy but still think it the best. They are, however, quite willing for others to try other ways; but they fear to have other ways, deemed inferior and impractical, tried on peoples who do not want them. It is the alleged forced expansion of communism which is today scaring most Americans into war.

But is it true that expanding communism is threatening our way of life? Or, on the contrary, is it the maintenance of our industrial methods which is threatening to keep the mass of the world's people not only below our own standard of living, but even below the life of ordinary decency and sheer survival? It is this aspect of world war which America is today refusing to discuss, indeed is often not permitted to discuss.

Most of us through education and lack of information firmly believe that the poverty and distress of the majority of human beings are primarily their own fault and perhaps can never be entirely alleviated. We are willing to do something in some vague "Point Four," provided the funds for this come out of public taxation and not out of private profits. But we say that even our great wealth is not able to support the world. When two answers are made to this we do not try to reply. The first answer is that a few centuries ago the aristocracy of the world believed that a standard of life such as American workers have today could not be achieved in any state without the ruin of its culture.

I was taught in high school, at the close of the last century, that labor unions were futile, strikes wrong, and increased wages would go mainly to waste and drunkenness. The second answer as to inevitable poverty for most men is that the colonial system helped cause poverty, that this system is now disappearing and that the remaining poverty and distress are not our fault and are falsely made to seem so by Russia.

Here emerges the kernel of the falsehood which is scaring America into war. Colonialism has not disappeared, even though its back is broken in India and China. American business, however, is desperately trying to maintain and restore where possible the essentials of colonialism under the name of Free Enterprise and Western Democracy, and is plunging the world into destruction with false ideals and misleading fears.

That is a grave charge and needs, I am quite aware, circumstantial proof. Let me indicate proof in this way: There are today at least eighteen main causes of World War and no one of them is Russia. On the contrary, they

are the great groups of essential raw material, and the land and labor necessary for their production, which the leading nations of the world need for their industry and their standard of living. These products are illustrated by the gold and diamonds from South Africa; copper from Rhodesia, uranium from the Congo, oil from the Middle East, tin and rubber from Malaya, beverages like tea from China, coffee from Brazil and cocoa from West Africa; drugs like opium and quinine from India; foods like sugar, chocolate, coconuts, fruits and spices from the whole tropical world; fibres like cotton, silk and hemp from our own South, China and India; and dozens of other drugs, dyestuffs and foods.

These materials, with few exceptions, are produced in tropical lands inhabited by colored peoples whose poverty and ignorance are not natural nor indigenous, but have been increased and made wider during the last three centuries by the determination of Europe and North America to rule the world for their own comfort, luxury and power.

Armed by scientific discovery and a new industrial technique, the white world, since the 17th century, has set itself to reduce colored labor to serfdom or slavery, to seize the land and natural resources of colonial and quasicolonial countries and so far as possible to rule these peoples by absolute military dictatorship, allowing them little education, no land and too little income for health or decency. Spain, followed by France and Holland, and succeeded by Great Britain, built up a domination of the world which became the foundation of modern civilization. Wealth, luxury, art and learning were thus sustained in the western world until its cultural accomplishment came to be regarded as the highest ideal in the universe: "Better fifty years of Europe than a cycle in Cathay!"

Logic taught us that eventually the revolt of the miserable victims of this world tyranny would cause its extinction. Revolt came early and still continues. But long before divided and ignorant colonial might could successfully storm the bastions of the west, those bastions themselves fell of their own presumption and overweight. The imperial thieves fell out over the division of the fabulous spoils of Asia, Africa and South America, and Europe approached suicide in three world wars, each of increased cost, destruction and human murder.

The Rich Fall Out; The Poor Feel Their Power

The rift in imperialism began when Germany and Italy, later Japan, and finally the United States, demanded a larger share of the spoils of imperial control of the colored world. They insisted on a redistribution of wealth and power. The ensuing World War effected such a redistribution. But it also weakened the intricate system of commercial control which had placed the real power of great modern states in the hands of those who controlled wealth—not simply national wealth but the most valuable materials of the whole earth.

The power of the rich in the late 18th and 19th centuries was curtailed by democratic control in the hands of the mass of the inhabitants; but this control was limited at home and of no avail in those parts of Asia, Africa and America which the organized industry of the imperial states dominated. Both the national and international organization of industry and commerce was not only undemocratic, but usually oligarchical, if not approaching absolute monarchy. The system placed so great power in the hands of those controlling home industry that they could and did reduce national democracy to the rule of wealth; or at most made home labor a minor partner with industry in the impoverishment, disease and

compulsory ignorance of the majority of the peoples of the earth.

The first World War shook this system to its foundations, not only by its cost, but because if filled many of the colored peoples with a fierce desire to escape from the coercion of Europe. In Eastern Europe, which under Western Europe leadership had sunk to quasi-colonial status, the result was a revolution which put socialists in control of Russia.

Socialism was an old, but indefinite and unsystematized theory of easing the monopoly of wealth and the oligarchical control of industry by substituting public welfare for private profit. The great but impractical theorists who had advocated such a change from the first rise of modern industry in the 15th century had seldom been able to agree on a definite program, and the few attempts at socialism had usually failed or been easily suppressed.

In the case of the Russian Revolution of 1917, however, a set of educated and devoted leaders appeared, determined to carry out the theories of Karl Marx. Marx, by long and thorough study of the Hegelian philosophy of science and by wide knowledge of actual working conditions, had tried to find a scientific foundation for the production and distribution of wealth. Lenin and his Russian followers were not entirely dogmatic. They doubted that the time was ripe or the Russians ready immediately to found a socialist state, and they tried to make some compromise and alliance with the economy of Western Europe. But Britain, France, Japan and the United States made the mistake of trying summarily and by force to suppress this revolution, using the armies of sixteen nations, together with spies, traitors and the worst type of hired mercenaries.

Without doubt this wide effort to stop the Revolution of 1917 would have succeeded for a time had not the whole system of European economy tottered so crazily in 1929 and after. Europe, the United States and Japan needed all their energies to restore their own solvency and rebuild international trade. But even then Britain and France were determined to dominate world industry and commerce as they had before the first World War. They were willing to admit the United States and Germany to junior partnership, but determined to ignore Italy and firmly excluded Japan.

This short-sighted effort led to three developments which changed the course of modern history. It gave the Soviet Union time to build an independent socialist state; it encouraged Japan to undertake her own colonial empire in Asia; and Italy and Germany, joined later by Japan, attempted to restore the European domination of labor, land and products in the colonial and semi-colonial areas of the world, but with one revolutionary change: France and the United States were now to be Junior Partners, and Germany was set to rule the world with the advice of Italy and Japan. There ensued long attempts at compromise— not touching the control of the world by Europe, but only concerning the division of power between the older empires and newer interlopers. Both sides tacitly agreed that the destruction of Russia and communism must follow their understanding.

But Western and Central Europe could find no basis of agreement and a second World War followed, which was at bottom caused by the rivalry among the great groups for control of the colonial products which I have named.

This war not only further wracked the world industrial system, but curiously enough, compelled Britain and America to make an alliance with the Soviet Union as the only method of conquering almost invincible Germany, Italy and Japan. They hesitated long and hoped until the end that Germany and the Soviet Union would annihilate each other while Western Europe and America were withholding or delaying their support of the hard-pressed Russian armies.

Germany and Japan were completely conquered at last, but what remained were the same causes of World War which ante-dated 1914: namely, those valuable and indispensable materials from colonial regions together with the cheap labor necessary to produce them, which must be seized and used for domestic industry and consumption if the pre-world war organization of industry and control of wealth was to continue. That it must continue, no Britisher nor American for a moment doubted.

U.S.A.—Colonialism's Last Stronghold

Consider for a moment our own country and its interest in colonial products or products of semi-colonial areas.

In 1930 we imported at least two billion dollars' worth of diamonds, silk, coffee, mineral oil, rubber, paper, copper, fibres, sugar, spices, vegetable oils and cocoa. They are all materials upon which not only our own industry but our present standards of living are based. We could scarcely be satisfied a day without abundant supply of them. Moreover we buy them cheap. We pay practically nothing for the land on which they are grown or found; we pay the colored laborer from 25 cents to a dollar a day and make him work. On the other hand the goods which we export to pay for these cheap colonial goods are priced at our own valuation because we control the monopoly of the only markets where colonials can buy machinery, tools and processed goods. We even prevent colonials from supplying their own needs and make them work for us.

This colonial trade is a source of vast profit to private enterprise because even the capital investment needed in colonial life often comes from taxes on citizens in the home country while private firms reap the profits. Thus British taxpayers built the great West African harbor of Takoradi, while private shippers use it. The United States Navy built the harbor at Monrovia, Liberia, from our tax money while the Firestone Company uses it for sizeable dividends.

Moreover this foreign trade with colonial countries is far more profitable than domestic industry. There are in colonies few if any labor unions; there is a minimum of taxation on foreign corporations; there are no wage floors or prohibition of child labor; freight charges are set by the foreign firms who monopolize transport and can make or break a local industry. Capital rushes for such investment if it is assured that there will be no danger of native presumption trying to control foreign capital. This is just what began to happen after the second World War. Not only was Russia, whose industries often paid 50% on investment to Germans, French and British, lost to western business, but also Poland, Czechoslovakia and much of the Balkan area.

Vast colonial regions began to break from European domination. Britain had to emancipate India, but before leaving she encouraged a resurgence of religious hate and made fast alliance with native capitalists, who continued to exploit the poor. The United States entered China as a welcomed friend but we were more interested in tea, silk, fibres, tungsten, oils and cotton than in people. So the wretched Chinese for ten awful years writhed in poverty, war and misery, bearing alone the world burden of Japanese imperialism until in one mighty surge they wrenched American guns right out of the hands of the scoundrel Chiang Kai-shek and drove his filthy outfit onto Formosa where our taxes still support it. Indonesia began to break the bonds of Dutch and British control; Southeast Asia revolted fiercely against their British and French masters. There were other signs of revolt in Africa, the South Seas, the Philippines, the Caribbean and South and Central America. The whole of Western Europe leaned toward control of wealth by democratic process.

It was at this point that world-wide propaganda, led by the United States, on a scale which put Hitler to shame, was started to make men believe that socialism led by a new Russian imperialism was starting a third world war and that America must curb the movement by unlimited force. As a matter of fact what was really beginning was the desperate American attempt to revive colonial imperialism with the United States in the saddle instead of Britain. . . .

Chapter IV

On Labor, Economics, and Politics

From the "disheartening loss of self-respect" experienced by young black servants to the unchecked power of businessmen who "rule everywhere," Du Bois's insights on labor, economics, and politics were piercing and widely applicable. He understood the importance of labor in social life, the essential role labor plays in economic systems, and the integral relationship both labor and economics have with politics. Du Bois wrote of the central importance of the right to vote and of the equally important need for the democratization of industry. His description of "the agitator," the herald of social change and prophet of social betterment, is reminiscent of Durkheim's discussion in *The Rules of Sociological Method* (1895) of progressive deviants who pave the way for a new morality. His discussion of (un)employment directly anticipates Mills's famous distinction between "troubles" and "issues." His persistent insistence that social equality and human freedom can be achieved only when democracy is extended to the economy is directly indebted to the writings of Karl Marx, but Du Bois embellishes Marx's work by incorporating matters of race and racism when necessary.

1. "Servants"

Published in 1899 in
The Philadelphia Negro

. . . Probably over one-fourth of the domestic servants of Philadelphia are Negroes, and conversely nearly one-third of the Negroes in the city are servants. This makes the Negro a central problem in any careful study of domestic service, and domestic service a large part of the Negro problems. The matter thus is so important that it has been made the subject of a special study appended to this work. A few general considerations only will be advanced here.

So long as entrance into domestic service involves a loss of all social standing and consideration, so long will domestic service be a social problem. The problem may vary in character with different countries and times, but there will always be some maladjustment in social relations when any considerable part of a population is required to get its support in a manner which the other part despises, or affects to despise. In the United States the problem is complicated by the fact that for years domestic service was performed by slaves, and afterward, up till to-day, largely by black freedmen—thus adding a despised race to a despised calling. Even when white servants increased in number they were composed of white foreigners, with but a small proportion of native Americans. Thus by long experience the United States has come to associate domestic service with some inferiority in race or training.

The effect of this attitude on the character of the service rendered, and the relation of mistress and maid, has been only too evident, and has in late years engaged the attention of some students and many reformers. These have pointed out how necessary and worthy a work the domestic performs, or could perform, if properly trained; that the health, happiness and efficiency of thousands of homes, which are training the future leaders of the republic, depend largely on their domestic service. This is true, and yet the remedy for present ills is not clear until we recognize how far removed the present commercial method of hiring a servant in market is from that which obtained at the time when the daughters of the family, or of the neighbor's family, helped in the housework. In other words, the industrial revolution of the century has affected domestic service along with other sorts of labor, by separating employer and employed into distinct classes. With the Negro the effect of this was not apparent so long as slavery lasted; the house servant remained an integral part of the master's family, with rights and duties. When emancipation broke this relation there went forth to hire a number of trained black servants, who were welcomed South and North; they liked their work, they knew no other kind, they understood it, and they made ideal servants. In Philadelphia twenty or thirty years ago there were plenty of this class of Negro servants and a few are still left.

A generation has, however, greatly altered the face of affairs. There were in the city, in 1890, 42,795 servants, and of these 10,235 were Negroes. Who are these Negroes? No longer members of Virginia households trained for domestic work, but principally young people who were using domestic service as a stepping-stone to something else; who worked as servants simply because they could get nothing else to do; who had received no training in service because they never expected to make it their life-calling. They, in common with their white fellow citizens, despised domestic service as a relic of slavery, and they longed to get other work as their fathers had longed to be free. In getting other work, however, they were not successful, partly on account of lack of ability, partly on account of the strong race prejudice against them. Consequently to-day the ranks of Negro servants, and that means largely the ranks of domestic service in general in Philadelphia, have received all those whom the harsh competition of a great city has pushed down, all whom a relentless color proscription has turned back from other chosen vocations; half-trained teachers and poorly equipped students who have not succeeded; carpenters and masons who may not work at their trades; girls with common school training, eager for the hard work but respectable standing of shop girls and factory hands, and proscribed by their color—in fact, all those young people who, by natural evolution in the case of the whites, would have stepped a grade higher than their fathers and mothers in the social scale, have in the case of the post-bellum generation of Negroes been largely forced back into the great mass of the listless and incompetent to earn bread and butter by menial service.

And they resent it; they are often discontented and bitter, easily offended and without interest in their work. Their attitude and complaint increases the discontent of their fellows who have little ability, and probably could not rise in the world if they might. And, above all, both the disappointed and the incompetents are alike ignorant of domestic service in nearly all its branches, and in this respect are a great contrast to the older set of Negro servants.

Under such circumstances the first far-sighted movement would have been to open such avenues of work and employment to young Negroes that only those best fitted for domestic work would enter service. Of course this is difficult to do even for the whites, and yet it is still the boast of America that, within certain limits, talent can choose the best calling for its exercise. Not so with Negro youth. On the contrary, the field for exercising their talent and ambition is, broadly speaking, confined to the dining room, kitchen and street. If now competition had drained off the talented and aspiring into other avenues, and eased the competition in this one vocation, then there would have been room for a second movement, namely, for training schools, which would fit the mass of Negro and white domestic servants for their complicated and important duties. Such a twin movement—the diversification of Negro industry and the serious training of domestic servants—would do two things: it would take the ban from the calling of domestic service by ceasing to make "Negro" and "servant" synonymous terms. This would make it possible for both whites and blacks to enter more freely into service without a fatal and disheartening loss of self-respect; secondly, it would furnish trained servants—a sad necessity to-day, as any housekeeper can testify. . . .

2. "The Value of Agitation"

Published in 1907 in *The Voice of the Negro*, Volume IV

There are those people in the world who object to agitation and one cannot wholly blame them. Agitation after all is unpleasant. It means that while you are going on peaceably and joyfully on your way some half-mad person insists upon saying things that you do not like to hear. They may be true but you do not like to hear them. You would rather wait till some convenient season; or you take up your newspaper and instead of finding pleasant notices about your friends and the present progress of the world, you read of some restless folks who

insist on talking about wrong and crime and unpleasant things. It would be much better if we did not have to have agitation; if we had a world where everything was going so well and it was unnecessary often to protest strongly, even wildly, of the evil and the wrong of the universe.

As a matter of fact, however, no matter how unpleasant the agitator is, and no matter how inconvenient and unreasonable his talk, yet we must ever have him with us. And why? Because this is a world where things are not all right. We are gifted with human nature which does not do the right or even desire the right always. So long as these things are true, then we are faced by this dilemma: either we must let the evil alone and refuse to hear of it or listen to it or we must try and right it. Now, very often it happens that the evil is there, the wrong has been done, and yet we do not hear of it—we do not know about it. Here then comes the agitator. He is the herald—he is the prophet—he is the man that says to the world: "There are evils which you do not know, but which I know and you must listen to them." Now, of course, there may be agitators who are telling the truth and there may be agitators who are telling untruths. Those who are not telling the truth may be lying or they may be mistaken. So that agitation in itself does not necessarily mean always the right and always reform.

Here then is some one who thinks that he has discovered some dangerous evil and wants to call the attention of good men of the world to it. If he does not persevere, we may perhaps pass him by. If he is easily discouraged, we may perhaps think that the evil which he thought he saw has been cured. But if he is sincere and if he is persistent, then there is but one thing for a person to do who wants to live in a world worth living in; that is, listen to him carefully, prove his tale and then try and right the wrong.

If we remember the history of all great reform movements, we remember that they have been preceded by agitation. Take for instance, the suppression of the slave trade. It was in a day when slavery could not be successfully attacked. But there was no doubt of the horrors of the slave trade. The best and worst of people alike admitted that. Here came a young man just graduated from college. By writing a prize essay he found himself interested in this great evil. He began to know and learn of things which other people did not know. Not that they knew nothing about them, but they had not brought together all the facts. One isolated person knew that fact and one knew this fact, but no one person knew both facts in juxtaposition. When they did become acquainted with all the facts he was sure that they must be moved to act. What then must he do? He must agitate. It was not pleasant—it was putting himself in jeopardy; he was called upon to lose friends in some cases, and in all cases to make himself unpleasant, insistent, persistent, telling of things that people did not want to hear about, because they were not interested in them. He must interest people in things in which they were not interested before, which is a hard task in this busy world; and yet, nevertheless, if Clarkson had not persisted, we would have much less than a chance to agitate for human rights today.

So it is with all great movements. They must be preceded by agitation. In the present status of the Negro it is particularly necessary that we today make the world realize what his position is—make them realize that he is not merely insisting on ornamental rights and neglecting plain duties, but that the rights we want are the rights that are necessary, inevitable before we can rightly do our duties.

Mrs. Gilman has a poem somewhere, where she speaks of that rule which is to be laid down in the great future state, "Unless a man works, he may not eat," and she says very aptly that "The cart is before the horse," because "unless a man eats he cannot work."

So to those people who are saying to black men today, "Do your duties first and then clamor for rights," we have a right to answer and to answer insistently: that the rights we are clamoring for are those that will enable us to do our duties. That we cannot possibly be asked to do any partial measure of our duty even, unless we can have those rights and have them now. We realize this. The great mass of people in the United States do not realize it. What then are we to do? We may sit in courteous and dumb self-forgetting silence until other people are interested and come to our rescue. But is it reasonable to suppose that this is going to happen before degeneration and destruction overtake us? This is a busy world. People are attending to their own affairs as they ought to.

The man that has a grievance is supposed to speak for himself. No one can speak for him—no one knows the thing as well as he does. Therefore it is reasonable to say that if the man does not complain that it is because he has no complaint. If a man does not express his needs, then it is because his needs are filled. And it has been our great mistake in the last decade that we have been silent and still and have not complained when it was our duty not merely to ourselves but to our country and to humanity in general to complain and to complain loudly. It is then high time that the Negro agitator should be in the land.

It is not a pleasant role to play. It is not always pleasant to nice ears to hear a man ever coming with his dark facts and unpleasant conditions. Nevertheless it is the highest optimism to bring forward the dark side of any human picture. When a man does this he says to the world: "Things are bad but it is worthwhile to let the world know that things are bad in order that they may become better. The real crushing pessimism takes hold of the world when people say things are so bad that they are not worth complaining of because they cannot be made better.

It is manifest that within the last year the whole race in the United States has awakened to the fact that they have lost ground and must start complaining and complain loudly. It is their business to complain.

This complaint should be made with reason and with strict regard to the truth, but nevertheless it should be made. And it is interesting to find even those persons who were deriding complaint a few years ago joining in the agitation today.

We of the Niagara Movement welcome them. We are glad of help from all sources. We are confirmed in our belief that if a man stand up and tell the thing he wants and point out the evil around him, that this is the best way to get rid of it. May we not hope then that we are going to have in the next century a solid front on the part of colored people in the United States, saying we want education for our children and we do not have it today in any large measure; we want full political rights and we never have had that; we want to be treated as human beings; and we want those of our race who stand on the threshold and within the veil of crime to be treated not as beasts, but as men who can be reformed or as children who can be prevented from going further in their career.

If we all stand and demand this insistently, the nation must listen to the voice of ten millions.

3. *"Of the Ruling of Men"*

Published in 1920 in *Darkwater*

. . . Who may be excluded from a share in the ruling of men? Time and time again the world has answered:

The Ignorant

The Inexperienced

The Guarded

The Unwilling

That is, we have assumed that only the intelligent should vote, or those who know how to rule men, or those who are not under benevolent guardianship, or those who ardently desire the right.

These restrictions are not arguments for the wide distribution of the ballot—they are rather reasons for restriction addressed to the self-interest of the present real rulers. We say easily, for instance, "The ignorant ought not to vote." We would say, "No civilized state should have citizens too ignorant to participate in government," and this statement is but a step to the fact: that no state is civilized which has citizens too ignorant to help rule it. Or, in other words, education is not a prerequisite to political control—political control is the cause of popular education.

Again, to make experience a qualification for the franchise is absurd: it would stop the spread of democracy and make political power hereditary, a prerequisite of a class, caste, race, or sex. It has of course been soberly argued that only white folk or Englishmen, or men, are really capable of exercising sovereign power in a modern state. The statement proves too much: only yesterday it was Englishmen of high descent, or men of "blood," or sovereigns "by divine right" who could rule. Today the civilized world is being ruled by the descendants of persons who a century ago were pronounced incapable of ever developing a self-ruling people. In every modern state there must come to the polls every generation, and indeed every year, men who are inexperienced in the solutions of the political problems that confront them and who must experiment in methods of ruling men. Thus and thus only will civilization grow.

Again, what is this theory of benevolent guardianship for women, for the masses, for Negroes—for "lesser breeds without the law"? It is simply the old cry of privilege, the old assumption that there are those in the world who know better what is best for others than those others know themselves, and who can be trusted to do this best.

In fact no one knows himself but that self's own soul. The vast and wonderful knowledge of this marvelous universe is locked in the bosoms of its individual souls. To tap this mighty reservoir of experience, knowledge, beauty, love, and deed we must appeal not to the few, not to some souls, but to all. The narrower the appeal, the poorer the culture; the wider the appeal the more magnificent are the possibilities. Infinite is human nature. We make it finite by choking back the mass of men, by attempting to speak for others, to interpret and act for them, and we end by acting for ourselves and using the world as our private property. If this were all, it were crime enough—but it is not all: by our ignorance we make the creation of the greater world impossible; we beat back a world built of the playing of dogs and laughter of children, the song of Black Folk and worship of Yellow, the love of women and strength of men, and try to express by a group of doddering ancients the Will of the World.

There are people who insist upon regarding the franchise, not as a necessity for the many, but as a privilege for the few. They say of persons and classes: "They do not need the ballot." This is often said of women. It is argued that everything which women with the ballot might do for themselves can be done for them; that they have influence and friends "at court," and that their enfranchisement would simply double the number of ballots. So, too, we are told that American Negroes can have done for them by other voters all that they could possibly do for themselves with the ballot and much more because the white voters are more intelligent.

Further than this, it is argued that many of the disfranchised people recognize these facts. "Women do not want the ballot" has been a very effective counter war-cry, so much so that many men have taken refuge in the declaration:

"When they want to vote, why, then—" So, too, we are continually told that the "best" Negroes stay out of politics.

Such arguments show so curious a misapprehension of the foundation of the argument for democracy that the argument must be continually restated and emphasized. We must remember that if the theory of democracy is correct, the right to vote is not merely a privilege, not simply a method of meeting the needs of a particular group, and least of all a matter of recognized want or desire. Democracy is a method of realizing the broadest measure of justice to all human beings. The world has, in the past, attempted various methods of attaining this end, most of which can be summed up in three categories:

The method of the benevolent tyrant.

The method of the select few.

The method of the excluded groups.

The method of intrusting the government of a people to a strong ruler has great advantages when the ruler combines strength with ability, unselfish devotion to the public good, and knowledge of what that good calls for. Such a combination is, however, rare and the selection of the right ruler is very difficult. To leave the selection to force is to put a premium on physical strength, chance, and intrigue; to make the selection a matter of birth simply transfers the real power from sovereign to minister. Inevitably the choice of rulers must fall on electors.

Then comes the problem, who shall elect. The earlier answer was: a select few, such as the wise, the best born, the able. Many people assume that it was corruption that made such aristocracies fail. By no means. The best and most effective aristocracy, like the best monarchy, suffered from lack of knowledge. The rulers did not know or understand the needs of the people and they could not find out, for in the last analysis only the man himself, however humble, knows his own condition. He may not know how to remedy it, he may not realize just what is the matter; but he knows when something hurts and he alone knows how that hurt feels. Or if sunk below feeling or comprehension or complaint, he does not even know that he is hurt, God help his country, for it not only lacks knowledge, but has destroyed the sources of knowledge.

So soon as a nation discovers that it holds in the heads and hearts of its individual citizens the vast mine of knowledge, out of which it may build a just government, then more and more it calls those citizens to select their rulers and to judge the justice of their acts.

Even here, however, the temptation is to ask only for the wisdom of citizens of a certain grade or those of recognized worth. Continually some classes are tacitly or expressly excluded. Thus women have been excluded from modern democracy because of the persistent theory of female subjection and because it was argued that their husbands or other male folks would look to their interests. Now, manifestly, most husbands, fathers, and brothers, will, so far as they know how or as they realize women's needs, look after them. But remember the foundation of the argument,—that in the last analysis only the sufferer knows his sufferings and that no state can be strong which excludes from its expressed wisdom the knowledge possessed by mothers, wives, and daughters. We have but to view the unsatisfactory relations of the sexes the world over and the problem of children to realize how desperately we need this excluded wisdom.

The same arguments apply to other excluded groups: if a race, like the Negro race, is excluded, then so far as that race is a part of the economic and social organization of the land, the feeling and the experience of that race are absolutely necessary to the realization of the broadest justice for all citizens. Or if the "submerged tenth" be excluded, then again, there is lost from the world an experience of untold value, and they must be raised rapidly to a place where they can speak for themselves. In the same way and for the same reason children must be educated, insanity prevented, and only those put under the guardianship of others who can in no way be trained to speak for themselves.

The real argument for democracy is, then, that in the people we have the source of that endless life and unbounded wisdom which the rulers of men must have. A given people today may not be intelligent, but through a democratic government that recognizes, not only the worth of the individual to himself, but the worth of his feelings and experiences to all, they can educate, not only the individual unit, but generation after generation, until they accumulate vast stores of wisdom. Democracy alone is the method of showing the whole experience of the race for the benefit of the future and if democracy tries to exclude women or Negroes or the poor or any class because of innate characteristics which do not interfere with intelligence, then that democracy cripples itself and belies its name.

From this point of view we can easily see the weakness and strength of current criticism of extension of the ballot. It is the business of a modern government to see to it, first, that the number of ignorant within its bounds is reduced to the very smallest number. Again, it is the duty of every such government to extend as quickly as possible the number of persons of mature age who can vote. Such possible voters must be regarded, not as sharers of a limited treasure, but as sources of new national wisdom and strength.

The addition of the new wisdom, the new points of view, and the new interests must, of course, be from time to time bewildering and confusing. Today those who have a voice in the body politic have expressed their wishes and sufferings. The result has been a smaller or greater balancing of their conflicting interests.

The appearance of new interests and complaints means disarrangement and confusion to the older equilibrium. It is, of course, the inevitable preliminary step to that larger equilibrium in which the interests of no human soul will be neglected. These interests will not, surely, be all fully realized, but they will be recognized and given as full weight as the conflicting interests will allow. The problem of government thereafter would be to reduce the necessary conflict of human interests to the minimum.

From such a point of view one easily sees the strength of the demand for the ballot on the part of certain disfranchised classes. When women ask for the ballot, they are asking, not for a privilege, but for a necessity. You may not see the necessity, you may easily argue that women do not need to vote. Indeed, the women themselves in considerable numbers may agree with you. Nevertheless, women do need the ballot. They need it to right the balance of a world sadly awry because of its brutal neglect of the rights of women and children. With the best will and knowledge, no man can know women's wants as well as women themselves. To disfranchise women is deliberately to turn from knowledge and grope in ignorance.

So, too, with American Negroes: the South continually insists that a benevolent guardianship of whites over blacks is the ideal thing. They assume that white people not only know better what Negroes need than Negroes themselves, but that they are anxious to supply these needs. As a result they grope in ignorance and helplessness. They cannot "understand" the Negro; they cannot protect him from cheating and lynching; and, in general, instead of loving guardianship we see anarchy and exploitation. If the Negro could speak for himself in the South instead of being spoken for, if he could defend himself instead of having to depend on the chance sympathy of white citizens, how much healthier a growth of democracy the South would have.

So, too, with the darker races of the world. No federation of the world, no true internation—can exclude the black and brown and yellow races from its counsels. They must equally and according to number act and be heard at the world's council. . . .

The principle of basing all government on the consent of the governed is undenied and undeniable. Moreover, the method of modern democracy has placed within reach of the modern state larger reserves of efficiency, ability, and even genius than the ancient or mediaeval state dreamed of. That this great work of the past can be carried further among all races and nations no one can reasonably doubt.

Great as are our human differences and capabilities there is not the slightest scientific reason for assuming that a given human being of any race or sex cannot reach normal, human development if he is granted a reasonable chance. This is, of course, denied. It is denied so volubly and so frequently and with such positive conviction that the majority of unthinking people seem to assume that most human beings are not human and have no right to human treatment or human opportunity. All this goes to prove that human beings are, and must be, woefully ignorant of each other. It always startles us to find folks thinking like ourselves. We do not really associate with each other, we associate with our ideas of each other, and few people have either the ability or courage to question their own ideas. None have more persistently and dogmatically insisted upon the inherent inferiority of women than the men with whom they come in closest contact. It is the husbands, brothers, and sons of women whom it has been most difficult to induce to consider women seriously or to acknowledge that women have rights which men are bound to respect. So, too, it is those people who live in closest contact with black folk who have most unhesitatingly asserted the utter impossibility of living beside Negroes who are not industrial or political slaves or social pariahs. All this proves that none are so blind as those nearest the thing seen, while, on the other hand, the history of the world is the history of the discovery of the common humanity of human beings among steadily-increasing circles of men.

If the foundations of democracy are thus seen to be sound, how are we going to make democracy effective where it now fails to function—particularly in industry? The Marxists assert that industrial democracy will automatically follow public ownership of machines and materials. Their opponents object that nationalization of machines and materials would not suffice because the mass of people do not understand the industrial process. They do not know:

What to do

How to do it

Who could do it best

or

How to apportion the resulting goods.

There can be no doubt but that monopoly of machines and materials is a chief source of the power of industrial tyrants over the common worker and that monopoly today is due as much to chance and cheating as to thrift and intelligence. So far as it is due to change and cheating, the argument for public ownership of capital is incontrovertible even though it involves some interference with long vested rights and inheritance. This is being widely recognized in the whole civilized world. But how about the accumulation of goods due to thrift and intelligence—would democracy in industry interfere here to such an extent as to discourage enterprise and make impossible the intelligent direction of the mighty and intricate industrial process of modern times?

The knowledge of what to do in industry and how to do it in order to attain the resulting goods rests in the hands and brains of the workers and managers, and the judges of the result are the public. Consequently it is not so much a question as to whether the world will admit democratic control here as how can such control be long avoided when the people once understand the fundamentals of industry. How can civilization persist in letting one person or a group of persons, by secret inherent power, determine what goods shall be made—whether bread or champagne, overcoats or silk socks? Can so vast a power be kept from the people?

But it may be opportunely asked: has our experience in electing public officials led us to think that we could run railways, cotton mills, and department stores by popular vote? The answer is clear: no, it has not, and the reason has been lack of interest in politics and the tyranny of the Majority. Politics have not touched the matters of daily life which are nearest the interests of the people—namely, work and wages; or if they have, they have touched it obscurely and indirectly. When voting touches the vital, everyday interests of all, nominations and elections will call for more intelligent activity. Consider too the vast unused and misused power of public rewards to obtain ability and genius for the service of the state. If millionaires can buy science and art, cannot the Democratic state outbid them not only with money but with the vast ideal of the common weal?

There still remains, however, the problem of the Majority.

What is the cause of the undoubted reaction and alarm that the citizens of democracy continually feel? It is, I am sure, the failure to feel the full significance of the change of rule from a privileged minority to that of an omnipotent majority, and the assumption that mere majority rule is the last word of government; that majorities have no responsibilities, that they rule by the grace of God. Granted that government should be based on the consent of the governed, does the consent of a majority at any particular time adequately express the consent of all? Has the minority, even though a small and unpopular and unfashionable minority, no right to respectful consideration?

I remember that excellent little high school text book, "Nordhoff's Politics," where I first read of government, saying this sentence at the beginning of its most important chapter: "The first duty of a minority is to become a majority." This is a statement which has its underlying truth, but it also has its dangerous falsehood; viz., any minority which cannot become a majority is not worthy of any consideration. But suppose that the out-voted minority is necessarily always a minority? Women, for instance, can seldom expect to be a majority; artists must always be the few; ability is always rare, and black folk in this land are but a tenth. Yet to tyrannize over such minorities, to browbeat and insult them, to call that government a democracy which makes majority votes an excuse for crushing ideas and individuality and self-development, is manifestly a peculiarly dangerous perversion of the real democratic ideal. It is right here, in its method and not in its object, that democracy in America and elsewhere has so often failed. We have attempted to enthrone any chance majority and make it rule by divine right. We have kicked and cursed minorities as upstarts and usurpers when their sole offense lay in not having ideas or hair like ours. Efficiency, ability, and genius found often no abiding place in such a soil as this. Small wonder that revolt has come and high-handed methods are rife, of pretending that policies which we favor or persons that we like have the anointment of a purely imaginary majority vote.

Are the methods of such a revolt wise, howsoever great the provocation and evil may be? If the absolute monarchy of majorities is galling and inefficient, is it any more inefficient than the absolute monarchy of individuals or privileged classes have been found to be in the past? Is the appeal from a numerous-minded despot to a smaller, privileged group or to one man likely to remedy matters permanently? Shall we step backward a thousand years because our present problem is baffling?

Surely not and surely, too, the remedy for absolutism lies in calling these same minorities to council. As the king-in-council succeeded the king by the grace of God, so in future democracies the toleration and encouragement of minorities and the willingness to consider as "men" the crankiest, humblest and poorest and blackest peoples, must be the real key to the consent of the governed. Peoples and governments will not in the future assume that because they have the brute power to enforce momentarily dominant ideas, it is best to do so without thoughtful conference with the ideas of smaller groups and individuals. Proportionate representation in physical and spiritual form must come.

That this method is virtually coming in vogue we can see by the minority groups of modern legislatures. Instead of the artificial attempts to divide all possible ideas and plans between two great parties, modern legislatures in advanced nations tend to develop smaller and smaller minority groups, while government is carried on by temporary coalitions. For a time we inveighed against this and sought to consider it a perversion of the only possible method of practical democracy. Today we are gradually coming to realize that government by temporary coalition of small and diverse groups may easily become the most efficient method of expressing the will of man and of setting the human soul free. The only hindrance to the faster development of this government by allied minorities is the fear of external war which is used again and again to melt these living, human, thinking groups into inhuman, thoughtless, and murdering machines.

The persons, then, who come forward in the dawn of the 20th century to help in the ruling of men must come with the firm conviction that no nation, race, or sex, has a monopoly of ability or ideas; that no human group is so small as to deserve to be ignored as a part, and as an integral and respected part, of the mass of men; that, above all, no group of twelve million black folk, even though they are at the physical mercy of a hundred million white majority, can be deprived of a voice in their government and of the right to self-development without a blow at the very foundations of all democracy and all human uplift; that the very criticism aimed today at universal suffrage is in reality a demand for power on the part of consciously efficient minorities,— but these minorities face a fatal blunder when they assume that less democracy will give them and their kind greater efficiency. However desperate the temptation, no modern nation can shut the gates of opportunity in the face of its women, its peasants, its laborers, or its socially damned. How astounded the future world-citizen will be to know that as late as 1918 great and civilized nations were making desperate endeavor to confine the development of ability and individuality to one sex,—that is, to one-half of the nation; and he will probably learn that similar effort to confine humanity to one race lasted a hundred years longer.

The doctrine of the divine right of majorities leads to almost humorous insistence on a dead level of mediocrity. It demands that all people be alike or that they be ostracized. At the same time its greatest accusation against rebels is this same desire to be alike: the suffragette is accused of wanting to be a man, the socialist is accused of envy of the rich, and the black man is accused of wanting to be white. That any one of these should simply want to be himself is to the average worshiper of the majority inconceivable, and yet of all worlds, may the good Lord deliver us from a world where everybody looks like his neighbor and thinks like his neighbor and is like his neighbor.

The world has long since awakened to a realization of the evil which a privileged few may exercise over the majority of a nation. So vividly has this truth been brought home to us that we have lightly assumed that a privileged and enfranchised majority cannot equally harm a nation. Insane, wicked, and wasteful as the tyranny of the few over the many may be, it is not more dangerous than the tyranny of the many over the few. Brutal physical revolution can, and usually does, end the tyranny of the few. But the spiritual losses from suppressed minorities may be vast and fatal and yet all unknown and unrealized because idea and dream and ability are paralyzed by brute force.

If, now, we have a democracy with no excluded groups, with all men and women enfranchised, what is such a democracy to do? How will it function? What will be its field of work?

The paradox which faces the civilized world today is that democratic control is everywhere limited in its control of human interests. Mankind is engaged in planting, forestry, and mining, preparing food and shelter, making clothes and machines, transporting goods and folk, disseminating news, distributing products, doing public and private personal service, teaching, advancing science, and creating art.

In this intricate whirl of activities, the theory of government has been hitherto to lay down only very general rules of conduct, marking the limits of extreme anti-social acts, like fraud, theft, and murder.

The theory was that within these bounds was Freedom—the Liberty to think and do and move as one wished. The real realm of freedom was found in experience to be much narrower than this in one direction and much broader in another. In matters of Truth and Faith and Beauty, the Ancient Law was inexcusably strait and modern law unforgivably stupid. It is here that the future and mighty fight for Freedom must and will be made. Here in the heavens and on the mountaintops, the air of Freedom is wide, almost limitless, for here, in the highest stretches, individual freedom harms no man, and, therefore, no man has the right to limit it.

On the other hand, in the valleys of the hard, unyielding laws of matter and the social necessities of time production, and human intercourse, the limits on our freedom are stern and unbending if we would exist and thrive. This does not say that everything here is governed by incontrovertible "natural" law which needs no human decision as to raw materials, machinery, prices, wages, news dissemination, education of children, etc.; but it does mean that decisions here must be limited by brute facts and based on science and human wants.

Today the scientific and ethical boundaries of our industrial activities are not in the hands of scientists, teachers, and thinkers; nor is the intervening opportunity for decision left in the control of the public whose welfare such decisions guide. On the contrary, the control of industry is largely in the hands of a powerful few, who decide for their own good and regardless of the good of others. The making of the rules of Industry, then, is not in the hands of All, but in the hands of the Few. The Few who govern industry envisage, not the wants of mankind, but their own wants. They work quietly, often secretly, opposing Law, on the one hand, as interfering with the "freedom of industry"; opposing, on the other hand, free discussion and open determination of the rules of work and wealth and wages, on the ground that harsh natural law brooks no interference by Democracy.

These things today, then, are not matters of free discussion and determination. They are strictly controlled. Who controls them? Who makes these inner, but powerful, rules? Few people know. Others assert and believe these rules are "natural"—a part of our inescapable physical environment. Some of them doubtless are; but most of them are just as clearly the dictates of self-interest laid down by the powerful private persons who today control industry. Just here it is that modern men demand that Democracy supplant skilfully concealed, but all too evident, Monarchy.

In industry, monarchy and the aristocracy rule, and there are those who, calling themselves democratic, believe that democracy can never enter here. Industry, they maintain, is a matter of technical knowledge and ability, and, therefore, is the eternal heritage of the few. They point to the failure of attempts at democratic control in industry, just as we used to point to Spanish-American governments, and they expose, not simply the failures of Russian Soviets,—they fly to arms to prevent that greatest experiment in industrial democracy which the world has yet seen. These are the ones who say: We must control labor or civilization will fail; we must control white labor in Europe and America; above all, we must control yellow labor in Asia and black labor in Africa and the South, else we shall have no tea, or rubber, or cotton. And yet,—and yet is it so easy to give up the dream of democracy? Must industry rule men or may men rule even industry? And unless men rule industry, can they ever hope really to make laws or educate children or create beauty?

That the problem of the democratization of industry is tremendous, let no man deny. We must spread that sympathy and intelligence which tolerates the widest individual freedom despite the necessary public control; we must learn to select for public office ability rather than mere affability. We must stand ready to defer to knowledge and science and judge by result rather than by method; and finally we must face the fact that the final distribution of goods—the question of wages and income is an ethical and not a mere mechanical problem and calls for grave public human judgment and not secrecy and closed doors. All this means time and development. It comes not complete by instant revolution of a day, nor yet by the deferred evolution of a thousand years—it comes daily, bit by bit and step by step, as men and women learn and grow and as children are trained in Truth.

These steps are in many cases clear: the careful, steady increase of public democratic ownership of industry, beginning with the simplest type of public utilities and monopolies, and extending gradually as we learn the way; the use of taxation to limit inheritance and to take the unearned increment for public use beginning (but not ending) with a "single tax" on monopolized land values; the training of the public in business technique by co-operation in buying and selling, and in industrial technique by the shop committee and manufacturing guild.

But beyond all this must come the Spirit— the Will to Human Brotherhood of all Colors, Races, and Creeds; the Wanting of the Wants of All. Perhaps the finest contribution of current Socialism to the world is neither its light nor its dogma, but the idea back of its one mighty word—Comrade!

4. *"Of Giving Work"*

Published in 1920 in *The Crisis*

"We give you people work and if we didn't, how would you live?"

The speaker was a southern white man. He was of the genus called "good." He had come down from the Big House to advise these Negroes, in the forlorn little church which crouched on the creek. He didn't come to learn, but to teach. The result was that he did not learn, and he saw only that blank, impervious gaze which colored people know how to assume; and that dark wall of absolute silence which they have a habit of putting up instead

of applause. He felt awkward, but he repeated what he had said, because he could not think of anything else to say:

"We give you people work, and if we didn't, how would you live?"

And then the old and rather ragged black man arose in the back of the church and came slowly forward and as he came, he said:

"And we gives you homes; and we gives you cotton; and we makes your land worth money; and we waits on you and gets your meals and cleans up your dirt. If we didn't do all those things for you, how would you live?"

The white man choked and got red, but the old black man went on talking:

"And what's more: we gives you a heap more than you gives us and we's getting mighty tired of the bargain—"

"I think we ought to give you fair wages," stammered the white man.

"And that ain't all," continued the old black man, "we ought to have something to say about your wages. Because if what *you* gives us gives *you* a right to say what we ought to get, then what *we* gives you gives *us* a right to say what *you* ought to get; and we're going to take that right *some day*."

The white man blustered:

"That's Bolshevism!" he shouted.

And then church broke up.

5. *"Business as Public Service"*

Published in 1929 in *The Crisis*

If six young persons start out upon their career, what is the object which they seek? Here is a singer. He seeks, of course, to sing songs well. Or a minister. He seeks to advance religious ideals. A teacher imparts truth and searches for it. A physician tries to heal and preserve health. A lawyer contends for law and justice. All this is clear for five of our boys;

but when it comes, for instance, to the grocer, we all say frankly the grocer seeks profit. We do not visualize, indeed many of us do not clearly know, of any service or ideal aim which the grocer follows, except that of personal profit. Of none of the other five employments mentioned do we for a moment make so narrow an object. The singer may receive high fees, but he protests that music is his life work. There may be physicians who will not spoil their night's rest for a call that involves no cash return; but they do not advertise this fact and continually we see physicians giving time and talent for nothing because they are interested. If a minister is called to a church that offers a higher salary he hastens to deny that the salary in itself was the main reason of his decision. No lawyer openly advertises for the highest paying client or openly neglects the cause of a poor unfortunate litigant.

Only the grocer of this group says frankly that he is trying to make money and that the more money he makes out of the grocery business the more successful he is. If he leaves the grocery store for the drygoods business he is regarded as having given full explanation when he says that he can make more in drygoods.

Now it is precisely this difference of attitude and opinion as to the aims of business and the aims of art and science that indicates where the trouble-spot of the modern economic world lies. For it is not true that the businessman, that industrial organization renders no public service. It is only true that public opinion ignores the high value of the real service of businessmen and judges them by a purely artificial and dangerous standard—this is, the private income they gain. This false standard is all the more dangerous because of the extraordinary opportunities of modern business. Invention, technical efficiency and discovery make industry and business an enthralling field. A very large portion of the keenest minds, best ability, and strongest characters goes into business and industry and yet

from these men and from their careers we strip or we seek to strip most of those ideals and restraints which lie around all other human services. There is no doubt of the service which the businessman, the industrial leader, gives to the world. They have transformed modern civilization and the only thing that makes the culture of today in any way greater than the culture of other days; the only respect in which we surpass Rome, Egypt, Babylon, is the extraordinary service of modern business in transforming raw materials, transporting goods to consumers, applying power, adapting the forces of nature and supplying regularly the multitudinous physical wants of modern men. We are right to compare this service with the service of the artist, the scientist and the worker for social uplift.

In the case of these other workers, however, the world deems their work well rewarded if it is well done and if they have enough to sustain life in such a way that the work can be well done. On the other hand, with the businessman, we have persuaded ourselves that the personal income which he is able to make from business transactions is his reward and we make no real attempt to proportion that reward according to the service which he renders his town, his country or mankind. Indeed if he can legally secure the income, we protect him in its enjoyment, even if he got it by gambling, robbery, and murder, or other actual disservice to civilization.

This more or less unconscious belief of the majority of thinking men has put tremendous power into the hands of businessmen. For income is power—power over goods, over the services of men, over the size of their wages, their homes, the conditions of their work and the direction and results of their work. Great income is great power. The ruling monarchs today are the men who control great income. Once birth and politics gave this control. Today business is the controlling power. The results are obvious. Businessmen rule everywhere. We find them ruling in religion: it is the businessman who says today what shall be taught and believed in churches. He rules in art and says what may and may not be designed and painted and put in monuments. It is the leaders of industry who determine what shall be regarded as truth in the history and economics and social studies which are taught in our schools and colleges. We tried to establish democratic government in England, France, the United States and elsewhere and we have done so over limited fields of endeavor; but we all know that the scope of democratic control is very small and that in the wider sphere of work and wages, income, rent, taxes, housing, streets, city and country life, health, amusements and recreation—it is organized and oligarchically guided industry and not democracy which rules.

So tremendous is this power of organized industry today that it transforms our ideals of right and wrong, of crime and morality. There is practically nothing that cannot be done and be called good if it returns large enough profit to the industrial doers. The result of this is a singular sense of contradiction, futility, often despair and certain unhappiness in all modern culture. Our world is wider, richer, more powerful, more spectacular than the worlds of the past, but it is illogical and unhappy, despite six thousand years of modern conscious development.

The reason for much of this muddle is plainly because the energy of the leading men of the world is diverted from seeking directly to serve mankind toward an endeavor to increase their incomes and garner the consequent tremendous social power to a degree which far surpasses their knowledge or ability to use it. It is the old story of monarchs mad with power.

Many men of many nations have tried to lay bare this sore spot of modern culture in an endeavor to heal it; but of all the nations today only Russia has made a determined and frontal attack upon the profit idea. This attack has been obscured and hindered by a thousand obstacles. The Bolshevik experiment may not succeed, but even if it does not succeed it is at least a facing of a plain, persistent, and threatening evil which all honest minds see. Russia says to the world that the object of business and industry, just like the object of art and science, is the service of the mass of mankind; and that there is no more room for private profit in the work of an engineer or a merchant than there is in the work of a teacher or a singer. In all cases and for all human effort the chief reward and the only real reward is the service rendered. In order that this service may be of the highest value to all men, the servant surely must be able to live in health, security and reasonable comfort and for this he needs a steady and assured income. He does not need great wealth; he certainly does not need an income which will tempt him to foolishly luxurious waste at the cost of poverty, ignorance and crime for others; and above all he does not need an income which will give him irresponsible power beyond his vision or grasp. He does need food and clothes and shelter and some experience of the real beauty of living. These things need never be dear or unattainable for the average man with ordinary exertion.

Any attempt to realize such an ideal whether in Russia, France, or America is naturally going to be fought. It is going to be fought by those people who wish to monopolize goods and the services of men for themselves regardless of the cost to others or of the public good. It is going to be fought by those otherwise unselfish persons who firmly believe that our present system of high income reward for ability is the only one suited to present human nature and that its surrender means wider distress and unhappiness than we see.

For this reason we are not only unwilling to contemplate radical economic change in our own land, but we are unwilling for Russia even to try to experiment in hers. We reel forward to increasing monopoly and concentrated wealth which continues to pile up for us new and staggering problems.

Conceive for a moment this our own land. We are rich in oil and iron, coal and water power, land and raw material. Yet the rights to and ownership of these gifts of God have been so distributed as private property among the captains of American industry that the cost of gasoline, steel, heat, electricity, cotton, wool, lumber and food is from twice to ten times as much to the average consumer as it would be under a more logical and far-sighted system.

On the other hand, the income of those who have monopolized land, oil, coal and iron and of those who are monopolizing water power for the production of electricity reaches dimensions almost inconceivable. The power of these modern industrial emperors surpasses anything that the ancient world dreamed of.

How to extricate ourselves from this situation and yet preserve to men the best and indispensable services of business and industry is the great problem of forward-looking modern men. It is not reasonable to insist that immoderate private income is the inevitable accompaniment or incentive to successful industry. It is not logical to admit that human beings who work for the work's sake when the object is beauty and truth can not be induced to work for the work's sake when the object is the food and clothes of millions. . . .

6. "Employment"

Published in 1930 in *The Crisis*

There still persists, the conviction that unemployment primarily and at bottom is the fault of the man who is without work. It may not be his fault under present circumstances but he surely must have been idle and careless in his youth, wasteful and thoughtless as a young man, to be found in his full manhood or in middle-age without work. This is cruelly untrue and leads to injustice and social disaster. It is especially untrue of colored workers and yet it is applied to them by whites and blacks. Whites suspect that the unemployed Negro thinks himself too good for menial work and the successful black man has a terrible faith in thrift and diligence.

The League for Independent Political Action has issued a little twelve-paged pamphlet on "Unemployment" written by Henry R. Mussey, which every Negro ought to read. We have had the tenets of an outworn and passing economic situation drilled into us: thrift and wage, property and income, work and wealth—all this is looked upon as the natural path of progress for a poor black laborer. As it becomes, under modern economic organization, increasingly impossible to realize this, even for white laborers, we are continually leaping to the conclusion that Negroes are the ones who are wrong and not the system; that our paupers and criminals and unsuccessful men are the victims of their own faithlessness and lack of foresight. True it is that the grandchildren of slaves will have an undue share of the lazy and unskilled. But our poverty and unemployment today is but partially due to that and this we must realize.

In truth there are, as Mr. Mussey points out, tens of millions of people in the United States who are perpetually in danger of losing their jobs, and the proportion of colored people among these is naturally very much larger than our proportion in the population. This is the natural result of slavery, caste, and prejudice.

Despite the effort of the President and his cabinet and now of the census to minimize the facts, there must be today five million people in the United States who want work and cannot get it. Unemployment, then, is not a matter to be cured simply by individual effort, or even by common effort.

Unemployment comes first through new inventions and improvements in the industrial process: a new machine, a new process, may forthwith put thousands of men out of employment; and it does not cure their desperate plight, even if later larger numbers of other men or of other generations receive new work with better wages, by learning a new technique.

There are, secondly, seasonal fluctuations in the number of workers wanted and this especially hits the colored agricultural laborer in the South and the colored day laborer in the North. There is also the cycle of business variation with panics and booms like those through which we are continually passing.

All these things cause inevitable unemployment no matter how thrifty the worker is and how carefully he may save.

What should be done about it? In the first place, we should know the truth about it, and not be systematically lied to by the United States Department of Labor and the United States Census. Secondly, there should be a national effort to distribute laborers where they can find jobs and this should apply to colored labor as well as white. It is not possible today, as it was a couple of generations ago, for any willing person to find work and it is idiotic to assume that it is.

Thirdly, private employers, if they realize that regularity of work is just as important as regularity of dividends, and indeed, far more so, may arrange their work to avoid periods of unemployment and not depend as they do today upon a starving surplus of labor which they can hire and fire as they will. This is being done in many plants but in practically none of them are Negroes employed and in nearly all only the highest class of skilled labor is benefited.

Public works, like road building and great projects of public improvement, can do something to help employment in times of depression. But above all, there should be employment insurance with its incidence so arranged that its cost will fall lightest on the employer who keeps his men at work regularly, and heaviest on the seasonal employer.

Finally, improvements in industry which lead to a replacement of labor by machines or to a substitution of new labor for old because of new technique, can only be compensated for by shorter working time for all labor without a reduction of wages. Otherwise, the private profit-maker mainly and the general consumer to some extent get all the advantage at crushing cost to the displaced worker who is forced into pauperism or crime. . . .

7. "Economic Disfranchisement"

Published in 1930 in *The Crisis*

THERE IS no universal suffrage in modern industry. So far as the government conducts industry, as in the case of the Post Office and, in some instances, the transportation system, universal political suffrage indirectly controls the industry. But there are great public services, like the railroad, the telephone, gas and electric lighting, the telegraph and others, where the industry, although public in nature, is private in ownership, and conducted by an autocracy, except insofar as public opinion and the granting of privileges and franchises gives remote control to the voters.

The disfranchisement, therefore, of the mass of workers in this case is the most extraordinary and vital disfranchisement in the modern world. When we talk of industrial democracy, we mean the increased right of the working people to determine the policies of great public services, either through direct public ownership or by private negotiation in the shape of shop committees, working agreements and the like.

What is the attitude of the Negro here? Most Negroes would have no attitude at all, so far as public ownership was concerned. They would not be interested; and yet, they are, or should be, tremendously interested. Take, for instance, the telephone service. It is well-nigh universal. The number of telephones in use by colored people runs into the millions. It is not possible that Negroes in the United States spend less than ten million dollars a year for telephone service, and they may spend three times as much as this. In the organization of work and trade a balance is always assumed between a service rendered or goods delivered, on one side, and a reciprocal service rendered and goods delivered, on the other. If the exchange is not direct it must be indirect, or the whole industrial combination fails. Yet in the case of the colored people and the telephone, there is no reciprocity. The Telephone Company in the North, almost without exception, employs no colored help whatsoever; no laborers, no telephone girls, no clerks, no officials. The whole service is absolutely closed to Negroes. In the South, a few colored men are employed as laborers and linemen, but not many.

Here, then, is a situation where a quasi-public institution absolutely refuses to let millions of citizens earn a decent living, while taxing them along with other citizens for this public service. This compulsory exclusion is, of course, not confined to colored people. It is exercised against Jews; it is exercised against various groups of foreign-born; it is exercised even against certain social classes among American-born citizens. But in the case of the Negroes we can see it openly, just as in those chemical experiments where an artificially colored liquid reveals diffusion and reaction.

What now must Negroes do? If this sort of thing goes on, then disfranchisement in industry is going to be a vital factor in their elimination from modern civilization. By consolidations and mergers, by holding companies and interlocking directorates, the great industries of the world are becoming integrated into vast private organizations, which means that the work of

the world—the skilled work, the best-paid work—in the vast majority of the cases, is subject to this social and racial exclusion, to this refusal to allow certain classes of men to earn a decent living.

It is an intolerable situation. Attempts have been made to correct it by appeal. In Chicago and in High Harlem, New York, these appeals have been effective in the case of small store chains, and even to a slight extent with a corporation like the Western Union Telegraph Company. But the Telephone Company remains adamant. The Gas Company is absolutely deaf and unsympathetic.

In this case there is only one thing to do, and that is for the Negro voters with intelligence and far-reaching memory to see that by their votes no further privileges and franchises are granted to these public-service companies; and to see that the work of these companies, just as far as possible and as soon as possible, is transferred to the government. Government ownership is the only solution for this present industrial disfranchisement of the Negro.

There are, of course, many other reasons and arguments for public ownership besides this personal and racial reason. But all these arguments simply bring home to the mass of people the fact that public service cannot be carried on endlessly for private advantage and private profit.

8. "Marxism and the Negro Problem"

Published in 1933 in *The Crisis*

... There are certain books in the world which every searcher for truth must know: the Bible, *Critique of Pure Reason, Origin of Species,* and Karl Marx's *Capital.*

Yet until the Russian Revolution, Karl Marx was little known in America. He was treated condescendingly in the universities, and regarded even by the intelligent public as a radical agitator whose curious and inconvenient theories it was easy to refute. Today, at last, we all know better, and we see in Karl Marx a colossal genius of infinite sacrifice and monumental industry, and with a mind of extraordinary logical keenness and grasp. We may disagree with many of the great books of truth that I have named, and with *Capital*, but they can never be ignored. . . .

The task which Karl Marx set himself was to study and interpret the organization of industry in the modern world. One of Marx's earlier works, *The Communist Manifesto*, issued in 1848. . . .

All will notice in this manifesto, phrases which have been used so much lately and so carelessly that they have almost lost their meaning. But behind them still is living and insistent truth. The *class struggle* of exploiter and exploited is a reality. The capitalist still today owns machines, materials, and wages with which to buy labor. The laborer even in America owns little more than his ability to work. A wage contract takes place between these two and the resultant manufactured commodity or service is the property of the capitalist.

Here Marx begins his scientific analysis based on a mastery of practically all economic theory before his time and on an extraordinary, thoroughgoing personal knowledge of industrial conditions over all Europe and many other parts of the world.

His final conclusions were never all properly published. He lived only to finish the first volume of this *Capital*, and the other two volumes were completed from his papers and notes by his friend Engels. The result is an unfinished work, extraordinarily difficult to read and understand and one which the master himself would have been first to criticize as not properly representing his mature and finished thought.

Nevertheless, that first volume, together with the fairly evident meaning of the others, lay down a logical line of thought. The gist of

that philosophy is that the value of products regularly exchanged in the open market depends upon the labor necessary to produce them; that capital consists of machines, materials and wages paid for labor; that out of the finished product, when materials have been paid for and the wear and tear and machinery replaced, and wages paid, there remains a surplus value. This surplus value arises from labor and is the difference between what is actually paid laborers for their wages and the market value of the commodities which the laborers produce. It represents, therefore, exploitation of the laborer, and this exploitation, inherent in the capitalistic system of production, is the cause of poverty, of industrial crises, and eventually of social revolution.

This social revolution, whether we regard it as voluntary revolt or the inevitable working of a vast cosmic law of social evolution, will be the last manifestation of the class struggle, and will come by inevitable change induced by the very nature of the conditions under which present production is carried on. It will come by the action of the great majority of men who compose the wage-earning proletariat, and it will result in common ownership of all capital, the disappearance of capitalistic exploitation, and the division of the products and services of industry according to human needs, and not according to the will of the owners of capital.

It goes without saying that every step of this reasoning and every presentation of supporting facts have been bitterly assailed. The labor theory of value has been denied; the theory of surplus value refuted; and inevitability of revolution scoffed at; while industrial crises—at least until this present one—have been defended as unusual exceptions proving the rule of modern industrial efficiency.

But with the Russian experiment and the World Depression most thoughtful men today are beginning to admit:

That the continued recurrence of industrial crises and wars based largely on economic rivalry, with persistent poverty, unemployment, disease and crime, are forcing the world to contemplate the possibilities of fundamental change in our economic methods; and that means thorough-going change, whether it be violent, as in France or Russia, or peaceful, as seems just as possible, and just as true to the Marxian formula, if it is fundamental change; in any case, Revolution seems bound to come.

Perhaps nothing illustrates this better than recent actions in the United States: our re-examination of the whole concept of Property; our banking moratorium; the extraordinary new agriculture bill; the plans to attack unemployment, and similar measures. Labor rather than gambling is the sure foundation of value and whatever we call it—exploitation, theft or business acumen—there is something radically wrong with an industrial system that turns out simultaneously paupers and millionaires and sets a world starving because it has too much food.

What now has all this to do with the Negro problem? First of all, it is manifest that the mass of Negroes in the United States belong distinctly to the working proletariat. Of every thousand working Negroes less than a hundred and fifty belong to any class that could possibly be considered bourgeois. And even this more educated and prosperous class has but small connections with the exploiters of wage and labor. Nevertheless, this black proletariat is not a part of the white proletariat. Black and white work together in many cases, and influence each other's rates of wages. They have similar complaints against capitalists, save that the grievances of the Negro worker are more fundamental and indefensible, ranging as they do, since the day of Karl Marx, from chattel slavery, to the worst paid, sweated, mobbed and cheated labor in any civilized land.

And while Negro labor in America suffers because of the fundamental inequities of the whole capitalistic system, the lowest and most

fatal degree of its suffering comes not from the capitalists but from fellow white laborers. It is white labor that deprives the Negro of his right to vote, denies him education, denies him affiliation with trade unions, expels him from decent houses and neighborhoods, and heaps upon him the public insults of open color discrimination. . . .

Under these circumstances, what shall we say of the Marxian philosophy and of its relation to the American Negro? We can only say, as it seems to me that the Marxian philosophy is a true diagnosis of the situation in Europe in the middle of the 19th Century despite some of its logical difficulties. But it must be modified in the United States of America and especially so far as the Negro group is concerned. The Negro is exploited to a degree that means poverty, crime, delinquency and indigence. And that exploitation comes not from a black capitalistic class but from the white capitalists and equally from the white proletariat. His only defense is such internal organization as will protect him from both parties, and such practical economic insight as will prevent inside the race group any large development of capitalistic exploitation.

Meantime, comes the Great Depression. It levels all in mighty catastrophe. The fantastic industrial structure of America is threatened with ruin. The trade unions of skilled labor are double-tongued and helpless. Unskilled and common white labor is too frightened at Negro competition to attempt united action. It only begs a dole. The reformist program of Socialism meets no response from the white proletariat because it offers no escape to wealth and no effective bar to black labor, and a mud-sill of black labor is essential to white labor's standard of living. The shrill cry of a few communists is not even listened to, because and solely because it seeks to break down barriers between black and white. There is not at present the slightest indication that a Marxian revolution based on a united class-conscious proletariat is anywhere on the American far horizon. Rather race antagonism and labor group rivalry are still undisturbed by world catastrophe. In the hearts of black laborers alone, therefore, lie those ideals of democracy in politics and industry which may in time make the workers of the world effective dictators of civilization.

9. "The Use of Capital"

Published in 1935 in *National Baptist Voice*

... Into this situation there come certain changes as the tribe grows in size and as its demands for goods and services vary. The greatest and most significant change is what we call the use of capital; that is, the preparation of goods, not for eating and wearing and enjoying, but to be used in further preparation of other goods. There is always some capital in a primitive tribe. Some of the seed of the corn is not eaten, but saved for further harvest, some of the iron is fashioned not for spear-heads, but for knives with which furniture can be made. As the amount and usefulness of this capital increases, the whole situation in the tribe is changed.

In a modern nation, consider for a moment the goods used as capital; that is, as agencies which produce other goods and services. Most of our buildings, all of our railroads, all of our multitudinous machines and engines, most of our ships and airplanes, all of our factories and stores and offices, most of our raw material, wheat, cotton, iron, steel, stone; indeed, the great bulk of the valuable and important things about us are not for direct use and enjoyment, but indirectly used to produce the things which we eat and wear and use directly. And think of the time consumed in making these goods. The appearance of this kind of goods which we call capital immediately brings changes in the idea of property.

Property, first, is a simple concept. A man makes his own arrows; his own fishing rods; his own clothes. They belong to him because he made them. On the other hand, he does not make the land upon which he works; and the primitive machines which he employs are usually made by several men working together. The land, therefore, is never conceived of as private property in a primitive tribe. The machines are looked upon as belonging to the community; while the individual tools and weapons are conceived of as belonging to the individual. When, now, the capital goods, the goods which are designed to make other goods, the tools and machines grow in number, to whom do they belong? This question was never settled in early industrial life or in later developments by decisions of abstract justice and right and considerations of the best interests of the community.

In such developments as accompanied the rise and fall of Rome, the descent of the barbarians, the wars and counter-wars which marked the growth of European nations, chance, power and cunning influenced the result. So that when we come to modern times, we find that not by design or purpose, not according to religion or ethics, but as a matter of fact, difficult or even impossible to explain; the land belonged to a few people; the machines and materials were monopolized by the rich and the mass of the workers without land and without capital, sold their toil for wages which were seldom above the amount necessary for their existence and reproduction. A great deal of bitter charge and invective have been brought against the rich and powerful who thus monopolize wealth. But this is not entirely fair. Most of the wealthy gained their power and resources by heritage, by opportunity, by hard work and especially by the public opinion of their times which encouraged and praised this acquisition of power.

Nevertheless, the excuses which then and now may be very properly made for capitalists and rich people do not at all alter the fact that the plight of the mass of workers is simply impossible and must be changed. Demands for such a change came in the Eighteenth and especially in the early Nineteenth Centuries. They were chiefly philanthropic demands, that is, they were appeals on the part of persons who knew the plight of the poor and who were sensitive to human welfare and who said: this sort of industry is not civilization; it is not in accordance with religion and it must be changed. But the difficulty was that here was a pattern set and hardened by the authority of hundreds of years. Most people, for instance, looked upon private ownership of land as a natural and God-given thing. They have no conception of the fact that during most of the years in which man has been civilized, private ownership of land was not only uncommon, but unthought of. Indeed, very largely, inconceivable. The source of the present ownership and monopoly of machines and raw materials is hard to extricate from a complicated industrial history.

There are those who insist that all property and all capital is theft and if we mean by theft the taking of goods for ourselves which others have produced, then it is true that property is theft; but we must remember that law, gospel and custom for a thousand years has called that sort of accumulation of property not only justifiable but as right and indispensable to the proper carrying on of industry. Today, therefore, we need not waste our time as to the past history and ethics of capital and industry, but we must, on the other hand, ask today; why is it that in a world where it is possible to raise enough food and manufacture enough clothing and build enough housing for the accommodation of all men, and in addition to this, give them services which will educate and amuse and develop them, when all this is undoubtedly possible and made possible by the reasonable amount of toil of the mass of men who can work, why is it, in spite of this that millions upon millions of workers can find no more to do, while other millions who do work cannot

get for their toil enough to sustain them and clothing and housing sufficient to protect them? And children and old people and the sick are faced with starvation. This is not merely a philosophy of envy. It need not lead to hatred and bloodshed, but it must lead to reform or civilization cannot go on . . . .

10. "The Release of Earl Browder"

Published in 1942 in the *Amsterdam News*

. . . Democracy is not, as so many of us are prone to think, simply the right of electing our rulers. It is not simply, as others think, the right of working people to have a voice in the conduct of industry. It is much more than this; it is a vaster and more inclusive ideal; it is the right to accumulate and use a great reservoir of human thought and experience, out of which a people may choose, not simply men and methods, but the wisest and best policies of government and conduct and have their choice all the more valuable because the sum of human knowledge is open freely to their understanding and inspection. It is here, in thought and concept, that real freedom lies. Freedom is not a mere matter of physical movement; that may be curtailed by geography. It is not just a matter of the election of officials; that may easily be frustrated by lack of candidates. It is not even economic freedom; for economic processes are to a degree subject to physical conditions. But there is a freedom of thought and planning, by which the world, if it has a broad basis of fact and knowledge of experience, can slowly and laboriously work out a way of life for the mass of men.

In free discussion and free investigation with the requisite intelligence to understand, lies the hope and the excuse of democracy. There must not be allowed to stand in the way of this freedom, either the Fear of the Satisfied or the Fury of the Distressed. It is natural that those people who are today living reasonably pleasant lives, under the present organization of industry, should be afraid even to discuss change, lest such change involve their disaster. It is perhaps even more reasonable that people whose lives by any standards of judgment are today not worth living; whose food is too little for health; whose shelter is too curtailed for decency; whose intelligence has had no adequate chance for development; that these in their fury should often want to tear down all that is, in the conviction that nothing could be worse than present conditions for millions upon millions of human beings. . . .

This is a great and strong nation. Its realization of the democratic ideal is the broadest ever attempted by man. Its standard of living for the working class is the highest in the world. Its economic and industrial technic is miraculous, yet our very accomplishment should make us neither foolish nor afraid. We know our own failures. Born in liberty we deliberately nourished slavery until it all but strangled us; we stood for human equality and let ourselves become a center of race prejudice and discrimination; we established free democratic elections and allowed them to degenerate into rule by one race, by political bosses and by great corporations. All this and more; but we know our faults and are going to correct them, lest government by the people and for the people perish from the earth. We are not afraid of criticism. We welcome discussion and we are not going to imprison any man of honest conviction because we fear the Truth. For this reason we rejoice at the freedom of Earl Browder.

11. "Human Rights for All Minorities"

Given as a speech in 1945
at a meeting of the East and West Association

. . . Democracy is not merely a distribution of power among a vast number of individuals. It is not merely majority rule based on the fact that the majority has the physical force to prevail. It is something far more fundamental than this. It rests upon the fact that, when we have proven knowledge, interpreted through the experience of a large number of individuals, it is possible through this pooled knowledge and experience to come to decisions much more fundamental and much more far-reaching than can be had in any other way. This is so clear and logical that it needs no proof, but rests on certain fundamental assumptions. The people participating effectively in this pool of democracy must be alive and well, they must know the world which they are interpreting, and they must know themselves.

It is here that frustration of democracy comes, particularly in the case of minorities. Manifestly, there can be no hope of effective functioning of democracy among people who have not enough to eat or to live decently, among people who are sick and ignorant. Nor can we assume that poverty, ignorance and disease are always the fault of those who suffer from them. If a minority does suffer because of these disadvantages, we know immediately where the remedy lies and what we are compelled to do if we want decency and justice in the world.

We know that colonies, as centers of this frustration of democracy, are the starting point of injustice and cruelty toward all groups of people who form minority groups and who at the same time, in a sense, are the majority of the peoples of the world. And they are part of this majority even though unjustly treated minorities do not actually occupy colonial status. Often they occupy quasi-colonial status, even though segregated in the slums of a large and prosperous nation which is leading civilization.

It is, then, this colonial status that forms an integral and fundamental part of modern civilization. We must not let words mislead us and think of the modern colony as the pioneer group of Grecian days or of European exploration, when people of one country went out in search of adventure or to earn a living in another country through trade. This kind of colony in modern days changed. Either it became an independent state with its own economic organization, or it became a part of the economic organization of the mother country. In this later case in our era it was that part of our economy which illustrated and carried out logically the conception of labor as a commodity.

We know the growth of classical economics in England in the nineteenth century: its conception of the self-regulating world market, of labor and land as purchasable commodities, and of gold as the only real money. But we do not remember nor try to learn that in back of the industrial revolution, out of the experiences of which classical economics arose, lay African slavery, and that it was through the purchase of slaves in open market, where there was no floor to the price of labor, that the conception of labor as a commodity, and not as the effort of human beings, arose and became an axiom in modern industry.

Without this African slave trade it is doubtful if European labor, or even the larger part of the labor of Asia or Africa which came under its sway, could have been reduced to the commodity status. But once labor, paid at the lowest conceivable price, became the basis of prosperity in America and England under the capitalist system, then a pattern was laid which gripped the world.

It led to land seizure and land monopoly in colonial regions and in civilized lands as a method of further reducing the price of labor and increasing the profits of investors.

Thus we must conceive of colonies in the nineteenth and twentieth centuries as not something far away from the centers of civilization; not as comprehending problems which are not our problems—the local problems of London, Paris and New York. They are not something which we can consider at our leisure but rather a part of our own present local economic organization. Moreover, while the center of the colonial system (and its form and pattern) is set in the localities which are called definitely colonies and are owned politically and industrially by imperial countries, we must remember also that in the organized and dominant states there are groups of people who occupy the quasi-colonial status: laborers who are settled in the slums of large cities; groups like Negroes in the United States who are segregated physically and discriminated against spiritually in law and custom; groups like the South American Indians who are the laboring peons, without rights or privileges, of large countries; and whole laboring classes in Asia and the South Seas who are legally part of imperial countries and, as a matter of fact, have their labor treated as a commodity at the lowest wage, and the land monopolized. All these people occupy what is really a colonial status and make the kernel and substance of the problem of minorities.

The connection of these colonial and quasi-colonial conditions within our economy is so strong and intricate that we seldom realize or study it. Remember that today we depend upon colonial and quasi-colonial workers for coffee, tea and cocoa; for sugar, rubber and the increasingly valuable vegetable oils; for minerals like gold, diamonds, copper and tin; for fibers like cotton, hemp and silk; for rice, spices, quinine and gum arabic. Indeed, for a mass of materials so inextricably part of our modern life that it would practically be impossible for us to get on without them. Yet all of these materials are raised by labor which does not receive in return enough income to keep it healthy, trained or effective, or even physically able to reproduce itself. In order to force this labor to work, it is systematically deprived of ownership of land and of a share in the free bounty of nature. It is kept in ignorance, first because intelligence would bring active or passive revolt against these conditions; and secondly because the cost of education would reduce the profits which are pouring into the coffers of the investors and into our mouths and on our backs.

This means that every civilized man is part and parcel of the colonial system and is depending for his welfare and convenience, not to mention his luxury, upon the degradation of the majority of men.

Not only this but policies of suppression and repression, common in colonies and in slums, easily transport themselves to treatment of other minorities, whose oppression is not due directly to economic causes. We have all seen how racial antipathy evolves policies of religious intolerance; how economic exploitation is transmuted into color prejudice; how any refusal to submit to dominant cultural patterns, current at the particular time, tends to bring into use the whole machinery of suppression, which is born of economic exploitation. This is the basic reason for coupling in this series of lectures, religious, geographic, racial and other problems, which find their essential unity in the oppression of the poor and ignorant in segregated parts of the world known as colonies and slums; and result in widespread denial of human rights. . . .

There is no question as to the path that ought to be followed and, in the long run, will be followed. This path is the path of economic reorganization and reform. It means the definite refusal any longer to follow the dictates of classical economics; the definite rejection of the myth of a self-regulating world market; the refusal longer to regard labor as a commodity, or land as a private monopoly. It means a definite rejection of the idea that any one commodity, like gold, must be the inevitable measure of exchange.

What then is the clear path of reform before us? It is not merely pity and philanthropy so much as the determination of men of goodwill who are cognizant of what social science has learned in the twentieth century, to insist on four truths:

1. Poverty is unnecessary.

2. Production of goods should be planned according to need and not for private profit.

3. Distribution of goods and services should be made according to reason and right and not by chance, birth or privilege.

4. Education and health should be free and compulsory.

I mean by this a denial of the old argument, which I learned in high school, that you could not have rational distribution of wealth because there was simply not enough of the things that human beings need, to go around.

Under that belief, the world tried to distribute its bounty to certain preferred peoples; to certain persons who were superior, or thought to be superior, or who called themselves superior. That myth has been definitely put on the shelf by science; and science today knows that there can be plenty in this world for the wants of its people; not enough, of course, for everybody to wear a mink coat, or to have two automobiles; not enough for everybody to have a town house and a country villa; but enough for everybody to have sufficient to eat and to wear, and comfortable, sanitary housing. If there is any lack of these things for anybody at any time, we know perfectly well that it is because some people have more than they need or some are not contributing to the world's work as they should. It is difficult today to get people to admit that before anybody has *cake*, all human beings should have *bread*. Nevertheless, that is the inevitable ideal to which we have got to come.

Secondly, production can be *planned*. Production must *not* depend upon the individual profit which any producer may get out of the production of anything that he makes or anything he does. Production must be carefully and scientifically planned, according to the rational needs of human beings. We are beginning to do this, but we are doing it with hesitation and with a feeling that the whole program of planned industry is merely an emergency. It is not. It is a perpetual imperative.

Third, the goods and services of the world should be distributed in accordance with a rational plan. It should not be a matter of birth, chance or of good luck. We have recently been regaled by the story of a bright young man who borrowed twenty-six thousand dollars, made five million dollars, and finally enriched himself circling the world. What we do not realize is that this sort of thing makes it the legal right of anybody to take advantage of chance and monopoly, and secure for himself the services and produce of vast numbers of workers while they starve. This should be not only illegal but *immoral*. The moral ideal of distribution of goods and services according to need and desert must eventually prevail if civilization endures.

Next, *health* should be compulsory; not something which has to be bought of private individuals or doled out by charity. Governments should establish regimes to which every individual has to submit in order to avoid, so far as possible, sickness and death.

Finally, education must not be a luxury for the few or propaganda for the privileged but a compulsory discipline for every human being, at public cost. Illiteracy must become a crime.

It is perfectly clear that if we have people who live decently with a healthy and agreeable amount of work; and who know the world, past and present, with the accumulated results of scientific research—we can then begin to have a real democracy.

One of the first results of such democracy will be greater areas of freedom and less compulsion. In basic natural law—the law of gravity, of atomic weights, of the movement of the stars and the rotation of seasons—there can be *no freedom*, no argument, only *law*. If a man

will eat, he must work—that is law and this law cannot be transgressed because a man is white-skinned, or because his father worked, or because he bet on the winner of the Derby. The attempt to flout this social law is disaster. On color and form, here is the freedom which is the true and inevitable child of democracy.

This is what real freedom means. With the doing away of poverty, needless sickness, premature death and investment in human degradation, we can have such freedom of expression as will let nobody tell any man whether he must believe in communism or capitalism, Christianity or Mohammedanism, but only the right freely to choose and follow his own beliefs.

This is the democracy which is the solution, and the only solution, to the problems of minorities and to the question of human rights for all men.

12. "We Must Know the Truth"

Published in 1947 in *The Worker*

I wish to lay down and defend, four propositions:

Poverty is unnecessary.
Colonies and quasi-colonial regions are the most poverty-stricken portions of the earth and most human beings live in them.
Socialism is an attack on poverty.
The United Nations is the greatest hope of abolishing colonialism and thus abolishing poverty in all the world.

Poverty is unnecessary. Most intelligent people today, even in civilized parts of the earth, believe that it is normal and necessary that most human beings should not have enough to eat and wear and insufficient shelter; and that because of this inevitable poverty most human beings must be ignorant, diseased and to a large extent criminal. The persons who believe this mythical witchcraft are ignorant of the plain teaching of science and industrial technique of science and industrial technique especially in the nineteenth and twentieth centuries.

Yet we know better or could know better if we would use the brains with which even the most stupid are endowed. To be specific, we know that the present floods in the Missouri and Mississippi Valleys are due simply to carelessness and greed: we could dam these waters, store them in reservoirs, and use them for cheap irrigation and power production for a cost not one-tenth as great as the toll of dead farmers, lost crops and property; and ruined, rich soil which is annually taken from corn and wheat fields and deposited in the Gulf of Mexico to obstruct shipping.

We know that annually many times as many persons die of tuberculosis, cancer and heart disease as need to if we would apply our present medical knowledge; and that the lost value of their work would pay to society much more than our present medical care costs us.

We know that the money which we refuse for schools and teachers does not amount to a tenth of what we are compelled to pay for police, jails, courts and insane asylums, to take wretched care of the crime of ignorant young people whom we neglect as children, leave in ignorance during youth and imprison and hang before they are thirty.

If we were really trying to relieve the wants of men, we would not have to destroy potatoes, burn corn, let food rot in warehouses or prevent men from buying wool where wool can be raised cheapest and best, in a land like this where most of our surface is empty unused space, and where wood, iron and coal are more plentiful than anywhere else on earth, it is simply a monument to our stupidity that we should have and continue to have a housing shortage.

In fine, while it was true a thousand years ago, that human toil and energy was unable to feed, clothe and shelter all mankind, this has not been the case since the beginning of the nineteenth century; and today, with what we know of natural forces; with the land and labor at our disposal, with the known technique of processing materials and transport of goods, there is no adequate reason why a single human being on earth should not have sufficient food, clothing and shelter for healthy life.

Colonies and quasi-colonial regions are the most poverty-stricken portions of the earth and most human beings live in them.

We have grown into the habit of regarding colonial questions as comparatively unimportant and far removed from our immediate domestic interests. We can easily correct this tragic error, if we remember that we have spent thousands of million dollars and killed millions of human beings, and maimed and crazed tens of millions more, mainly because of jealousy and greed arising primarily over the control of labor, land and materials of colonial peoples.

The basic reason for this is the fact that most of the goods and materials which we need for living in civilized lands comes from the land and labor of colonial people. Colonial peoples are not simply those who live and work in lands called colonies, but all those who live under colonial conditions. This comprehends nearly all Asia and Africa, most of South America and vast areas in the islands of the sea.

Most human beings live in such lands, and here poverty reaches a level which men in Europe and North America simply cannot conceive. Four hundred million people in India live on an average income of $25 a year per family; the millions of China average no more than $30 perhaps; the peoples of Africa probably do not average $20 a year, while South America and the Caribbean area hardly average $50.

This spells poverty at its harshest and crudest; and I repeat it is unnecessary, and largely deliberate on the part of the master nations of the world.

How can this happen? There is still in the minds of many men the explanation of laziness and congenital stupidity as the cause of the poverty of so-called backward peoples. In fact such people work harder than the people in cultured lands. They furnish an astounding proportion of the necessary goods and materials of the world, although this is largely concealed by the price system, through which we measure value by the market price.

These prices are set by those who manipulate markets for their own advantage. Consider, on the basis of human needs, and not at the price paid, what we get from colonies: sugar, rice, spices, rubber, fruit, coffee, tea, cocoa, vegetable, oils, cotton, wool, flax, quinine, diamonds, gold, copper, tin, hides.

Does it make these materials less basically valuable, because after the application to them of special techniques of manufacture, the manufacturers and financiers can put so high a price on the finished product that no colonial can buy it?

Of the dollar which you pay for a box of chocolates, the cocoa farmer in West Africa gets three cents: yet chocolate is cocoa boiled with sugar and sold with fancy forms and wrappings. We are part of colonial exploitation, whenever we buy a pound of coffee and pay the machine which grinds it three times as much as the man who raises it.

Socialism is an attack on poverty.

We can by our knowledge, by the use of our democratic power, prevent the concentration of political and economic power in the hands of the monopolists who rule colonies and make them the cesspools that they are.

These exploiters live in civilized lands and get their power by consent of the people living there. Many of these people are poor workers, but are deprived of their rightful democratic control by social forces and groups whose power comes from colonial exploitation.

Every leading land on earth is moving toward some form of socialism, so as to restrict the power of wealth, introduce democratic methods in industry, and stop the persistence of poverty and its children, ignorance, disease and crime.

The United Nations is the greatest hope of abolishing colonialism and thus abolishing poverty in all the world. . . .

We must understand industrial profit; we must know what wealth is and what it means; we must stand back of democracy in industry and better methods of production and a more just distribution of wealth.

We must not let ourselves be scared and intimidated by the fear of being called Communist, by the smearing of Henry Wallace, by lies printed about Russia for the last thirty years or by the word-spread attempt of a monopolized and privately owned press to keep the peoples of the world from knowing the truth about work and income.

In order to support the United Nations and its wider objects and duties we must know the truth and the truth will make us free.

13. "America's Pressing Problems"

Published in 1952 in *In Battle For Peace: The Story of my 83rd Birthday*

. . . Our industry is today controlled, by one thousand individuals and is conducted primarily for their profit and power. This does not exclude a great deal which is for the progress of America and the world, but human progress is not its main object nor its sole result. The American philosophy brought over from pioneer days was that individual success was necessarily social uplift, and today large numbers of Americans firmly believe that the success of monopolized industry controlled by an oligarchy is the success of this nation. It is not; and the high standard of living in the

United States and its productive capacity is not due to monopoly and private profit, but has come in spite of this and indicates how much higher standards of living might have been reached not only in America but throughout the world, if the bounty of the United States and its industrial planning had been administered for the progress of the masses instead of the power and luxury of the few.

The power of private corporate wealth in the United States has throttled democracy and this was made possible by the color caste which followed Reconstruction after the Civil War. When the Negro was disfranchised in the South, the white South was and is owned increasingly by the industrial North. Thus, caste which deprived the mass of Negroes of political and civil rights and compelled them to accept the lowest wage, lay underneath the vast industrial profit of the years 1890 to 1900 when the greatest combinations of capital took place.

The fight of Negroes for democracy in these years was the main movement of the kind in the United States. They began to gain the sympathy and cooperation of those liberal whites who succeeded the abolitionists and who now realized that physical emancipation of a working class must be followed by political and economic emancipation or means nothing. For more than a half century this battle of a group of black and white Americans for the abolition of color caste has gone on and made striking progress: the American Negro is beginning to vote, to be admitted to labor unions and to be granted many civil rights. But the mischief and long neglect of democracy has already spread throughout the nation. A large percentage of eligible voters do not go to the polls. Democracy has no part in industry, save through the violence or threatened violence of the strike. No great American industry admits that it could or should be controlled by those who do its work. But unless democratic methods enter industry, democracy fails to function in other

paths of life. Our political life is admittedly under the control of organized wealth and while the socialized organization of all our work proceeds, its management remains under oligarchical control and its objects are what that oligarchy decide. They may be beneficial decisions, they may be detrimental, but in no case are they arrived at by democratic methods.

The claim of the United States that it represents democracy in contrast to fascism or communism is patently false. Fascism is oligarchy in control of a socialized state which is run for the benefit of the oligarchs and their friends. Communism is a socialized state conducted by a group of workers for the benefit of the mass of the people. There may be little difference in the nature of the controls exercised in the United States, fascist Germany and the Soviet republics. There is a world of difference in the objects of that control. In the United States today the object is to center and increase the power of those who control organized wealth and they seek to prove to Americans that no other system is so successful in human progress. But instead of leaving proof of this to the free investigation of science, the reports of a free press, and the discussion of the public platform, today in the United States, organized wealth owns the press and chief news-gathering organs and is exercising increased control over the schools and making public discussion and even free thinking difficult and often impossible.

The cure for this and the way to change the socially planned United States into a welfare state is for the American people to take over the control of the nation in industry as well as government. This is proceeding gradually. Many Americans are not aware of this, but it is true: we conduct the post office; we are in the express and banking business; we have built the great Tennessee Valley river-control system; we exercise control in varying degrees over railroads, radio, city planning, air and water traffic; in a thousand other ways, social control for general welfare is growing and must grow in our country. But knowledge of this, of its success and of its prevalence in other lands, does not reach the mass of people. They are today being carried away by almost hysterical propaganda that the freedoms which they have and such individual initiative as remains are being threatened and that a Third World War is the only remedy. . . .

14. "There Must Come a Vast Social Change in the United States"

Published in 1951 in the *National Guardian*

. . . We must ask why is it that this rich world is poor? Why is it, that with all the wealth nature furnishes free, and all the power lying at our fingertips, the men who work hardest get the lowest income? Why is it that the men who think most clearly and constructively have often the hardest time making a decent living, while thousands who lie and cheat and steal get power and wealth? Why is it those who own the land and crops; the machines and capital; the buildings and clothing and food, are not always those who work and save and sacrifice, but too often those who scheme and contrive and rig the market; or sit at ease spending what somebody else earned?

There are fundamental questions as to work and wealth which all men must face; all schools teach and all honest pulpits discuss. Does a man's income consist of what he makes? No. Not even in primitive times was this true. And today the simplest work of production from catching a fish to building Boulder Dam is a complicated social effort involving from 10 to 10,000 workers, planners, managers and thinkers, and using even so-called "unemployed" housewives and

mothers, it lasts so long in time and is so intricate and complicated in technique that no mathematical formula can possibly show exactly what each worker contributes to the final value.

Only reason and justice can in the end determine income, to each according to his need and from each what he best can do, is the high ideal, enunciated before the Russian Revolution was thought of. This ideal the Soviet Union admits it has not yet attained, but declares its firm purpose to reach it. While the United States not only denies the justice of this aim but bluntly orders that it must not even be attempted.

We have got our economy upside down, our reward for work backside foremost and our brains so addled that if anyone dares question this insanity of our modern civilization we yell "subversive" and scare all fools out of their few wits.

If sincere dislike of this state of affairs is communism, then by the living God, no force of army, nor power of wealth, nor smartness of intellect will ever stop it. Denial of this right to think will manufacture communists faster than you can jail or kill them. Nothing will stop such communism but something better than communism. If our present policies are examples of free enterprise and individual initiative, they initiate crime and suffering as well as wealth; if this is the American way of life, God save America!

There is no way in the world for us to preserve the ideals of a democratic America, save by drastically curbing the present power of concentrated wealth, by assuming ownership of some natural resources, by administering many of our key industries and by socializing our services for public welfare. This need not mean the adoption of the communism of the Soviet Union, nor the socialism of Britain, nor even of the near-socialism of France, Italy or Scandinavia; but either in some way or to some degree, we socialize our economy, restore the New Deal and inaugurate the welfare state or we descend into a military fascism which will kill all dreams of Democracy or the abolition of poverty and ignorance; or of peace instead of war.

There must come vast social change in the United States; a change not violent, but by the will of the people; certain and inexorable, carried out "with malice toward none but charity for all"; with meticulous justice to the rich and thrifty and complete sympathy for the poor, the sick and the ignorant; with freedom and democracy for America, and on earth peace, good will toward men.

Chapter V

On Women

"The meaning of the twentieth century," wrote Du Bois in 1915, "is the freeing of the individual soul." When Du Bois wrote these words, he was not talking about the black man's soul and its bondage to the white man's system of subjugation. He wasn't even talking about men at all. He was concerned with the historical plight of women. Just as Friedrich Engels, who was fixated on class antagonism, could still acknowledge in *The Origin of the Family, Private Property, and the State* (1884) that the first class fissure in history was between men and women, so too did Du Bois, who was fixated on racial antagonism, acknowledge the transcending oppression of women at the hands of men: "the soul longest in slavery and still in the most disgusting and indefensible slavery is the soul of womanhood." Echoing Charlotte Perkins Gilman's *Women and Economics* (1898), Du Bois stressed that a woman needs "economic independence" and "the right of motherhood at her own discretion." An early male feminist, Du Bois wrote of the black female experience with eloquence, and in "the Freedom of Womanhood" (1924) he recognized the unique historical and libratory role of black women, nearly eighty years before Patricia Hill Collins's *Black Feminist Thought* (2000).

1. "The Black Mother"

Published in 1912 in *The Crisis*

The people of America, and especially the people of the Southern states, have felt so keen an appreciation of the qualities of motherhood in the Negro that they have proposed erecting a statue in the national capital to the black mammy. The black nurse of slavery days may receive the tribute of enduring bronze from the master class.

But this appreciation of the black mammy is always of the foster mammy, not of the mother in her home, attending to her own babies. And as the colored mother has retreated to her own home, the master class has cried out against her. "She is thriftless and stupid," the white mother says, "when she refuses to nurse my baby and stays with her own. She is bringing her daughter up beyond her station when she trains her to be a teacher instead of sending her into my home to act as nursemaid to my little boy and girl. I will never enter her street, heaven forbid. A colored street is taboo, and she no longer deserves my approval when she refuses to leave her home and enter mine."

Let us hope that the black mammy, for whom so many sentimental tears have been shed, has disappeared from American life. She existed under a false social system that deprived her of husband and child. Thomas Nelson Page, after—with wet eyelids—recounting the virtues

145

of his mammy, declared petulantly that she did not care for her own children. Doubtless this was true. How could it have been otherwise? But just so far as it was true it was a perversion of motherhood.

Let the present-day mammies suckle their own children. Let them walk in the sunshine with their own toddling boys and girls and put their own sleepy little brothers and sisters to bed. As their girls grow to womanhood, let them see to it that, if possible, they do not enter domestic service in those homes where they are unprotected, and where their womanhood is not treated with respect. In the midst of immense difficulties, surrounded by caste, and hemmed in by restricted economic opportunity, let the colored mother of today build her own statue, and let it be the four walls of her own unsullied home.

2. "Woman Suffrage"

Published in 1915 in *The Crisis*

This month 200,000 Negro voters will be called upon to vote on the question of giving the right of suffrage to women. *The Crisis* sincerely trusts that everyone of them will vote *Yes*. But *The Crisis* would not have them go to the polls without having considered every side of the question. Intelligence in voting is the only real support of democracy. For this reason we publish with pleasure Dean Kelly Miller's article against woman suffrage. We trust that our readers will give it careful attention and that they will compare it with that marvelous symposium which we had the pleasure to publish in our August number. Meantime, Dean Miller will pardon us for a word in answer to his argument.

Briefly put, Mr. Miller believes that the bearing and rearing of the young is a function which makes it practically impossible for women to take any large part in general, industrial and public affairs; that women are weaker than men; that women are adequately protected under man's suffrage; that no adequate results have appeared from woman suffrage and that office-holding by women is "risky."

All these arguments sound today ancient. If we turn to easily available statistics we find that instead of the women of this country or of any other country being confined chiefly to child-bearing they are as a matter of fact engaged and engaged successfully in practically every pursuit in which men are engaged. The actual work of the world today depends more largely upon women than upon men. Consequently this man-ruled world faces an astonishing dilemma: either Woman the Worker is doing the world's work successfully or not. If she is not doing it well why do we not take from her the necessity of working? If she is doing it well why not treat her as a worker with a voice in the direction of work?

The statement that woman is weaker than man is sheer rot: It is the same sort of thing that we hear about "darker races" and "lower classes." Difference, either physical or spiritual, does not argue weakness or inferiority. That the average woman is spiritually different from the average man is undoubtedly just as true as the fact that the average white man differs from the average Negro; but this is no reason for disfranchising the Negro or lynching him. It is inconceivable that any person looking upon the accomplishments of women today in every field of endeavor, realizing their humiliating handicap and the astonishing prejudices which they face and yet seeing despite this that in government, in the professions, in sciences, art and literature and the industries they are leading and dominating forces and growing in power as their emancipation grows,—it is inconceivable that any fair-minded person could for a moment talk about a "weaker" sex. The sex of Judith, Candace,

Queen Elizabeth, Sojourner Truth and Jane Addams was the merest incident of human function and not a mark of weakness and inferiority.

To say that men protect women with their votes is to overlook the flat testimony of the facts. In the first place there are millions of women who have no natural men protectors: the unmarried, the widowed, the deserted and those who have married failures. To put this whole army incontinently out of court and leave them unprotected and without voice in political life is more than unjust, it is a crime.

There was a day in the world when it was considered that by marriage a woman lost all her individuality as a human soul and simply became a machine for making men. We have outgrown that idea. A woman is just as much a thinking, feeling, acting person after marriage as before. She has opinions and she has a right to have them and she has a right to express them. It is conceivable, of course, for a country to decide that its unit of representation should be the family and that one person in that family should express its will. But by what possible process of rational thought can it be decided that the person to express that will should always be the male, whether he be genius or drunkard, imbecile or captain of industry? The meaning of the twentieth century is the freeing of the individual soul; the soul longest in slavery and still in the most disgusting and indefensible slavery is the soul of womanhood. God give her increased freedom this November! . . .

3. "The Damnation of Women"

Published in 1920 in *Darkwater*

I remember four women of my boyhood: my mother, cousin Inez, Emma, and Ide Fuller. They represented the problem of the widow, the wife, the maiden, and the outcast. They were, in color, brown and light-brown, yellow with brown freckles, and white. They existed not for themselves, but for men; they were named after the men to whom they were related and not after the fashion of their own souls.

They were not beings, they were relations and these relations were enfilmed with mystery and secrecy. We did not know the truth or believe it when we heard it. Motherhood! What was it? We did not know or greatly care. My mother and I were good chums. I liked her. After she was dead I loved her with a fierce sense of personal loss.

Inez was a pretty, brown cousin who married. What was marriage? We did not know, neither did she, poor thing! It came to mean for her a litter of children, poverty, a drunken, cruel companion, sickness, and death. Why?

There was no sweeter sight than Emma,— slim, straight, and dainty, darkly flushed with the passion of youth; but her life was a wild, awful struggle to crush her natural, fierce joy of love. She crushed it and became a cold, calculating mockery.

Last there was that awful outcast of the town, the white woman, Ide Fuller. What she was, we did not know. She stood to us as embodied filth and wrong,—but whose filth, whose wrong?

Grown up I see the problem of these women transfused; I hear all about me the unanswered call of youthful love, none the less glorious because of its clean, honest, physical passion. Why unanswered? Because the youth are too poor to marry or if they marry, too poor to have children. They turn aside, then, in three directions: to marry for support, to what men call shame, or to that which is more evil than nothing. It is an unendurable paradox; it must be changed or the bases of culture will totter and fall.

The world wants healthy babies and intelligent workers. Today we refuse to allow the combination and force thousands of intelligent workers to go childless at a horrible expenditure of moral force, or we damn them if they break our idiotic conventions. Only at the sacrifice of intelligence and the chance to do their best work can the majority of modern women bear children. This is the damnation of women.

All womanhood is hampered today because the world on which it is emerging is a world that tries to worship both virgins and mothers and in the end despises motherhood and despoils virgins.

The future woman must have a life work and economic independence. She must have knowledge. She must have the right of motherhood at her own discretion. The present mincing horror at free womanhood must pass if we are ever to be rid of the bestiality of free manhood; not by guarding the weak in weakness do we gain strength, but by making weakness free and strong.

The world must choose the free woman or the white wraith of the prostitute. Today it wavers between the prostitute and the nun. Civilization must show two things: the glory and beauty of creating life and the need and duty of power and intelligence. This and this only will make the perfect marriage of love and work.

> *God is Love,*
> *Love is God;*
> *There is no God but Love*
> *And Work is His Prophet!*

All this of woman,—but what of black women?

The world that wills to worship womankind studiosly forgets its darker sisters. They seem in a sense to typify that veiled Melancholy:

> *"Whose saintly visage is too bright*
> *To hit the sense of human sight,*
> *And, therefore, to our weaker view*
> *O'er-laid with black."*

Yet the world must heed these daughters of sorrow, from the primal black All-Mother of men down through the ghostly throng of mighty womanhood, who walked in the mysterious dawn of Asia and Africa; from Neith, the primal mother of all, whose feet rest on hell, and whose almighty hands uphold the heavens; all religion, from beauty to beast, lies on her eager breasts; her body bears the stars, while her shoulders are necklaced by the dragon; from black Neith down to

> *"That starr'd Ethiop queen who strove*
> *To set her beauty's praise above*
> *The sea-nymphs,"*

through dusky Cleopatras, dark Candaces, and darker, fiercer Zinghas, to our own day and our own land,—in gentle Phillis; Harriet, the crude Moses; the sybil, Sojourner Truth; and the martyr, Louise De Mortie.

The father and his worship is Asia; Europe is the precocious, self-centered, forward-striving child; but the land of the mother is and was Africa. In subtle and mysterious way, despite her curious history, her slavery, polygamy, and toil, the spell of the African mother pervades her land. Isis, the mother, is still titular goddess, in thought if not in name, of the dark continent. Nor does this all seem to be solely a survival of the historic matriarchate through which all nations pass,—it appears to be more than this,—as if the great black race in passing up the steps of human culture gave the world, not only the Iron Age, the cultivation of the soil, and the domestication of animals, but also, in peculiar emphasis, the mother-idea.

"No mother can love more tenderly and none is more tenderly loved than the Negro mother," writes Schneider. Robin tells of the slave who bought his mother's freedom instead of his own. Mungo Park writes: "Everywhere in Africa, I have noticed that no greater affront can be offered a Negro than insulting his mother. 'Strike me,' cries a Mandingo to his enemy, 'but revile not my mother!'" And the Krus and Fantis say the same. The peoples on the Zambezi and the great lakes cry in sudden fear or joy: "O, my mother!" And the Herero swears (endless oath) "By my mother's tears!" "As the mist in the swamps," cries the Angola Negro, "so lives the love of father and mother."

A student of the present Gold Coast life describes the work of the village headman, and adds: "It is a difficult task that he is set to, but in this matter he has all-powerful helpers in the female members of the family, who will be either the aunts or the sisters or the cousins or the nieces of the headman, and as their interests are identical with his in every particular, the good women spontaneously train up their children to implicit obedience to the headman, whose rule in the family thus becomes a simple and an easy matter. 'The hand that rocks the cradle rules the world.' What a power for good in the native state system would the mothers of the Gold Coast and Ashanti become by judicious training upon native lines!"

Schweinfurth declares of one tribe: "A bond between mother and child which lasts for life is the measure of affection shown among the Dyoor" and Ratzel adds:

"Agreeable to the natural relation the mother stands first among the chief influences affecting the children. From the Zulus to the Waganda, we find the mother the most influential counsellor at the court of ferocious sovereigns, like Chaka or Mtesa; sometimes sisters take her place. Thus even with chiefs who possess wives by hundreds the bonds of blood are the strongest and that the woman, though often heavily burdened, is in herself held in no small esteem among the Negroes is clear from the numerous Negro queens, from the medicine women, from the participation in public meetings permitted to women by many Negro peoples."

As I remember through memories of others, backward among my own family, it is the mother I ever recall,—the little, far-off mother of my grandmothers, who sobbed her life away in song, longing for her lost palm-trees and scented waters; the tall and bronzen grandmother, with beaked nose and shrewish eyes, who loved and scolded her black and laughing husband as he smoked lazily in his high oak chair; above all, my own mother, with all her soft brownness,—the brown velvet of her skin, the sorrowful black-brown of her eyes, and the tiny brown-capped waves of her midnight hair as it lay new parted on her forehead. All the way back in these dim distances it is mothers and mothers of mothers who seem to count, while fathers are shadowy memories.

Upon this African mother-idea, the westward slave trade and American slavery struck like doom. In the cruel exigencies of the traffic in men and in the sudden, unprepared emancipation the great pendulum of social equilibrium swung from a time, in 1800,—when America had but eight or less black women to every ten black men,—all too swiftly to a day, in 1870,—when there were nearly eleven women to ten men in our Negro population. This was but the outward numerical fact of social dislocation; within lay polygamy, polyandry, concubinage, and moral degradation, They fought against all this desperately, did these black slaves in the West Indies, especially among the half-free artisans; they set up their ancient household gods, and when Toussaint and Cristophe founded their kingdom in Haiti, it was based on old African tribal ties and beneath it was the mother-idea.

The crushing weight of slavery fell on black women. Under it there was no legal marriage, no legal family, no legal control over children. To be sure, custom and religion replaced here and there what the law denied, yet one has but to read advertisements like the following to see the hell beneath the system:

"One hundred dollars reward will be given for my two fellows, Abram and Frank. Abram has a wife at Colonel Stewart's, in Liberty County, and a mother at Thunderbolt, and a sister in Savannah.

"WILLIAM ROBERTS."

"Fifty dollars reward—Ran away from the subscriber a Negro girl named Maria. She is of a copper color, between thirteen and fourteen years of age—bareheaded and barefooted. She is small for her age—very sprightly and very likely. She stated she was going to see her mother at Maysville.

"SANFORD THOMSON."

"Fifty dollars reward—Ran away from the subscriber his Negro man Pauladore, commonly called Paul. I understand General R. Y. Hayne has purchased his wife and children from H. L. Pinckney, Esq., and has them now on his plantation at Goose Creek, where, no doubt, the fellow is frequently lurking.

"T. DAVIS."

The Presbyterian synod of Kentucky said to the churches under its care in 1835: "Brothers and sisters, parents and children, husbands and wives, are torn asunder and permitted to see each other no more. These acts are daily occurring in the midst of us. The shrieks and agony often witnessed on such occasions proclaim, with a trumpet tongue, the iniquity of our system. There is not a neighborhood where these heartrending scenes are not displayed. There is not a village or road that does not behold the sad procession of manacled outcasts whose mournful countenances tell that they are exiled by force from all that their hearts hold dear."

A sister of a president of the United States declared: "We Southern ladies are complimented with the names of wives, but we are only the mistresses of seraglios."

Out of this, what sort of black women could be born into the world of today? There are those who hasten to answer this query in scathing terms and who say lightly and repeatedly that out of black slavery came nothing decent in womanhood; that adultery and uncleanness were their heritage and are their continued portion.

Fortunately so exaggerated a charge is humanly impossible of truth. The half-million women of Negro descent who lived at the beginning of the 19th century had become the mothers of two and one-fourth million daughters at the time of the Civil War and five million granddaughters in 1910. Can all these women be vile and the hunted race continue to grow in wealth and character? Impossible. Yet to save from the past the shreds and vestiges of self-respect has been a terrible task. I most sincerely doubt if any other race of women could have brought its fineness up through so devilish a fire.

Alexander Crummell once said of his sister in the blood: "In her girlhood all the delicate tenderness of her sex has been rudely outraged. In the field, in the rude cabin, in the press-room, in the factory she was thrown into the companionship of coarse and ignorant men. No chance was given her for delicate reserve or tender modesty. From her childhood she was the doomed victim of the grossest passion. All the virtues of her sex were utterly ignored. If the instinct of chastity asserted itself, then she had to fight like a tiger for the ownership and possession of her own person and ofttimes had to suffer pain and lacerations for her virtuous self-assertion. When she reached maturity, all the tender instincts of her womanhood were ruthlessly violated. At the age of marriage,—always prematurely anticipated under slavery—she was mated as the stock of the plantation were mated, not to be the companion of a loved and chosen husband, but to be the breeder of human cattle for the field or the auction block."

Down in such mire has the black motherhood of this race struggled,—starving its own wailing offspring to nurse to the world their swaggering masters; welding for its children chains which affronted even the moral sense of an unmoral world. Many a man and woman in the South have lived in wedlock as holy as Adam and Eve and brought forth their brown and golden children, but because the darker woman was helpless, her chivalrous and whiter mate could cast her off at his pleasure and publicly sneer at the body he had privately blasphemed.

I shall forgive the white South much in its final judgment day: I shall forgive its slavery, for slavery is a world-old habit; I shall forgive its fighting for a well-lost cause, and for remembering that struggle with tender tears; I shall forgive its so-called "pride of race," the passion of its hot blood, and even its dear, old, laughable strutting and posing; but one thing I shall never forgive, neither in this world nor the world to come: its wanton and continued and persistent insulting of the black womanhood which it sought and seeks to prostitute to its lust. I cannot forget that it is such Southern gentlemen into whose hands smug Northern hypocrites of today are seeking to place our women's eternal destiny,—men who insist upon withholding from my mother and wife and daughter those signs and appellations of courtesy and respect which elsewhere he withholds only from bawds and courtesans.

The result of this history of insult and degradation has been both fearful and glorious. It has birthed the haunting prostitute, the brawler, and the beast of burden; but it has also given the world an efficient womanhood, whose strength lies in its freedom and whose chastity was won in the teeth of temptation and not in prison and swaddling clothes.

To no modern race does its women mean so much as to the Negro nor come so near to the fulfilment of its meaning. As one of our women writes: "Only the black woman can say 'when and where I enter, in the quiet, undisputed dignity of my womanhood, without violence and without suing or special patronage, then and there the whole Negro race enters with me.'"

They came first, in earlier days, like foam flashing on dark, silent waters,—bits of stern, dark womanhood here and there tossed almost carelessly aloft to the world's notice. First and naturally they assumed the panoply of the ancient African mother of men, strong and black, whose very nature beat back the wilderness of oppression and contempt. Such a one was that cousin of my grandmother, whom western Massachusetts remembers as "Mum Bett." Scarred for life by a blow received in defense of a sister, she ran away to Great Barrington and was the first slave, or one of the first, to be declared free under the Bill of Rights of 1780. The son of the judge who freed her, writes:

"Even in her humble station, she had, when occasion required it, an air of command which conferred a degree of dignity and gave her an ascendancy over those of her rank, which is very unusual in persons of any rank or color. Her determined and resolute character, which enabled her to limit the ravages of Shay's mob, was manifested in her conduct and deportment during her whole life. She claimed no distinction, but it was yielded to her from her superior experience, energy, skill, and sagacity. Having known this woman as familiarly as I knew either of my parents, I cannot believe in the moral or physical inferiority of the race to which she belonged. The degradation of the African must have been otherwise caused than by natural inferiority."

It was such strong women that laid the foundations of the great Negro church of today, with its five million members and ninety millions of dollars in property. One of the early mothers of the church, Mary Still, writes thus quaintly, in the forties:

"When we were as castouts and spurned from the large churches, driven from our knees, pointed at by the proud, neglected by the careless, without a place of worship, Allen, faithful to the heavenly calling, came forward and laid the foundation of this connection. The women, like the women at the sepulcher, were early to aid in laying the foundation of the temple and in helping to carry up the noble structure and in the name of their God set up their banner; most of our aged mothers are gone from this to a better state of things. Yet some linger still on their staves, watching with intense interest the ark as it moves over the tempestuous waves of opposition and ignorance. . . .

"But the labors of these women stopped not here, for they knew well that they were subject to affliction and death. For the purpose of mutual aid, they banded themselves together in society capacity, that they might be better able to administer to each others' sufferings and to soften their own pillows. So we find the females in the early history of the church abounding in good works and in acts of true benevolence."

From such spiritual ancestry came two striking figures of wartime,—Harriet Tubman and Sojourner Truth.

For eight or ten years previous to the breaking out of the Civil War, Harriet Tubman was a constant attendant at anti-slavery conventions, lectures, and other meetings; she was a black woman of medium size, smiling countenance, with her upper front teeth gone, attired in coarse but neat clothes, and carrying always an old-fashioned reticule at her side. Usually as soon as she sat down she would drop off in sound sleep.

She was born a slave in Maryland, in 1820, bore the marks of the lash on her flesh; and had been made partially deaf, and perhaps to some degree mentally unbalanced by a blow on the head in childhood. Yet she was one of the most important agents of the Underground Railroad and a leader of fugitive slaves. She

ran away in 1849 and went to Boston in 1854, where she was welcomed into the homes of the leading abolitionists and where every one listened with tense interest to her strange stories. She was absolutely illiterate, with no knowledge of geography, and yet year after year she penetrated the slave states and personally led North over three hundred fugitives without losing a single one. A standing reward of $10,000 was offered for her, but as she said: "The whites cannot catch us, for I was born with the charm, and the Lord has given me the power." She was one of John Brown's closest advisers and only severe sickness prevented her presence at Harper's Ferry.

When the war cloud broke, she hastened to the front, flitting down along her own mysterious paths, haunting the armies in the field, and serving as guide and nurse and spy. She followed Sherman in his great march to the sea and was with Grant at Petersburg, and always in the camps the Union officers silently saluted her.

The other woman belonged to a different type,—a tall, gaunt, black, unsmiling sybil, weighted with the woe of the world. She ran away from slavery and giving up her own name took the name of Sojourner Truth. She says: "I can remember when I was a little, young girl, how my old mammy would sit out of doors in the evenings and look up at the stars and groan, and I would say, 'Mammy, what makes you groan so?' And she would say, 'I am groaning to think of my poor children; they do not know where I be and I don't know where they be. I look up at the stars and they look up at the stars!'"

Her determination was founded on unwavering faith in ultimate good. Wendell Phillips says that he was once in Faneuil Hall, when Frederick Douglass was one of the chief speakers. Douglass had been describing the wrongs of the Negro race and as he proceeded he grew more and more excited and finally ended by saying that they had no hope of justice from the whites, no possible hope except in their own right arms. It must come to blood! They must fight for themselves. Sojourner Truth was sitting, tall and dark, on the very front seat facing the platform, and in the hush of feeling when Douglass sat down she spoke out in her deep, peculiar voice, heard all over the hall:

"Frederick, is God dead?"

Such strong, primitive types of Negro womanhood in America seem to some to exhaust its capabilities. They know less of a not more worthy, but a finer type of black woman wherein trembles all of that delicate sense of beauty and striving for self-realization, which is as characteristic of the Negro soul as is its quaint strength and sweet laughter. George Washington wrote in grave and gentle courtesy to a Negro woman, in 1776, that he would "be happy to see" at his headquarters at any time, a person "to whom nature has been so liberal and beneficial in her dispensations." This child, Phillis Wheatley, sang her trite and halting strain to a world that wondered and could not produce her like. Measured today her muse was slight and yet, feeling her striving spirit, we call to her still in her own words:

"Through thickest glooms look back,
immortal shade."

Perhaps even higher than strength and art loom human sympathy and sacrifice as characteristic of Negro womanhood. Long years ago, before the Declaration of Independence, Kate Ferguson was born in New York. Freed, widowed, and bereaved of her children before she was twenty, she took the children of the streets of New York, white and black, to her empty arms, taught them, found them homes, and with Dr. Mason of Murray Street Church established the first modern Sunday School in Manhattan.

Sixty years later came Mary Shadd up out of Delaware. She was tall and slim, of that ravishing dream-born beauty,—that twilight of the races which we call mulatto. Well-educated, vivacious, with determination shining from her sharp eyes, she threw herself singlehanded into the great Canadian pilgrimage when thousands of hunted black men hurried northward and crept beneath the protection of the lion's paw. She became teacher, editor, and lecturer; tramping afoot through winter snows, pushing without blot or blemish through crowd and turmoil to conventions and meetings, and finally becoming recruiting agent for the United States government in gathering Negro soldiers in the West.

After the war the sacrifice of Negro women for freedom and uplift is one of the finest chapters in their history. Let one life typify all: Louise De Mortie, a free-born Virginia girl, had lived most of her life in Boston. Her high forehead, swelling lips, and dark eyes marked her for a woman of feeling and intellect. She began a successful career as a public reader. Then came the War and the Call. She went to the orphaned colored children of New Orleans,—out of freedom into insult and oppression and into the teeth of the yellow fever. She toiled and dreamed. In 1887 she had raised money and built an orphan home and that same year, in the thirty-fourth of her young life, she died, saying simply: "I belong to God."

As I look about me today in this veiled world of mine, despite the noisier and more spectacular advance of my brothers, I instinctively feel and know that it is the five million women of my race who really count. Black women (and women whose grandmothers were black) are today furnishing our teachers; they are the main pillars of those social settlements which we call churches; and they have with small doubt raised three-fourths of our church property. If we have today, as seems likely, over a billion dollars of accumulated goods, who shall say how much of it has been wrung from the hearts of servant girls and washer-women and women toilers in the fields? As makers of two million homes these women are today seeking in marvelous ways to show forth our strength and beauty and our conception of the truth.

In the United States in 1910 there were 4,931,882 women of Negro descent; over twelve hundred thousand of these were children, another million were girls and young women under twenty, and two and a half-million were adults. As a mass these women were unlettered,—a fourth of those from fifteen to twenty-five years of age were unable to write. These women are passing through, not only a moral, but an economic revolution. Their grandmothers married at twelve and fifteen, but twenty-seven per cent of these women today who have passed fifteen are still single.

Yet these black women toil and toil hard. There were in 1910 two and a half million Negro homes in the United States. Out of these homes walked daily to work two million women and girls over ten years of age,—over half of the colored female population as against a fifth in the case of white women. These, then, are a group of workers, fighting for their daily bread like men; independent and approaching economic freedom! They furnished a million farm laborers, 80,000 farmers, 22,000 teachers, 600,000 servants and washerwomen, and 50,000 in trades and merchandizing.

The family group, however, which is the ideal of the culture with which these folk have been born, is not based on the idea of an economically independent working mother. Rather its ideal harks back to the sheltered harem with the mother emerging at first as nurse and homemaker, while the man remains the sole breadwinner. What is the inevitable result of the clash of such ideals and such facts in the colored group? Broken families.

Among native white women one in ten is separated from her husband by death, divorce, or desertion. Among Negroes the ratio is one in seven. Is the cause racial? No, it is economic,

because there is the same high ratio among the white foreign-born. The breaking up of the present family is the result of modern working and sex conditions and it hits the laborers with terrible force. The Negroes are put in a peculiarly difficult position, because the wage of the male breadwinner is below the standard, while the openings for colored women in certain lines of domestic work, and now in industries, are many. Thus while toil holds the father and brother in country and town at low wages, the sisters and mothers are called to the city. As a result the Negro women outnumber the men nine or ten to eight in many cities, making what Charlotte Gilman bluntly calls "cheap women."

What shall we say to this new economic equality in a great laboring class? Some people within and without the race deplore it. "Back to the homes with the women," they cry, "and higher wage for the men." But how impossible this is has been shown by war conditions. Cessation of foreign migration has raised Negro men's wages, to be sure—but it has not only raised Negro women's wages, it has opened to them a score of new avenues of earning a living. Indeed, here, in microcosm and with differences emphasizing sex equality, is the industrial history of labor in the 19th and 20th centuries. We cannot abolish the new economic freedom of women. We cannot imprison women again in a home or require them all on pain of death to be nurses and housekeepers.

What is today the message of these black women to America and to the world? The uplift of women is, next to the problem of the color line and the peace movement, our greatest modern cause. When, now, two of these movements—woman and color—combine in one, the combination has deep meaning.

In other years women's way was clear: to be beautiful, to be petted, to bear children. Such has been their theoretic destiny and if perchance they have been ugly, hurt, and barren, that has been forgotten with studied silence. In partial compensation for this narrowed destiny the white world has lavished its politeness on its womankind,—its chivalry and bows, its uncoverings and courtesies—all the accumulated homage disused for courts and kings and craving exercise. The revolt of white women against this preordained destiny has in these latter days reached splendid proportions, but it is the revolt of an aristocracy of brains and ability,—the middle class and rank and file still plod on in the appointed path, paid by the homage, the almost mocking homage, of men.

From black women of America, however, (and from some others, too, but chiefly from black women and their daughters' daughters) this gauze has been withheld and without semblance of such apology they have been frankly trodden under the feet of men. They are and have been objected to, apparently for reasons peculiarly exasperating to reasoning human beings. When in this world a man comes forward with a thought, a deed, a vision, we ask not, how does he look,—but what is his message? It is of but passing interest whether or not the messenger is beautiful or ugly,—the *message* is the thing. This, which is axiomatic among men, has been in past ages but partially true if the messenger was a woman. The world still wants to ask that a woman primarily be pretty and if she is not, the mob pouts and asks querulously, "What else are women for?" Beauty "is its own excuse for being," but there are other excuses, as most men know, and when the white world objects to black women because it does not consider them beautiful, the black world of right asks two questions: "What is beauty?" and, "Suppose you think them ugly, what then? If ugliness and unconventionality and eccentricity of face and deed do not hinder men from doing the world's work and reaping the world's reward, why should it hinder women?"

Other things being equal, all of us, black and white, would prefer to be beautiful in face

and form and suitably clothed; but most of us are not so, and one of the mightiest revolts of the century is against the devilish decree that no woman is a woman who is not by present standards a beautiful woman. This decree the black women of America have in large measure escaped from the first. Not being expected to be merely ornamental, they have girded themselves for work, instead of adorning their bodies only for play. Their sturdier minds have concluded that if a woman be clean, healthy, and educated, she is as pleasing as God wills and far more useful than most of her sisters. If in addition to this she is pink and white and straight-haired, and some of her fellow-men prefer this, well and good; but if she is black or brown and crowned in curled mists (and this to us is the most beautiful thing on earth), this is surely the flimsiest excuse for spiritual incarceration or banishment.

The very attempt to do this in the case of Negro Americans has strangely over-reached itself. By so much as the defective eyesight of the white world rejects black women as beauties, by so much the more it needs them as human beings,—an enviable alternative, as many a white woman knows. Consequently, for black women alone, as a group, "handsome is that handsome does" and they are asked to be no more beautiful than God made them, but they are asked to be efficient, to be strong, fertile, muscled, and able to work. If they marry, they must as independent workers be able to help support their children, for their men are paid on a scale which makes sole support of the family often impossible.

On the whole, colored working women are paid as well as white working women for similar work, save in some higher grades, while colored men get from one-fourth to three-fourths less than white men. The result is curious and three-fold: the economic independence of black women is increased, the breaking up of Negro families must be more frequent, and the number of illegitimate children is decreased more slowly among them than other evidences of culture are increased, just as was once true in Scotland and Bavaria.

What does this mean? It forecasts a mighty dilemma which the whole world of civilization, despite its will, must one time frankly face: the unhusbanded mother or the childless wife. God send us a world with woman's freedom and married motherhood inextricably wed, but until He sends it, I see more of future promise in the betrayed girl-mothers of the black belt than in the childless wives of the white North, and I have more respect for the colored servant who yields to her frank longing for motherhood than for her white sister who offers up children for clothes. Out of a sex freedom that today makes us shudder will come in time a day when we will no longer pay men for work they do not do, for the sake of their harem; we will pay women what they earn and insist on their working and earning it; we will allow those persons to vote who know enough to vote, whether they be black or female, white or male; and we will ward race suicide, not by further burdening the over-burdened, but by honoring motherhood, even when the sneaking father shirks his duty.

> "Wait till the lady passes," said a Nashville white boy.

> "She's no lady; she's a nigger," answered another.

So some few women are born free, and some amid insult and scarlet letters achieve freedom; but our women in black had freedom thrust contemptuously upon them. With that freedom they are buying an untrammeled independence and dear as is the price they pay for it, it will in the end be worth every taunt and groan. Today the dreams of the mothers are coming true. We have still our poverty and degradation, our lewdness and our cruel toil; but we have, too, a vast group of women of Negro blood who for strength of character, cleanness of soul, and

unselfish devotion of purpose, is today easily the peer of any group of women in the civilized world. And more than that, in the great rank and file of our five million women we have the up-working of new revolutionary ideals, which must in time have vast influence on the thought and action of this land.

For this, their promise, and for their hard past, I honor the women of my race. Their beauty,—their dark and mysterious beauty of midnight eyes, crumpled hair, and soft, full-featured faces—is perhaps more to me than to you, because I was born to its warm and subtle spell; but their worth is yours as well as mine. No other women on earth could have emerged from the hell of force and temptation which once engulfed and still surrounds black women in America with half the modesty and womanliness that they retain. I have always felt like bowing myself before them in all abasement, searching to bring some tribute to these long-suffering victims, these burdened sisters of mine, whom the world, the wise, white world, loves to affront and ridicule and wantonly to insult. I have known the women of many lands and nations,—I have known and seen and lived beside them, but none have I known more sweetly feminine, more unswervingly loyal, more desperately earnest, and more instinctively pure in body and in soul than the daughters of my black mothers. This, then,—a little thing—to their memory and inspiration.

4. "The Freedom of Womanhood"

Published in 1924 in *The Gift of Black Folk*

> *The emancipation of woman is, of course, but one phase of the growth of democracy. It deserves perhaps separate treatment because it is an interesting example of the way in which the Negro has helped American democracy.*

In the United States in 1920 there were 5,253,695 women of Negro descent; over twelve hundred thousand of these were children, another twelve hundred thousand were girls and young women under twenty, and two and a half million were adults. As a mass these women have but the beginnings of education,—twelve percent of those from sixteen to twenty years of age were unable to write, and twenty-eight percent of those twenty-one years of age and over. These women are passing through, not only a moral, but an economic revolution. Their grandmothers married at twelve and fifteen, but in 1910 twenty-seven percent of these women who had passed fifteen were still single.

Yet these black women toil and toil hard. There were in 1910 two and a half million Negro homes in the United States. Out of these homes walked daily to work two million women and girls over ten years of age,—one half of the colored female population as against a fifth in the case of white women. These, then, are a group of workers, fighting for their daily bread like men; independent and approaching economic freedom! They furnished a million farm laborers, 80,000 farmers, 22,000 teachers, 600,000 servants and washerwomen, and 50,000 in trades and merchandizing. In 1920, 38.9% of colored women were at work as contrasted with 17.2% of native white women. Of the colored women 39% were farming and 50% in service.

The family group, however, which is the ideal of the culture into which these folk have been born, is not based on the idea of an economically independent working mother. Rather its ideal harks back to the sheltered harem with the mother emerging at first as nurse and homemaker, while the man remains the sole breadwinner. Thus the Negro woman more than the women of any other group in America is the protagonist in the fight for an economically independent womanhood in modern countries. Her fight has not been willing or for the most part conscious but it has, nevertheless, been curiously effective in its influence on the working world.

This matter of economic independence is, of course, the central fact in the struggle of women for equality. In the earlier days the slave woman was found to be economically as efficient as the man. Moreover, because of her production of children she became in many ways more valuable; but because she was a field hand the slave family differed from the free family. The children were brought up very largely in common on the plantation, there was comparatively small parental control or real family life and the chief function of the woman was working and not making a home. We can see here pre-figured a type of social development toward which the world is working again for similar and larger reasons. In our modern industrial organization the work of women is being found as valuable as that of men. They are consequently being taken from the home and put into industry and the rapidity by which this process is going on is only kept back by the problem of the child; and more and more the community is taking charge of the education of children for this reason.

In America the work of Negro women has not only pre-figured this development but it has had a direct influence upon it. The Negro woman as laborer, as seamstress, as servant and cook, has come into competition with the white male laborer and with the white woman worker. The fact that she could and did replace the white man as laborer, artisan and servant, showed the possibility of the white woman doing the same thing, and led to it. Moreover, the usual sentimental arguments against women at work were not brought forward in the case of Negro womanhood. Nothing illustrates this so well as the speech of Sojourner Truth before the second National Woman Suffrage Convention, in 1852.

Sojourner Truth came from the lowest of the low, a slave whose children had been sold away from her, a hard, ignorant worker without even a name, who came to this meeting of white women and crouched in a corner against the wall. "Don't let her speak," was repeatedly said to the presiding officer. "Don't get our cause mixed up with abolition and 'niggers'." The discussion became warm, resolutions were presented and argued. Much was said of the superiority of man's intellect, the general helplessness of women and their need for courtesy, the sin of Eve, etc. Most of the white women, being "perfect ladies," according to the ideals of the time, were not used to speaking in public and finally to their dismay the black woman arose from the corner. The audience became silent.

Sojourner Truth was an Amazon nearly six feet high, black, erect and with piercing eyes, and her speech in reply was to the point:

"Dat man ober dar say dat women needs to be helped into carriages, and lifted ober ditches, and to have the best places every whar. Nobody eber help me into carriages, or ober mud puddles, or gives me any best place" (and raising herself to her full height and her voice to a pitch like rolling thunder, she asked), "and ai'n't I a woman? Look at me! Look at my arm!" (And she bared her right arm to the shoulder, showing her tremendous muscular power.) "I have plowed, and planted, and gathered into barns, and no man could head me—and ai'n't I a woman? I could work as much and eat as much as a man (when I could get it), and bear de lash as well—and ai'n't I a woman? I have borne thirteen chilern and seen 'em mos'all sold off into slavery, and when I cried out with a mother's grief, none but Jesus heard—and ai'n't I a woman? Den dey talks 'bout dis ting in de head—what dis dey call it?" ("Intellect," whispered some one near.) "Dat's it honey. What's dat got to do with women's rights or niggers' rights? If my cup won't hold but a pint and yourn holds a quart, wouldn't ye be mean not to let me have my little half-measure full?" . . . She ended by asserting that "If de fust woman God ever made was strong enough to turn the world upside down, all

'lone, dese togedder" (and she glanced her eye over us,) "ought to be able to turn it back and get it right side up again, and now dey is asking to do it, de men better let 'em. . . . "

"Amid roars of applause, she turned to her corner, leaving more than one of us with streaming eyes and hearts beating with gratitude. She had taken us up in her strong arms and carried us safely over the slough of difficulty, turning the whole tide in our favor. I have never in my life seen anything like the magical influence that subdued the mobbish spirit of the day and turned the jibes and sneers of an excited crowd into notes of respect and admiration. Hundreds rushed up to shake hands, and congratulate the glorious old mother and bid her God speed on her mission of 'testifying again concerning the wickedness of this 'ere people'."[1]

Again and in more concrete ways the Negro woman has influenced America and that is by her personal contact with the family—its men, women and children. As housekeeper, maid and nurse—as confidante, adviser and friend, she was often an integral part of the white family life of the South, and transmitted her dialect, her mannerisms, her quaint philosophy and her boundless sympathy.

Beyond this she became the concubine. It is a subject scarcely to be mentioned today with our conventional morals and with the bitter racial memories swirling about this institution of slavery. Yet the fact remains stark, ugly, painful, beautiful.

Let us regard it dispassionately, remembering that the concubine is as old as the world and that birth is a biological fact. It is usual to speak of the Negro as being the great example of the unassimiliated group in American life. This, of course, is flatly untrue; probably of the strains of blood longest present in America since the discovery by Columbus, the Negro has been less liable to absorption than other groups; but this does not mean that he has not been absorbed and that his blood has not been spread throughout the length and breadth of the land.

"We southern ladies are complimented with the names of wives; but we are only the mistresses of seraglios," said a sister of President Madison; and a Connecticut minister who lived 14 years in Carolina said: "As it relates to amalgamation, I can say, that I have been in respectable families (so-called), where I could distinguish the family resemblance in the slaves who waited upon the table. I once hired a slave who belonged to his own uncle. It is so common for the female slaves to have white children, that little is ever said about it. Very few inquiries are made as to who the father is."[2]

One has only to remember the early histories of cities like Charleston and New Orleans to see what the Negro concubine meant and how she transfigured America. Paul Alliot said in his reflections of Louisiana in 1803: "The population of that city counting the people of all colors is only twelve thousand souls. Mulattoes and Negroes are openly protected by the Government. He who strikes one of those persons, even though he had run away from him, would be severely punished. Also twenty whites could be counted in the prisons of New Orleans against one man of color. The wives and daughters of the latter are much sought after by the white men, and white women at times esteem well-built men of color." The same writer tells us that few white men marry, preferring to live with their slaves or with women of color. . . .

Whatever judgment we may pass upon all this and however we may like or dislike it, the fact remains that the colored slave women became the medium through which two great races were united in America. Moreover it is the fashion to assume that all this was merely infiltration of white blood into the black; but we must remember it was just as surely infiltration of black blood into white America and not even an extraordinary drawing of the color line against all visible Negro blood has ever been able to trace its true limits.

There is scarcely an American, certainly none of the South and no Negro American, who does not know in his personal experience of Americans of Negro descent who either do not know or do not acknowledge their African ancestry. This is their right, if they do know, and a matter of but passing importance if they do not. But without doubt the spiritual legacy of Africa has been spread through this mingling of blood. . . .

We have noted then the Negro woman in America as a worker tending to emancipate all women workers; as a mother nursing the white race and uniting the black and white race; as a conspirator urging forward emancipation in various sorts of ways; and we have finally only to remember that to-day the women of America who are doing humble but on the whole the most effective work in the social uplift of the lowly, not so much by money as by personal contact, are the colored women. Little is said or known about it but in thousands of churches and social clubs, in missionary societies and fraternal organizations, in unions like the National Association of Colored Women, these workers are founding and sustaining orphanages and old folk homes; distributing personal charity and relief; visiting prisoners; helping hospitals; teaching children; and ministering to all sorts of needs. Their work, as it comes now and then in special cases to the attention of individuals of the white world, forms a splendid bond of encouragement and sympathy, and helps more than most realize in minimizing racial difficulties and encouraging human sympathy.[3]

Notes

1. Testimony of the presiding officer, Mrs. Frances D. Gage, in "*Narrative of Sojourner Truth*," 1884, pp. 134–5.

2. Goodell, *Slave Code*, p. III.

3. Cf. Annual Reports National Association of Colored Women; Atlanta University Publications, No. 14.

Chapter VI

On Religion

Du Bois attended church regularly as a child, and his early writings were infused with Christian verbiage. One of his most famous poems, "Credo," first published in 1904, declares a belief in God as well as the Devil. He wrote a collection of prayers, *Prayers for Dark People,* published after his death in 1980. Yet by the time Du Bois was thirty, he had lost his Christian faith and subscribed to an unapologetic agnosticism for the rest of his life. In his autobiography (1968) he dismissed religious beliefs as "fairy tales," praising the Soviet Union for educating its children sans "religious lies." Though religiously inactive as an adult, he still recognized the importance of religion, particularly for the black community. From short stories depicting Jesus as a black man, to socio-historical analyses of slave religion, from surveys on black ministers to critiques of white Christian racism, Du Bois wrote an enormous amount on religion, always emphasizing the role of the black church as a communal stronghold. As he wrote in "The Problem of Amusement" (1897): "The Negro church is not simply an organism for the propagation of religion; it is the center of the social, intellectual, and religious life of an organized group of people."

1. "The Function of the Negro Church"

Published in 1899 in *The Philadelphia Negro*

The Negro church is the peculiar and characteristic product of the transplanted African, and deserves especial study. As a social group the Negro church may be said to have antedated the Negro family on American soil; as such it has preserved, on the one hand, many functions of tribal organization, and on the other hand, many of the family functions. Its tribal functions are shown in its religious activity, its social authority and general guiding and co-ordinating work; its family functions are shown by the fact that the church is a centre of social life and intercourse; acts as newspaper and intelligence bureau, is the centre of amusements—indeed, is the world in which the Negro moves and acts. So far-reaching are these functions of the church that its organization is almost political. . . .

2. Extraordinary methods are used and efforts made to maintain and increase the membership of the various churches. To be a popular church with large membership means ample revenues, large social influence and a leadership among the colored people unequaled in power and effectiveness. Consequently people are attracted to the church by sermons, by music and by entertainments; finally, every year a revival is held, at which considerable numbers

161

of young people are converted. All this is done in perfect sincerity and without much thought of merely increasing membership, and yet every small church strives to be large by these means and every large church to maintain itself or grow larger. The churches thus vary from a dozen to a thousand members.

3. Without wholly conscious effort the Negro church has become a centre of social intercourse to a degree unknown in white churches even in the country. The various churches, too, represent social classes. At St. Thomas' one looks for the well-to-do Philadelphians, largely descendants of favorite mulatto house-servants, and consequently well-bred and educated, but rather cold and reserved to strangers or newcomers; at Central Presbyterian one sees the older, simpler set of respectable Philadelphians with distinctly Quaker characteristics—pleasant but conservative; at Bethel may be seen the best of the great laboring class—steady, honest people, well dressed and well fed, with church and family traditions; at Wesley will be found the new arrivals, the sight-seers and the strangers to the city—hearty and easy-going people, who welcome all comers and ask few questions; at Union Baptist one may look for the Virginia servant girls and their young men; and so on throughout the city. Each church forms its own social circle, and not many stray beyond its bounds. Introductions into that circle come through the church, and thus the stranger becomes known. All sorts of entertainments and amusements are furnished by the churches: concerts, suppers, socials, fairs, literary exercises and debates, cantatas, plays, excursions, picnics, surprise parties, celebrations. Every holiday is the occasion of some special entertainment by some club, society or committee of the church; Thursday afternoons and evenings, when the servant girls are free, are always sure to have some sort of entertainment. Sometimes these exercises are free, sometimes an admission fee is charged, sometimes refreshments or articles are on sale. The favorite entertainment is a

concert with solo singing, instrumental music, reciting, and the like. Many performers make a living by appearing at these entertainments in various cities, and often they are persons of training and ability, although not always. So frequent are these and other church exercises that there are few Negro churches which are not open four to seven nights in a week and sometimes one or two afternoons in addition.

Perhaps the pleasantest and most interesting social intercourse takes place on Sunday; the weary week's work is done, the people have slept late and had a good breakfast, and sally forth to church well dressed and complacent. The usual hour of the morning service is eleven, but people stream in until after twelve. The sermon is usually short and stirring, but in the larger churches elicits little response other than an "Amen" or two. After the sermon the social features begin; notices on the various meetings of the week are read, people talk with each other in subdued tones, take their contributions to the altar, and linger in the aisles and corridors long after dismission to laugh and chat until one or two o'clock. Then they go home to good dinners. Sometimes there is some special three o'clock service, but usually nothing save Sunday-school, until night. Then comes the chief meeting of the day; probably ten thousand Negroes gather every Sunday night in their churches. There is much music, much preaching, some short addresses; many strangers are there to be looked at; many beaus bring out their belles, and those who do not gather in crowds at the church door and escort the young women home. The crowds are usually well behaved and respectable, though rather more jolly than comports with a puritan idea of church services.

In this way the social life of the Negro centres in his church—baptism, wedding and burial, gossip and courtship, friendship and intrigue—all lie in these walls. What wonder that this central club house tends to become more and more luxuriously furnished, costly in appointment and easy of access!

4. It must not be inferred from all this that the Negro is hypocritical or irreligious. His church is, to be sure, a social institution first, and religious afterwards, but nevertheless, its religious activity is wide and sincere. In direct moral teaching and in setting moral standards for the people, however, the church is timid, and naturally so, for its constitution is democracy tempered by custom. Negro preachers are often condemned for poor leadership and empty sermons, and it is said that men with so much power and influence could make striking moral reforms. This is but partially true. The congregation does not follow the moral precepts of the preacher, but rather the preacher follows the standard of his flock, and only exceptional men dare seek to change this. And here it must be remembered that the Negro preacher is primarily an executive officer, rather than a spiritual guide. If one goes into any great Negro church and hears the sermon and views the audience, one would say: either the sermon is far below the calibre of the audience, or the people are less sensible than they look; the former explanation is usually true. The preacher is sure to be a man of executive ability, a leader of men, a shrewd and affable president of a large and intricate corporation. In addition to this he may be, and usually is, a striking elocutionist; he may also be a man of integrity, learning, and deep spiritual earnestness; but these last three are sometimes all lacking, and the last two in many cases. Some signs of advance are here manifest: no minister of notoriously immoral life, or even of bad reputation, could hold a large church in Philadelphia without eventual revolt. Most of the present pastors are decent, respectable men; there are perhaps one or two exceptions to this, but the exceptions are doubtful, rather than notorious. On the whole then, the average Negro preacher in this city is a shrewd manager, a respectable man, a good talker, a pleasant companion, but neither learned nor spiritual, nor a reformer.

The moral standards are therefore set by the congregations, and vary from church to church in some degree. . . .

2. "Of the Faith of the Fathers"

Published in 1903 in The Souls of Black Folk

It was out in the country, far from home, far from my foster home, on a dark Sunday night. The road wandered from our rambling loghouse up the stony bed of a creek, past wheat and corn, until we could hear dimly across the fields a rhythmic cadence of song,—soft, thrilling, powerful, that swelled and died sorrowfully in our ears. I was a country schoolteacher then, fresh from the East, and had never seen a Southern Negro revival. To be sure, we in Berkshire were not perhaps as stiff and formal as they in Suffolk of olden time; yet we were very quiet and subdued, and I know not what would have happened those clear Sabbath mornings had some one punctuated the sermon with a wild scream, or interrupted the long prayer with a loud Amen! And so most striking to me, as I approached the village and the little plain church perched aloft, was the air of intense excitement that possessed that mass of black folk. A sort of suppressed terror hung in the air and seemed to seize us,— a pythian madness, a demoniac possession, that lent terrible reality to song and word. The black and massive form of the preacher swayed and quivered as the words crowded to his lips and flew at us in singular eloquence. The people moaned and fluttered, and then the gaunt-cheeked brown woman beside me suddenly leaped straight into the air and shrieked like a lost soul, while round about came wail and groan and outcry, and a scene of human passion such as I had never conceived before.

Those who have not thus witnessed the frenzy of a Negro revival in the untouched backwoods of the South can but dimly realize the religious feeling of the slave; as described, such scenes appear grotesque and funny, but as seen they are awful. Three things characterized this religion of the slave,—the Preacher, the Music, and the Frenzy. The preacher is the most unique personality developed by the Negro on American soil. A leader, a politician, an orator, a "boss," an intriguer, an idealist,—all these he is, and ever, too, the centre of a group of men, now twenty, now a thousand in number. The combination of a certain adroitness with deep-seated earnestness, of tact with consummate ability, gave him his preeminence, and helps him maintain it. The type, of course, varies according to time and place, from the West Indies in the sixteenth century to New England in the nineteenth, and from the Mississippi bottoms to cities like New Orleans or New York.

The Music of Negro religion is that plaintive rhythmic melody, with its touching minor cadences, which, despite caricature and defilement, still remains the most original and beautiful expression of human life and longing yet born on American soil. Sprung from the African forests, where its counterpart can still be heard, it was adapted, changed, and intensified by the tragic soul-life of the slave, until, under the stress of law and whip, it became the one true expression of a people's sorrow, despair, and hope.

Finally the Frenzy of "Shouting," when the Spirit of the Lord passed by, and, seizing the devotee, made him mad with supernatural joy, was the last essential of Negro religion and the one more devoutly believed in than all the rest. It varied in expression from the silent rapt countenance or the low murmur and moan to the mad abandon of physical fervor,—the stamping, shrieking, and shouting, the rushing to and fro and wild waving of arms, the weeping and laughing, the vision and the trance. All this is nothing new in the world, but old as

religion, as Delphi and Endor. And so firm a hold did it have on the Negro, that many generations firmly believed that without this visible manifestation of the God there could be no true communion with the Invisible.

These were the characteristics of Negro religious life as developed up to the time of Emancipation. Since under the peculiar circumstances of the black man's environment they were the one expression of his higher life, they are of deep interest to the student of his development, both socially and psychologically. Numerous are the attractive lines of inquiry that here group themselves. What did slavery mean to the African savage? What was his attitude toward the World and Life? What seemed to him good and evil,—God and Devil? Whither went his longings and strivings, and wherefore were his heart-burnings and disappointments? Answers to such questions can come only from a study of Negro religion as a development, through its gradual changes from the heathenism of the Gold Coast to the institutional Negro church of Chicago.

Moreover, the religious growth of millions of men, even though they be slaves, cannot be without potent influence upon their contemporaries. The Methodists and Baptists of America owe much of their condition to the silent but potent influence of their millions of Negro converts. Especially is this noticeable in the South, where theology and religious philosophy are on this account a long way behind the North, and where the religion of the poor whites is a plain copy of Negro thought and methods. The mass of "gospel" hymns which has swept through American churches and well-nigh ruined our sense of song consists largely of debased imitations of Negro melodies made by ears that caught the jingle but not the music, the body but not the soul, of the Jubilee songs. It is thus clear that the study of Negro religion is not only a vital part of the history of the Negro in America, but no uninteresting part of American history.

The Negro church of to-day is the social centre of Negro life in the United States, and the most characteristic expression of African character. Take a typical church in a small Virginia town: it is the "First Baptist"—a roomy brick edifice seating five hundred or more persons, tastefully finished in Georgia pine, with a carpet, a small organ, and stained-glass windows. Underneath is a large assembly room with benches. This building is the central club-house of a community of a thousand or more Negroes. Various organizations meet here,—the church proper, the Sunday-school, two or three insurance societies, women's societies, secret societies, and mass meetings of various kinds. Entertainments, suppers, and lectures are held beside the five or six regular weekly religious services. Considerable sums of money are collected and expended here, employment is found for the idle, strangers are introduced, news is disseminated and charity distributed. At the same time this social, intellectual, and economic centre is a religious centre of great power. Depravity, Sin, Redemption, Heaven, Hell, and Damnation are preached twice a Sunday after the crops are laid by; and few indeed of the community have the hardihood to withstand conversion. Back of this more formal religion, the Church often stands as a real conserver of morals, a strengthener of family life, and the final authority on what is Good and Right.

Thus one can see in the Negro church to-day, reproduced in microcosm, all the great world from which the Negro is cut off by color-prejudice and social condition. In the great city churches the same tendency is noticeable and in many respects emphasized. A great church like the Bethel of Philadelphia has over eleven hundred members, an edifice seating fifteen hundred persons and valued at one hundred thousand dollars, an annual budget of five thousand dollars, and a government consisting of a pastor with several assisting local preachers, an executive and legislative board, financial boards and tax collectors; general church meetings for making laws; subdivided groups led by class leaders, a company of militia, and twenty-four auxiliary societies. The activity of a church like this is immense and far-reaching, and the bishops who preside over these organizations throughout the land are among the most powerful Negro rulers in the world.

Such churches are really governments of men, and consequently a little investigation reveals the curious fact that, in the South, at least, practically every American Negro is a church member. Some, to be sure, are not regularly enrolled, and a few do not habitually attend services; but, practically, a proscribed people must have a social centre and that centre for this people is the Negro church. The census of 1890 showed nearly twenty-four thousand Negro churches in the country, with a total enrolled membership of over two and a half millions, or ten actual church members to every twenty eight persons, and in some Southern states one in every two persons. Besides these there is the large number who, while not enrolled as members, attend and take part in many of the activities of the church. There is an organized Negro church for every sixty black families in the nation, and in some States for every forty families, owning, on an average, a thousand dollars' worth of property each, or nearly twenty-six million dollars in all.

Such, then, is the large development of the Negro church since Emancipation. The question now is, What have been the successive steps of this social history and what are the present tendencies? First, we must realize that no such institution as the Negro church could rear itself without definite historical foundations. These foundations we can find if we remember that the social history of the Negro did not start in America. He was from a definite social environment—the polygamous clan life under the headship of the chief and the potent influence of the priest. His religion was nature-worship, with profound belief in invisible surrounding influences, good and bad, and his worship was through incantation and sacrifice. The first rude change in this life was the slave ship and the West Indian sugar-fields. The plantation organization replaced the clan and tribe, and the white master replaced the chief with far greater and more despotic powers. Forced and long-continued toil became the rule of life, the old ties of blood relationship and kinship disappeared, and instead of the family appeared a new polygamy and polyandry, which, in some cases, almost reached promiscuity. It was a terrific social revolution, and yet some traces were retained of the former group life, and the chief remaining institution was the Priest or Medicine-man. He early appeared on the plantation and found his function as the healer of the sick, the interpreter of the Unknown, the comforter of the sorrowing, the supernatural avenger of wrong, and the one who rudely but picturesquely expressed the longing, disappointment, and resentment of a stolen and oppressed people. Thus, as bard, physician, judge, and priest, within the narrow limits allowed by the slave system, rose the Negro preacher, and under him the first church was not at first by any means Christian nor definitely organized; rather it was an adaptation and mingling of heathen rites among the members of each plantation, and roughly designated as Voodooism. Association with the masters, missionary effort and motives of expediency gave these rites an early veneer of Christianity, and after the lapse of many generations the Negro church became Christian.

Two characteristic things must be noticed in regard to the church. First, it became almost entirely Baptist and Methodist in faith; secondly, as a social institution it antedated by many decades the monogamic Negro home. From the very circumstances of its beginning, the church was confined to the plantation, and

consisted primarily of a series of disconnected units; although, later on, some freedom of movement was allowed, still this geographical limitation was always important and was one cause of the spread of the decentralized and democratic Baptist faith among the slaves. At the same time, the visible rite of baptism appealed strongly to their mystic temperament. To-day the Baptist Church is still largest in membership among Negroes, and has a million and a half communicants. Next in popularity came the churches organized in connection with the white neighboring churches, chiefly Baptist and Methodist, with a few Episcopalian and others. The Methodists still form the second greatest denomination, with nearly a million members. The faith of these two leading denominations was more suited to the slave church from the prominence they gave to religious feeling and fervor. The Negro membership in other denominations has always been small and relatively unimportant, although the Episcopalian and Presbyterians are gaining among the more intelligent classes to-day, and the Catholic Church is making headway in certain sections. After Emancipation, and still earlier in the North, the Negro churches largely severed such affiliations as they had had with the white churches, either by choice or by compulsion. The Baptist churches became independent, but the Methodists were compelled early to unite for purposes of episcopal government. This gave rise to the great African Methodist Church, the greatest Negro organization in the world, to the Zion Church and the Colored Methodist, and to the black conferences and churches in this and other denominations.

The second fact noted, namely, that the Negro church antedates the Negro home, leads to an explanation of much that is paradoxical in this communistic institution and in the morals of its members. But especially it leads us to regard this institution as peculiarly the expression of the inner ethical life of a people in a sense seldom true elsewhere. Let us turn, then, from the outer physical development of the church to the more important inner ethical life of the people who compose it. The Negro has already been pointed out many times as a religious animal—a being of that deep emotional nature which turns instinctively toward the supernatural. Endowed with a rich tropical imagination and a keen, delicate appreciation of Nature, the transplanted African lived in a world animate with gods and devils, elves and witches; full of strange influences,—of Good to be implored, of Evil to be propitiated. Slavery, then, was to him the dark triumph of Evil over him. All the hateful powers of the Under-world were striving against him, and a spirit of revolt and revenge filled his heart. He called up all the resources of heathenism to aid,—exorcism and witchcraft, the mysterious Obi worship with its barbarious rites, spells, and blood-sacrifice even, now and then, of human victims. Weird midnight orgies and mystic conjurations were invoked, the witch-woman and the voodoo-priest became the centre of Negro group life, and that vein of vague superstition which characterizes the unlettered Negro even to-day was deepened and strengthened.

In spite, however, of such success as that of the fierce Maroons, the Danish blacks, and others, the spirit of revolt gradually died away under the untiring energy and superior strength of the slave masters. By the middle of the eighteenth century the black slave had sunk, with hushed murmurs, to his place at the bottom of a new economic system, and was unconsciously ripe for a new philosophy of life. Nothing suited his condition then better than the doctrines of passive submission embodied in the new newly learned Christianity. Slave masters early realized this, and cheerfully aided religious propaganda within certain bounds. The long system of repression and degradation of the Negro tended to emphasize the elements of his character which made him

a valuable chattel: courtesy became humility, moral strength degenerated into submission, and the exquisite native appreciation of the beautiful became an infinite capacity for dumb suffering. The Negro, losing the joy of this world, eagerly seized upon the offered conceptions of the next; the avenging Spirit of the Lord enjoining patience in this world, under sorrow and tribulation until the Great Day when He should lead His dark children home,—this became his comforting dream. His preacher repeated the prophecy, and his bards sang,—

"Children, we all shall be free
When the Lord shall appear!"

This deep religious fatalism, painted so beautifully in "Uncle Tom," came soon to breed, as all fatalistic faiths will, the sensualist side by side with the martyr. Under the lax moral life of the plantation, where marriage was a farce, laziness a virtue, and property a theft, a religion of resignation and submission degenerated easily, in less strenuous minds, into a philosophy of indulgence and crime. Many of the worst characteristics of the Negro masses of to-day had their seed in this period of the slave's ethical growth. Here it was that the Home was ruined under the very shadow of the Church, white and black; here habits of shiftlessness took root, and sullen hopelessness replaced hopeful strife.

With the beginning of the abolition movement and the gradual growth of a class of free Negroes came a change. We often neglect the influence of the freedman before the war, because of the paucity of his numbers and the small weight he had in the history of the nation. But we must not forget that his chief influence was internal,—was exerted on the black world; and that there he was the ethical and social leader. Huddled as he was in a few centres like Philadelphia, New York, and New Orleans, the masses of the freedmen sank into poverty and listlessness; but not all of them. The free Negro leader early arose and his chief characteristic was intense earnestness and deep feeling on the slavery question. Freedom became to him a real thing and not a dream. His religion became darker and more intense, and into his ethics crept a note of revenge, into his songs a day of reckoning close at hand. The "Coming of the Lord" swept this side of Death, and came to be a thing to be hoped for in this day. Through fugitive slaves and irrepressible discussion this desire for freedom seized the black millions still in bondage, and became their one ideal of life. The black bards caught new notes, and sometimes even dared to sing,—

> "O Freedom, O Freedom, O Freedom
>   over me!
> Before I'll be a slave
> I'll be buried in my grave,
> And go home to my Lord
> And be free."

For fifty years Negro religion thus transformed itself and identified itself with the dream of Abolition, until that which was a radical fad in the white North and an anarchistic plot in the white South had become a religion to the black world.

Thus, when Emancipation finally came, it seemed to the freedman a literal Coming of the Lord. His fervid imagination was stirred as never before, by the tramp of armies, the blood and dust of battle, and the wail and whirl of social upheaval. He stood dumb and motionless before the whirlwind: what had he to do with it? Was it not the Lord's doing, and marvellous in his eyes? Joyed and bewildered with what came, he stood awaiting new wonders till the inevitable Age of Reaction swept over the nation and brought the crisis of to-day.

It is difficult to explain clearly the present critical stage of Negro religion. First, we must remember that living as the blacks do in close contact with a great modern nation, and sharing, although imperfectly, the soul-life of that nation, they must necessarily be affected more or less directly by all the religious and ethical forces that are to-day moving the United States. These questions and movements are, however, overshadowed and dwarfed by the (to them) all-important question of their civil, political, and economic status. They must perpetually discuss the "Negro Problem,"—must live, move, and have their being in it, and interpret all else in its light or darkness. With this come, too, peculiar problems of their inner life,—of the status of women, the maintenance of Home, the training of children, the accumulation of wealth, and the prevention of crime. All this must mean a time of intense ethical ferment, of religious heart-searching and intellectual unrest. From the double life every American Negro must live, as a Negro and as an American, as swept on by the current of the nineteenth while yet struggling in the eddies of the fifteenth century,—from this must arise a painful self-consciousness, an almost morbid sense of personality and a moral hesitancy which is fatal to self-confidence. The worlds within and without the Veil of Color are changing, and changing rapidly, but not at the same rate, not in the same way; and this must produce a peculiar wrenching of the soul, a peculiar sense of doubt and bewilderment. Such a double life, with double thoughts, double duties, and double social classes, must give rise to double words and double ideals, and tempt the mind to pretence or revolt, to hypocrisy or radicalism.

In some such doubtful words and phrases can one perhaps most clearly picture the peculiar ethical paradox that faces the Negro of to-day and is tingeing and changing his religious life. Feeling that his rights and his dearest ideals are being trampled upon, that the public conscience is ever more deaf to his righteous appeal, and that all the reactionary forces of prejudice, greed, and revenge are daily gaining new strength and fresh allies, the Negro faces no enviable dilemma. Conscious of his impotence, and pessimistic, he often becomes bitter and vindictive; and his religion, instead of a worship, is a complaint and a curse, a wail rather than a hope, a sneer rather than a faith. On the other hand, another type of mind, shrewder and keener and more tortuous too, sees in the very strength of the anti-Negro movement its patent weaknesses, and with Jesuitic casuistry is deterred by no ethical considerations in the endeavor to turn this weakness to the black man's strength. Thus we have two great and hardly reconcilable streams of thought and ethical strivings; the danger of the one lies in anarchy, that of the other in hypocrisy. The one type of Negro stands almost ready to curse God and die, and the other is too often found a traitor to right and a coward before force; the one is wedded to ideals remote, whimsical, perhaps impossible of realization; the other forgets that life is more than meat and the body more than raiment. But, after all, is not this simply the writhing of the age translated into black, the triumph of the Lie which today, with its false culture, faces the hideousness of the anarchist assassin?

To-day the two groups of Negroes, the one in the North, the other in the South, represent these divergent ethical tendencies, the first tending toward radicalism, the other toward hypocritical compromise. It is no idle regret with which the white South mourns the loss of the old-time Negro,—the frank, honest, simple old servant who stood for the earlier religious age of submission and humility. With all his laziness and lack of many elements of true manhood, he was at least open-hearted, faithful, and sincere. To-day he is gone, but who is to blame for his going? Is it not those very persons who mourn for him? Is it not the tendency, born of Reconstruction and Reaction, to found a society on lawlessness and deception, to tamper with the moral fibre of a naturally honest

and straightforward people until the whites threaten to become ungovernable tyrants and the blacks criminals and hypocrites? Deception is the natural defence of the weak against the strong, and the South used it for many years against its conquerors; to-day it must be prepared to see its black proletariat turn that same two-edged weapon against itself. And how natural this is! The death of Denmark Vesey and Nat Turner proved long since to the Negro the present hopelessness of physical defence. Political defence is becoming less and less available, and economic defence is still only partially effective. But there is a patent defence at hand,—the defence of deception and flattery, of cajoling and lying. It is the same defence which peasants of the Middle Age used and which left its stamp on their character for centuries. To-day the young Negro of the South who would succeed cannot be frank and outspoken, honest and self-assertive, but rather he is daily tempted to be silent and wary, politic and sly; he must flatter and be pleasant, endure petty insults with a smile, shut his eyes to wrong; in too many cases he sees positive personal advantage in deception and lying. His real thoughts, his real aspirations, must be guarded in whispers; he must not criticise, he must not complain. Patience, humility, and adroitness must, in these growing black youth, replace impulse, manliness, and courage. With this sacrifice there is an economic opening, and perhaps peace and some prosperity. Without this there is riot, migration, or crime. Nor is this situation peculiar to the Southern United States, is it not rather the only method by which undeveloped races have gained the right to share modern culture? The price of culture is a Lie.

On the other hand, in the North the tendency is to emphasize the radicalism of the Negro. Driven from his birthright in the South by a situation at which every fibre of his more outspoken and assertive nature revolts, he finds himself in a land where he can scarcely earn a decent living amid the harsh competition and the color discrimination. At the same time, through schools and periodicals, discussions and lectures, he is intellectually quickened and awakened. The soul, long pent up and dwarfed, suddenly expands in new-found freedom. What wonder that every tendency is to excess, radical complaint, radical remedies, bitter denunciation or angry silence. Some sink, some rise. The criminal and the sensualist leave the church for the gambling-hell and the brothel, and fill the slums of Chicago and Baltimore; the better classes segregate themselves from the group-life of both white and black, and form an aristocracy, cultured but pessimistic, whose bitter criticism stings while it points out no way of escape. They despise the submission and subserviency of the Southern Negroes, but offer no other means by which a poor and oppressed minority can exist side by side with its masters. Feeling deeply and keenly the tendencies and opportunities of the age in which they live, their souls are bitter at the fate which drops the Veil between; and the very fact that this bitterness is natural and justifiable only serves to intensify it and make it more maddening.

Between the two extreme types of ethical attitude which I have thus sought to make clear wavers the mass of the millions of Negroes, North and South; and their religious life and activity partake of this social conflict within their ranks. Their churches are differentiating,—now into groups of cold, fashionable devotees, in no way distinguishable from similar white groups save in color of skin; now into large social and business institutions catering to the desire for information and amusement of their members, warily avoiding unpleasant questions both within and without the black world, and preaching in effect if not in word: *Dum vivimus, vivamus.*

But back of this still broods silently the deep religious feeling of the real Negro heart, the stirring, unguided might of powerful human souls who have lost the guiding star of the past and seek in the great night a new religious ideal. Some day the Awakening will come, when the pent-up vigor of ten million souls shall sweep irresistibly toward the Goal, out of the Valley of the Shadow of Death, where all that makes life worth living— Liberty, Justice, and Right—is marked "For White People Only."

3. "Immortality"

Published in 1929 in *We Believe in Immortality*

My thought on personal immortality is easily explained. I do not know. I do not see how any one could know. Our whole basis of knowledge is so relative and contingent that when we get to argue concerning ultimate reality and the real essence of life and the past and the future, we seem to be talking without real data and getting nowhere. I have every respect for people who believe in the future life, but I cannot accept their belief or their wish as knowledge. Equally, I am not impressed by those who deny the possibility of future life. I have no knowledge of the possibilities of this universe and I know of no one who has.

4. "Missions and Mandates"

Published in 1945 in *Color and Democracy*

. . . The Christian Church in America today is almost completely separated along the color line, just as are the army, the navy, the nursing service, and even the blood banks. In many cases where moral opposition is needed, the Church became strangely silent and complacent. . . .

We must add to this that the Church as organized in modern civilized countries has become the special representative of the employing and exploiting classes. It has become mainly a center of wealth and social exclusiveness, and by this very fact, wherever you find a city of large and prosperous churches, such as Atlanta, Georgia, or Dallas, Texas, or Minneapolis, Minnesota, you find cities where the so-called best people, the educated, intelligent, and well-to-do, are critical of democracy, suspicious of the labor movement, bitter against Soviet Russia, and indifferent to the Negro problem, because their economic interests have put them in opposition to forward movements and the teachers and preachers whom they hire have fed them on that kind of prejudice, or maintained significant silence.

Notwithstanding this, it is all too clear today that if we are to have a sufficient motive for the uplift of backward peoples, for the redemption and progress of colonials, such a motive can be found only in the faith and ideals of organized religion; and the great task that is before us is to join this belief and the consequent action with the scientific knowledge and efficient techniques of economic reform.

It would be unfair to myself, and perhaps to others, if I did not frankly say that my attitude toward organized religion is distinctly critical. I cannot believe that any chosen body of people or special organization of mankind has received a direct revelation of ultimate truth which is denied to earnest scientific effort. I admit readily that it would be most satisfactory if instead of occupying a little island of knowledge in the midst of vast stretches of unknown truth, we could with conviction and utter faith plant ourselves on a completely revealed knowledge of the ends and aims of the universe. But no matter how satisfying this would be, it does not therefore follow that it is true, or that those who assert it and believe in it have the right to persecute and condemn those who cannot accept urgent desire, or myth and fairy tale, as valid truth. It may well be that God has revealed ultimate knowledge to babes and

sucklings, but that is no reason why I, one who does not believe this miracle, should surrender to infants the guidance of my mind and effort. No light of faith, no matter how kindly and beneficent, can in a world of reason guide human beliefs to truth unless it is continually tested by pragmatic fact.

On the other hand, I must just as frankly acknowledge that the majority of the best and earnest people of this world are today organized in religious groups, and that without the co-operation of the richness of their emotional experience, and the unselfishness of their aims, science stands helpless before crude fact and selfish endeavor. The reason for this religious majority may be inexperience and lack of education; it may be divine grace and human sin. Whatever it is, the fact is unquestionable today.

Is there not, then, a chance to find common ground for a program of human betterment which seeks by means of known and tested knowledge the ideal ends of faith? This would involve on the part of the Church a surrender of dogma to the extent of being willing to work for human salvation this side of eternity, and to admit the possibility of vast betterment here and now—a path the Church has often followed. The Church should in colonies voluntarily adopt a self-denying ordinance: not to stress doctrine or dogma until social uplift in education, health, and economic organization have progressed far enough to enable colonial peoples intelligently and independently to compare the religion offered with their inherited cultures. This would involve on the part of science the admission that what we know is greatly exceeded by what we do not know, and that there may be realms in time and space of infinitely more importance than the problems of this small world. Nevertheless, a realistic program of making this world better *now* ought to combine the efforts of Church and science, of missionary effort and social reform. . . .

Chapter VII

On Crime

Du Bois was one of the first criminologists to reject genetic theories of criminal behavior, favoring instead a sociological approach, emphasizing matters of history, politics, economics, and other related social phenomena. In his appraisal of black crime rates, he documented the lingering results of slavery upon black culture, the pernicious effects of segregation and slums, the daily humiliations of racism, the state's demand for young convict labor, and the grossly unequal systems of justice for whites and blacks. Antedating Jeffrey Reiman's thesis in *The Rich Get Richer and the Poor Get Prison* (1998) by nearly a century, Du Bois asserted in *The Philadelphia Negro* (1899) that black criminality must be viewed in its relation to institutional racism and class inequality: "in convictions by human courts the rich always are favored somewhat at the expense of the poor, the upper classes at the expense of the unfortunate classes, and whites at the expense of Negroes." Like Ida B. Wells, Du Bois was an anti-lynching crusader, and his writings and speeches on lynching exposed to the world the degree to which white American justice and morality were severely diseased.

1. "The Negro Criminal"

Published in 1899 in *The Philadelphia Negro*

. . . From his earliest advent the Negro, as was natural, has figured largely in the criminal annals of Philadelphia. Only such superficial study of the American Negro as dates his beginning with 1863 can neglect this past record of crime in studying the present. Crime is a phenomenon of organized social life, and is the open rebellion of an individual against his social environment. Naturally then, if men are suddenly transported from one environment to another, the result is lack of harmony with the new conditions; lack of harmony with the new physical surroundings leading to disease and death or modification of physique; lack of harmony with social surroundings leading to crime. Thus very early in the history of the colony characteristic complaints of the disorder of the Negro slaves is heard. . . .

Throughout the land there has been since the war a large increase in crime, especially in cities. This phenomenon would seem to have sufficient cause in the increased complexity of life, in industrial competition, and the rush of great numbers to the large cities. It would therefore be natural to suppose that the Negro would also show this increase in criminality and, as in the case of all lower classes, that he would show it in greater degree. His evolution has, however, been marked by some peculiarities.

For nearly two decades after emancipation he took little part in many of the great social movements about him for obvious reasons. His migration to city life, therefore, and his sharing in the competition of modern industrial life, came later than was the case with the mass of his fellow citizens. The Negro began to rush to the cities in large numbers after 1880, and consequently the phenomena attendant on that momentous change of life are tardier in his case. His rate of criminality has in the last two decades risen rapidly, and this is a parallel "phenomenon to the rapid rise of the white criminal record two or three decades ago. Moreover, in the case of the Negro there were special causes for the prevalence of crime: he had lately been freed from serfdom, he was the object of stinging oppression and ridicule, and paths of advancement open to many were closed to him. Consequently the class of the shiftless, aimless, idle, discouraged and disappointed was proportionately larger. . . .

A Special Study in Crime[1]

Let us now take the 541 Negroes who have been the perpetrators of the serious crimes charged to their race during the last ten years and see what we may learn. These are all criminals convicted after trial for periods varying from six months to forty years. It seems plain in the first place that the 4 per cent of the population of Philadelphia having Negro blood furnished from 1885 to 1889, 14 per cent of the serious crimes, and from 1890 to 1895, 22½ per cent. This of course assumes that the convicts in the penitentiary represent with a fair degree of accuracy the crime committed. The assumption is not wholly true; in convictions by human courts the rich always are favored somewhat at the expense of the poor, the upper classes at the expense of the unfortunate classes, and whites at the expense of Negroes. We know for instance that certain

crimes are not punished in Philadelphia because the public opinion is lenient, as for instance embezzlement, forgery, and certain sorts of stealing; on the other hand a commercial community is apt to punish with severity petty thieving, breaches of the peace, and personal assault or burglary. It happens, too, that the prevailing weakness of ex-slaves brought up in the communal life of the slave plantation, without acquaintanceship with the institution of private property, is to commit the very crimes which a great centre of commerce like Philadelphia especially abhors. We must add to this the influences of social position and connections in procuring whites pardons or lighter sentences. It has been charged by some Negroes that color prejudice plays some part, but there is no tangible proof of this, save perhaps that there is apt to be a certain presumption of guilt when a Negro is accused, on the part of police, public and judge.[2] All these considerations modify somewhat our judgment of the moral status of the mass of Negroes. And yet, with all allowances, there remains a vast problem of crime.

The chief crimes for which these prisoners were convicted were:

Theft	243
Serious assaults on persons	139
Robbery and burglary	85
Rape	24
Other sexual crimes	23
Homicide	16
All other crimes	11
Total	541

. . . Let us now turn from the crime to the criminals. 497 of them (91.87 per cent) were males and 44 (8.13 per cent) were females. 296 (54.71 per cent) were single, 208 (34.45 per cent) were married, and 37 (6.84 per cent) were widowed. In age they were divided as follows:

Age	Number	Percentage	
15-19	58	10.73	66.92
20-24	170	56.19	
25-29	132		
30-39	132	24.03	34.08
40-49	34	6.29	
50-59	10	1.85	
60 and over	5	.91	
Total	541	100	

The mass of criminals are, it is easy to see, young single men under thirty. . . .

Altogether 21 per cent were natives of Philadelphia; 217 were born in the North, and 309, or 57 per cent, were born in the South. Two-thirds of the Negroes of the city, judging from the Seventh Ward, were born outside the city, and this part furnishes 79 per cent of the serious crime. 54 per cent were born in the South and this part furnishes 57 per cent of the crime, or more, since many giving their birthplace as in the North were really born in the South.

The total illiteracy of this group reaches 26 per cent or adding in those who can read and write imperfectly, 34 per cent compared with 18 per cent for the Negroes of the city in 1890. In other words the illiterate fifth of the Negro population furnished a third of the worst criminals. . . .

. . . A study of statistics seems to show that the crime and pauperism of the Negroes exceeds that of the whites; that in the main, nevertheless, it follows in its rise and fall the fluctuations shown in the records of the whites, *i. e.,* if crime increases among the whites it increases among Negroes, and *vice versa*, with this peculiarity, that among the Negroes the change is always exaggerated—the increase greater, the decrease more marked in nearly all cases. This is what we would naturally expect: we have here the record of a low social class, and as the condition of a lower class is by its very definition worse than that of a higher, so the situation of the Negroes is worse as respects crime and poverty than that of the mass of whites. Moreover, any change in social conditions is bound to affect the poor and unfortunate more than the rich and prosperous. We have in all probability an example of this in the increase of crime since 1890; we have had a period of financial stress and industrial depression; the ones who have felt this most are the poor, the unskilled laborers, the inefficient and unfortunate, and those with small social and economic advantages: the Negroes are in this class, and the result has been an increase in Negro crime and pauperism; there has also been an increase in the crime of the whites, though less rapid by reason of their richer and more fortunate upper classes.

So far, then, we have no phenomena which are new or exceptional, or which present more than the ordinary social problems of crime and poverty—although these, to be sure, are difficult enough. Beyond these, however, there are problems which can rightly be called Negro problems: they arise from the peculiar history and condition of the American Negro. The first peculiarity is, of course, the slavery and emancipation of the Negroes. That their emancipation has raised them economically and morally is proven by the increase of wealth and co-operation, and the decrease of poverty and crime between the period before the war and the period since; nevertheless, this was manifestly no simple process: the first effect of emancipation was that of any sudden social revolution: a strain upon the strength and resources of the Negro, moral, economic and physical, which drove many to the wall. For this reason the rise of the Negro in this city is a series of rushes and backslidings rather than a continuous growth. The second great peculiarity of the situation of the Negroes is the fact of immigration; the great numbers of raw recruits who have from time to time precipitated themselves upon the Negroes of the city and shared their small industrial opportunities, have made reputations which, whether good or bad, all their race must share; and finally whether they failed or succeeded in the strong competition, they themselves must soon prepare to face a new immigration.

Here then we have two great causes for the present condition of the Negro: Slavery and emancipation with their attendant phenomena of ignorance, lack of discipline, and moral weakness; immigration with its increased competition and moral influence. To this must be added a third as great—possibly greater in influence than the other two, namely the environment in which a Negro finds himself—the world of custom and thought in which he must live and work, the physical surrounding of house and home and ward, the moral encouragements and discouragements which he encounters. We dimly seek to define this social environment partially when we talk of color prejudice—but this is but a vague characterization; what we want to study is not a vague thought or feeling but its concrete manifestations. We know pretty well what the surroundings are of a young white lad, or a foreign immigrant who comes to this great city to join in its organic life. We know what influences and limitations surround him, to what he may attain, what his companionships are, what his encouragements are, what his drawbacks.

This we must know in regard to the Negro if we would study his social condition. His strange social environment must have immense effect on his thought and life, his work and crime, his wealth and pauperism. That this environment differs and differs broadly from the environment of his fellows, we all know, but we do not know just how it differs. The real foundation of the difference is the wide-spread feeling all over the land, in Philadelphia as well as in Boston and New Orleans, that the Negro is something less than an American and ought not to be much more

than what he is. Argue as we may for or against this idea, we must as students recognize its presence and its vast effects. . . .

For the last ten or fifteen years young Negroes have been pouring into this city at the rate of a thousand a year; the question is then what homes they find or make, what neighbors they have, how they amuse themselves, and what work they engage in? Again, into what sort of homes are the hundreds of Negro babies of each year born? Under what social influences do they come, what is the tendency of their training, and what places in life can they fill? To answer all these questions is to go far toward finding the real causes of crime and pauperism among this race; the next two chapters, therefore, take up the question of environment.

Notes

1. For the collection of the material here compiled, I am indebted to Mr. David N. Fell, Jr., a student of the Senior Class, Wharton School, University of Pennsylvania, in the year '96–'97. As before noted the figures in this Section refer to the number of prisoners received at the Eastern Penitentiary, and not to the total prison population at any particular time.

2. Witness the case of Marion Stuyvesant accused of the murder of the librarian, Wilson, in 1897.

2. "The Relations of Negroes to Whites in the South"

Published in 1901 in *Annals of the American Academy of Political and Social Sciences*

. . . Moreover the political status of the Negro in the South is closely connected with the question of Negro crime. There can be no doubt that crime among Negroes has greatly increased in the last twenty years and that there has appeared in the slums of great cities a distinct criminal class among the blacks. In explaining this unfortunate developement we must note two things, (1) that the inevitable result of emancipation was to increase crime and criminals, and (2) that the police system of the South was primarily designed to control slaves. As to the first point we must not forget that under a strict slave régime there can scarcely be such a thing as crime. But when these variously constituted human particles are suddenly thrown broadcast on the sea of life, some swim, some sink, and some hang suspended, to be forced up or down by the chance currents of a busy hurrying world. So great an economic and social revolution as swept the South in '63 meant a weeding out among the Negroes of the incompetents and vicious—the beginning of a differentiation of social grades. Now a rising group of people are not lifted bodily from the ground like an inert solid mass, but rather stretch upward like a living plant with its roots still clinging in the mold. The appearance, therefore, of the Negro criminal was a phenomenon to be awaited, and while it causes anxiety it should not occasion surprise.

Here again the hope for the future depended peculiarly on careful and delicate dealing with these criminals. Their offenses at first were those of laziness, carelessness and impulse rather than of malignity or ungoverned viciousness. Such misdemeanors needed discriminating treatment, firm but reformatory, with no hint of injustice and full proof of guilt. For such dealing with criminals, white or black, the South had no machinery, no adequate jails or reformatories and a police system arranged to deal with blacks alone, and which tacitly assumed that every white man was *ipso facto* a member of that police. Thus grew up a double system of justice which erred on the white side by undue leniency and the practical immunity of red-handed criminals, and erred on the black side by undue severity, injustice and lack of discrimination. For, as I have said, the police system of the South was originally designed to keep track of all Negroes, not simply of criminals, and when

the Negroes were freed and the whole South was convinced of the impossibility of free Negro labor, the first and almost universal device was to use the courts as a means of re-enslaving the blacks. It was not then a question of crime but rather of color that settled a man's conviction on almost any charge. Thus Negroes came to look upon courts as instruments of injustice and oppression, and upon those convicted in them as martyrs and victims.

When now the real Negro criminal appeared and, instead of petty stealing and vagrancy, we began to have highway robbery, burglary, murder and rape, it had a curious effect on both sides [of] the color line; the Negroes refused to believe the evidence of white witnesses or the fairness of white juries, so that the greatest deterrent to crime, the public opinion of one's own social caste was lost and the criminal still looked upon as crucified rather than hanged. On the other hand the whites, used to being careless as to the guilt or innocence of accused Negroes, were swept in moments of passion beyond law, reason and decency. Such a situation is bound to increase crime and has increased it. To natural viciousness and vagrancy is being daily added motives of revolt and revenge which stir up all the latent savagery of both races and make peaceful attention to economic development often impossible.

But the chief problem in any community cursed with crime is not the punishment of the criminals but the preventing of the young from being trained to crime. And here again the peculiar conditions of the South have prevented proper precautions. I have seen twelve-year-old boys working in chains on the public streets of Atlanta, directly in front of the schools, in company with old and hardened criminals; and this indiscriminate mingling of men, women and children makes the chain-gangs perfect schools of crime and debauchery. The struggle for reformatories which has gone on in Virginia, Georgia and other states is the one encouraging sign of the awakening of some communities to the suicidal results of this policy.

It is the public schools, however, which can be made outside the homes the greatest means of training decent self-respecting citizens. We have been so hotly engaged recently in discussing trade schools and the higher education that the pitiable plight of the public school system in the South has almost dropped from view. Of every five dollars spent for public education in the State of Georgia the white schools get four dollars and the Negro one dollar, and even then the white public school system, save in the cities, is bad and cries for reform. If this be true of the whites, what of the blacks? I am becoming more and more convinced as I look upon the system of common school training in the South that the national government must soon step in and aid popular education in some way. To-day it has been only by the most strenuous efforts on the part of the thinking men of the South that the Negro's share of the school fund has not been cut down to a pittance in some half dozen states, and that movement not only is not dead but in many communities is gaining strength. What in the name of reason does this nation expect of a people poorly trained and hard pressed in severe economic competition, without political rights and with ludicrously inadequate common school facilities? What can it expect but crime and listlessness, offset here and there by the dogged struggles of the fortunate and more determined who are themselves buoyed by the hope that in due time the country will come to its senses? . . .

3. "Notes on Negro Crime, Particularly in Georgia"

Published in 1904 by
the Atlanta University Press

11. Causes of Negro Crime

This study is too incomplete to lead us to many definite conclusions. Yet certain causes

of crime among Negroes today seem clear. They may be briefly classified as follows:

A.—*Faults of the Negroes.*

1. Abuse of their new freedom and tendency toward idleness and vagrancy.

2. Loose ideas of property, petty pilfering.

3. Unreliability, lying and deception.

4. Exaggerated ideas of personal rights, irritability and suspicion.

5. Sexual looseness, weak family life and poor training of children; lack of respect for parents.

6. Lack of proper self-respect; low or extravagant ideals.

7. Poverty, low wages and lack of accumulated property.

8. Lack of thrift and prevalence of the gambling spirit.

9. Waywardness of the "second generation."

10. The use of liquor and drugs.

All these faults are real and important causes of Negro crime. They are not racial traits but due to perfectly evident historic causes: slavery could not survive as an institution and teach thrift; and its great evil in the United States was its low sexual morals; emancipation meant for the Negroes poverty and a great stress of life due to sudden change. These and other considerations explain Negro crime. They do not excuse it however and a great burden of pressing reform from within lies upon the Negro's shoulders. Especially is this true with regard to the atrocious crime of rape. This is not to be sure a crime peculiar to the Negro race. An Englishman tells us that in Jamaica justice has been dealt out impartially; and this has not resulted in "impudence" on the part of the blacks towards the whites.

Indeed, when reasonably treated they are remarkably courteous,—more so than the average Teuton. Attacks by black men on white women are absolutely unknown; a young white woman is safe anywhere, the only terror being from white sailors. There are offenses against black women and children, but not whites. He infers from this that the danger of such attacks on white women, if it exists in the United States, is not really due to race. For his own part he is sure that the evil, where it exists, is augmented by the state of frenzy with which it is met.*

But granting this and making allowance for all exaggeration in attributing this crime to Negroes, there still remain enough well authenticated cases of brutal assault on women by black men in America to make every Negro bow his head in shame. Negroes must recognize their responsibility for their own worst classes and never let resentment against slander allow them even to seem to palliate an awful deed. This crime must at all hazards stop. Lynching is awful, and injustice and caste are hard to bear; but if they are to be successfully attacked they must cease to have even this terrible justification.

B.—Faults of the whites

1. The attempt to enforce a double standard of justice in the courts, one for Negroes and one for whites.

2. The election of judges for short terms, making them subservient to waves of public opinion in a white electorate.

3. The shirking of jury duty by the best class of whites, leaving the dealing out of justice to the most ignorant and prejudiced.

4. Laws so drawn as to entangle the ignorant, as in the case of laws for labor contracts, and to leave wide discretion as to punishment in the hands of juries and petty officials.

5. Peonage and debt-slavery as methods of securing cheap and steady labor.

6. The tendency to encourage ignorance and subserviency among Negroes instead of intelligence, ambition and independence.

7. The taking of all rights of political self-defense from the Negro either by direct law, or custom, or by the "white primary" system.

8. The punishment of crime as a means of public and private revenue rather than as a means of preventing the making of criminals.

9. The rendering of the chastity of Negro women difficult of defense in law or custom against the aggressions of white men.

10. Enforcing a caste system in such a way as to humiliate Negroes and kill their self-respect.

. . . There is much difference of opinion on many of the points enumerated above, but it certainly seems clear that absolutely impartial courts; the presence of intelligent Negroes on juries when Negroes are tried; the careful defense of ignorance in law and custom; the absolute doing away with every vestige of involuntary servitude except in prisons under absolute state control, and for the reformation of the prisoner; the encouraging of intelligent, ambitious, and independent black men; the granting of the right to cast an untramelled vote to intelligent and decent Negroes; the unwavering defense of all women who want to be decent against indecent approach, and an effort to increase rather than to kill the self respect of Negroes, it seems certain that such a policy would make quickly and decidedly for the decrease of Negro criminality in the South and in the land.

---

*Sidney Olivier, in the *British Friend*, Dec., 1904.

The arguments against this are often strongly urged; it is said that whites and Negroes differ so in standards of culture that courts must discriminate; that partially forced labor is necessary in the South; that intelligent Negroes become impudent fault-finders and disturb a delicate situation; that the South cannot in self-defense permit Negro suffrage; that Negro women are unchaste; and that the Negro must be "kept down" at all hazards. To all this it can only be said: These arguments have been used against every submerged class since the world began, and history has repeatedly proven them false. . . .

Resolutions. The following resolutions were adopted before the conference adjourned:

The Ninth Atlanta Conference, after a study of crime among Negroes in Georgia, has come to these conclusions:

Amount of Crime

1. The amount of crime among Negroes in this state is very great. This is a dangerous and threatening phenomenon. It means that large numbers of the freedmen's sons have not yet learned to be law-abiding citizens and steady workers, and until they do so the progress of the race, of the South, and of the nation will be retarded.

Causes of Crime

2. The causes of this state of affairs seem clear:

First. The mass of the Negroes are in a transient stage between slavery and freedom. Such a period of change involves physical strain, mental bewilderment and moral weakness. Such periods of stress have among all people

given rise to crime and a criminal class. *Secondly.* Race prejudice in so far as it narrows the opportunities open to Negroes and teaches them to lose self-respect and ambition by arbitrary caste proscriptions is a potent cause of carelessness, disorder and crime. *Thirdly.* Negroes have less legal protection than others against unfair aggression upon their rights, liberty and prosperity. This is particularly true of Negro women, whose honor and chastity have in this state very little protection against the force and influence of white men, particularly in the country districts and small towns. *Fourthly.* Laws as to vagrancy, disorder, contracts for work, chattel mortgages and crop-liens are so drawn as to involve in the coils of the law the ignorant, unfortunate and careless Negroes, and lead to their degradation and undue punishment, when their real need is inspiration, knowledge and opportunity. *Fifthly.* Courts usually administer two distinct sorts of justice: one for whites and one for Negroes; and this custom, together with the fact that judge and court officials are invariably white and elected to office by the influence of white votes alone, makes it very difficult for a Negro to secure justice in court when his opponent is white. *Sixthly.* The methods of punishment of Negro criminals is calculated to breed crime rather than stop it. Lynching spreads among black folk the firmly fixed idea that few accused Negroes are really guilty; the leasing of convicts, even the present system of state control, makes the state traffic in crime for the sake of revenue instead of seeking to reform criminals for the sake of moral regeneration; and finally the punishment of Negro criminals is usually unintelligent: they are punished according to the crime rather than according to their criminal record; little discrimination is made between old and young, male and female, hardened thug and careless mischief-maker; and the result is that a single sentence to the chaingang for a trivial misdemeanor usually makes the victim a confirmed criminal for life. . . .

4. "Morals and Manners"

Published in 1914 by
the Atlanta University Press

1. Southern whites are not arrested and punisht for smaller misdemeanors.

2. The number of foreigners in the South is very small.

3. The Negroes suffer from race discrimination.

The criminologist passes no judgment on the right or wrong of this discrimination. He simply recognizes it as a fact; but he knows:

(a) That many economic forces of the South depend largely on the courts for a supply of labor.

(b) That public opinion in the South exaggerates the guilt of Negroes in certain crimes and enforces itself thru police, jury, magistrate and judge.

(c) That southern public opinion over-looks and unduly minimizes certain other Negro misdemeanors, which lead to immorality and crime.

Of the truth of these statements there can be no reasonable doubt in the mind of any careful student.

In crimes against society (unchastity, perjury and violating United States laws) the Negro is less seldom committed than whites. This is because his crimes against chastity, when his own race are victims, are seldom punisht properly in the South. His proportion of crimes against property are larger, due to his past economic history. His proportion of crimes against the person are greatest because right here, in his personal contact with his fellows, prejudice and discrimination, exasperation and revolt show themselves most frequently; and also because his masses are reaching the brawling stage of self-assertion.

While the proportions vary the actual number of those committed for bigamy, perjury, arson, adultery and violating United States laws is small. Of the more frequent delinquencies, vagrancy, drunkenness, and fraud show the Negroes less guilty than whites. The cases of disorder are but a little larger than the Negro's proportion. The cases of stealing are more seriously in excess, but this excess is hardly more than would be expected from the heritage of slavery, the custom of partial payment in kind and very low wages contrasted with rapidly expanding wants. The cases of rape, altho absolutely few in number, are relatively large, but here the influence of racial prejudice is large: Any insult or suspected insult to white women by a Negro in the South is liable to be denominated and punisht as attempted rape. How much real guilt therefore lies back of the figures can only be conjectured. The really dangerous excess of Negro crime would appear to be in assault and homicide, fighting and killing. Here again interpretation is difficult: How much of these are aggressions on whites, repelling of white aggressions on Negroes, and brawling among Negroes themselves? Undoubtedly the majority of cases belong to the last category, but a very large and growing number come under the other heads and must be set down to the debit of the race problem.

Any Negro tried for perjury, assault, robbery, rape, homicide, arson, burglary, larceny or fraud is going to get a severer penalty in the South than a white man similarly charged. This the white community judges to be necessary and its decisions are carried out by police forces, police magistrates and juries drawn from the white classes whose racial prejudices are strongest. The higher judges tend toward greater independence but even they must stand in fear of the white electorate, whose power is exercised at short intervals.

Next to this stands the fact that in the South road-building, mining, brickmaking, lumbering and to some extent agriculture depend largely on convict labor. The demand for such labor is strong and increasing. The political power of the lessees is great and the income to the city and state is tempting. The glaring brutalities of the older lease system are disappearing but the fact still remains that the state is supplying a demand for degraded labor and especially for life and long term laborers and that almost irresistibly the police forces and sheriffs are pusht to find black criminals in suitable quantities.

If this is so, many ask, how can crime in the North be explained? Northern Negro crime is different in character and cause. It arises from:

(a)   A sudden change from country to city life.

(b)   Segregation in slums.

(c)   Difficulty of obtaining employment.

The proof of (a) is seen among the whites: Massachusetts and Iowa are of similar grade of culture, yet Massachusetts, a state of towns and cities, has 846 annual commitments per 100,000 of population while Iowa, a state of farms, has 402. Thus prejudice and economic demand account for much of the excess of Negro crime. But they do not account for all of it. Another factor as shown by the census is: *Ignorance.* Of native white criminals ninety-three per cent could read and write; of foreigners seventy-eight per cent; of Negroes only sixty-two per cent. This minimum of education it is the duty of the state to furnish; and since this is not done, the Negro, more than any other criminal element has the legitimate

but costly excuse of sheer ignorance. Another factor is: *Neglect of the young.* The South sent to prison in 1904 sixteen hundred children of both races under twenty years of age, nine hundred and fifty of whom were under fifteen years of age. Yet, North and South Carolina, Alabama, Mississippi, Texas, and Oklahoma made no provision whatsoever for juvenile delinquents among Negroes; and Florida, Georgia, Louisiana, Tennessee and West Virginia had each one small institution with from thirteen to fifty-four inmates. Probably a thousand delinquent Negro children in the South to-day are being trained in prisons by companionship with the worst grown criminals. And this thing has been going on for years.

This is the more serious because Negro crime is peculiarly the crime of the young. The following table is explicit:

AGES BY PERCENTAGES

	Native Whites	Negroes
Under 20 years of age	10	19
20–30 years	35	52
30 years and over	55	29

The cause of this youthful crime is:

(1)   The difficulty of adjusting the young to a caste system.

(2)   The poor home training.

(3)   The demand for strong young convict labor.

Other causes of crime not shown in these figures are:

(1)   Poverty.

(2)   Discouragement arising from lawless treatment and withdrawal of civil and political rights.

(3)   Lack of self-respect under a caste system.

What now is the remedy for Negro crime?

1. Justice in southern courts; Negroes on the police force and in the jury box.

2. Abolition of the economic demand for criminals in the South.

3. Better housing and free chance to work in the North.

4. National aid to Negro education.

5. Better wages.

6. Full civil and political rights for Negroes, on the same basis as they are granted to whites.

There is a theory held by many persons and often openly exprest, that Negroes are especially guilty of crimes against white women. The facts do not bear this out. In the West Indies, with an overwhelming preponderance of Negroes in the population, such crimes are practically unknown. In the United States lynching has long been excused by many as the only cure for these crimes. But of 2855 lynch law murders done, between 1885 and 1913, the accusation of assault on women was made in only 706 or 24.4 per cent, less than a fourth, of these cases. It is moreover fair to assume that in these 706 alleged cases the proportion of guilty persons was small.

It must be remembered that in a condition of inflamed racial hatred, where sexual intercourse between colored men and white women is regarded as a crime in many sections under any circumstances and where fear and suspicion are in the air, the general accusation of rape may include much that is not criminal at all. Personal insult of all degrees, wrongful suspicion, lying and disguise, accident, self defense, circumstantial evidence, burglary in a woman's room, exaggeration, illicit relations and sheer mental suggestion may all go to swell the charge of rape.

5. "Lynched by Years, 1885-1914"

Published in 1915 in *The Crisis*

LYNCHED BY YEARS, 1885-1914			
1885	78	1900	107
1886	71	1901	107
1887	80	1902	86
1888	95	1903	86
1889	95	1904	83
1890	90	1905	61
1891	121	1906	64
1892	155	1907	60
1893	154	1908	93
1894	134	1909	73
1895	112	1910	65
1896	80	1911	63
1897	122	1912	63
1898	102	1913	79
1899	84	1914	69
Total			2,732

These lynchings produce the usual little pleasantries with which the American nation is so familiar. Murder, for instance, sounds very awful and yet we must remember that one of those lynched for murder was killed in defense of a colored woman's honor. In another case a marshal had already shot a man whom he was about to arrest. The man then killed him and was promptly lynched. In two Florida cases proof that the lynched men were innocent came after they were dead. Blood hounds and posses have been responsible for desperate resistance on the part of men afterward lynched, and in one case the man who had been respited on account of doubt of his guilt was promptly killed by the mob.

The so-called assaults were to a considerable extent fights where the white man was worsted. One constable received a flesh wound and his assailant was lynched, whereupon the constable promptly recovered. Another white man suffered the indignity of being struck by a hoe, and still another of having his chin bitten off. The assailants in both cases were killed with great enthusiasm.

Attacks on property are most irritating, and one boy who stole a pair of shoes suffered the same fate as a man who stole a couple of mules. Mules are quite valuable in Mississippi. In the very recent lynchings in Louisiana it would seem that the search for a missing $500 was the chief motive. The burning of a barn in Mississippi resulted in two lynchings.

The chivalry of southern white manhood toward colored women has been particularly conspicuous this season. Two men raped a colored girl in Oklahoma. One was killed by her brother and their friends thereupon *lynched the girl*! A Mississippi mob killed a wife along with her husband, leaving a four-year-old child motherless, while in another case a colored woman who had the impudence to refuse to allow her home to be searched was summarily dealt with.

On the other hand, white womanhood received its usual protection. An impudent porter pushed a white woman off the sidewalk and was lynched. In two cases colored men were found in white women's rooms. They were immediately charged with "attempted" rape and killed.

Human bonfires have been made in three or four cases: one in Georgia, one in Mississippi, and one in Louisiana. In Louisiana the victim was a nice old man of the "uncle" type which the white South particularly loves. A theatrical company playing "Potash and Perlmutter" made an excursion to the entertainment and several society women were present.

All this goes to show how peculiarly fitted the United States is for moral leadership of the world. . . .

Chapter VIII

On Education

When Du Bois first ventured into the South to attend college at Fisk University, he spent two summer breaks teaching elementary school in small black communities in rural Tennessee, an experience of which he eloquently wrote in *The Souls of Black Folk* (1903). Ever since his experience in those Tennessee hills, he thought and wrote extensively about the nature of education. One of his many public disagreements with Booker T. Washington concerned the of education of black people: Should they be predominantly trained in vocational skills or exposed to broader educational cultivation? Du Bois favored the latter, as he wrote in Chapter 5 of *The Souls of Black Folk*: "The function of the university is not simply to teach breadwinning . . . it is, above all, to be the organ of that fine adjustment between real life and the growing knowledge of life, an adjustment which forms the secret of civilization." One of his most famous and controversial concepts related to the education of black people was that of the "Talented Tenth," an idea elaborated upon in one of the selections printed below.

1. "The Talented Tenth"

Published in 1903 in *The Negro Problem*

The Negro race, like all races, is going to be saved by its exceptional men. The problem of education, then, among Negroes must first of all deal with the Talented Tenth; it is the problem of developing the Best of this race that they may guide the Mass away from the contamination and death of the Worst, in their own and other races. Now the training of men is a difficult and intricate task. Its technique is a matter for educational experts, but its object is for the vision of seers. If we make money the object of man-training, we shall develop money-makers but not necessarily men; if we make technical skill the object of education, we may possess artisans but not, in nature, men. Men we shall have only as we make manhood the object of the work of the schools—intelligence, broad sympathy, knowledge of the world that was and is, and of the relation of men to it—this is the curriculum of that Higher Education which must underlie true life. On this foundation we may build bread winning, skill of hand and quickness of brain, with never a fear lest the child and man mistake the means of living for the object of life.

If this be true—and who can deny it—three tasks lay before me; first to show from the past that the Talented Tenth as they have risen among American Negroes have been worthy of leadership; secondly, to show how these men may be educated and developed; and thirdly, to show their relation to the Negro problem.

You misjudge us because you do not know us. From the very first it has been the educated and intelligent of the Negro people that have led and elevated the mass, and the sole obstacles that nullified and retarded their efforts were slavery and race prejudice; for what is slavery but the legalized survival of the unfit and the nullification of the work of natural internal leadership? Negro leadership, therefore, sought from the first to rid the race of this awful incubus that it might make way for natural selection and the survival of the fittest. In colonial days came Phillis Wheatley and Paul Cuffe striving against the bars of prejudice; and Benjamin Banneker, the almanac maker, voiced their longings when he said to Thomas Jefferson, "I freely and cheerfully acknowledge that I am of the African Race, and in colour which is natural to them, of the deepest dye; and it is under a sense of the most profound gratitude to the Supreme Ruler of the Universe, that I now confess to you that I am not under that state of tyrannical thraldom and inhuman captivity to which too many of my brethren are doomed, but that I have abundantly tasted of the fruition of those blessings which proceed from that free and unequalled liberty with which you are favored, and which I hope you will willingly allow, you have mercifully received from the immediate hand of that Being from whom proceedeth every good and perfect gift.

"Suffer me to recall to your mind that time, in which the arms of the British crown were exerted with every powerful effort, in order to reduce you to a state of servitude; look back, I entreat you, on the variety of dangers to which you were exposed; reflect on that period in which every human aid appeared unavailable, and in which even hope and fortitude wore the aspect of inability to the conflict, and you cannot but be led to a serious and grateful sense of your miraculous and providential preservation, you cannot but acknowledge, that the present freedom and tranquility which

you enjoy, you have mercifully received, and that a peculiar blessing of heaven.

"This, sir, was a time when you clearly saw into the injustice of a state of Slavery, and in which you had just apprehensions of the horrors of its condition. It was then that your abhorrence thereof was so excited, that you publicly held forth this true and invaluable doctrine, which is worthy to be recorded and remembered in all succeeding ages: 'We hold these truths to be self evident, that all men are created equal; that they are endowed with certain inalienable rights, and that among these are life, liberty and the pursuit of happiness.'"

Then came Dr. James Derham, who could tell even the learned Dr. Rush something of medicine, and Lemuel Haynes, to whom Middlebury gave an honorary A.M. in 1804. These and others we may call the Revolutionary group of distinguished Negroes—they were persons of marked ability, leaders of a Talented Tenth, standing conspicuously among the best of their time. They strove by word and deed to save the color line from becoming the line between the bond and free, but all that they could do was nullified by Eli Whitney and the Curse of Gold. So they passed into forgetfulness.

But their spirit did not wholly die; here and there in the early part of the century came other exceptional men. Some were natural sons of unnatural fathers and were given often a liberal training and thus a race of educated mulattoes sprang up to plead for the black men's rights. There was Ira Aldridge, whom all Europe loved to honor; there was that voice crying in the Wilderness, David Walker, and saying:

"I declare it does appear to me as though some nations think God is asleep, or that he made the Africans for nothing else but to dig their mines and work their farms, or they cannot believe history, sacred or profane. I ask every man who has a heart, and is blessed with the privilege of believing—Is not God a God of justice to all his creatures? Do you say he is?

Then if he gives peace and tranquility to tyrants and permits them to keep our fathers, our mothers, ourselves and our children in eternal ignorance and wretchedness to support them and their families, would he be to us a God of Justice? I ask, O, ye Christians, who hold us and our children in the most abject ignorance and degradation that ever a people were afflicted with since the world began—I say if God gives you peace and tranquility, and suffers you thus to go on afflicting us, and our children, who have never given you the least provocation—would he be to us a God of Justice? If you will allow that we are men, who feel for each other, does not the blood of our fathers and of us, their children, cry aloud to the Lord of Sabaoth against you for the cruelties and murders with which you have and do continue to afflict us?"

This was the wild voice that first aroused Southern legislators in 1829 to the terrors of abolitionism.

In 1831 there met that first Negro convention in Philadelphia, at which the world gaped curiously but which bravely attacked the problems of race and slavery, crying out against persecution and declaring that "Laws as cruel in themselves as they were unconstitutional and unjust, have in many places been enacted against our poor, unfriended and unoffending brethren (without a shadow of provocation on our part), at whose bare recital the very savage draws himself up for fear of contagion—looks noble and prides himself because he bears not the name of Christian." Side by side this free Negro movement, and the movement for abolition, strove until they merged into one strong stream. Too little notice has been taken of the work which the Talented Tenth among Negroes took in the great abolition crusade. From the very day that a Philadelphia colored man became the first subscriber to Garrison's "Liberator," to the day when Negro soldiers made the Emancipation Proclamation possible, black leaders worked shoulder to shoulder with white men in a movement, the success of which would have been impossible without them. There was Purvis and Remond, Pennington and Highland Garnet, Sojourner Truth and Alexander Crummell, and above all, Frederick Douglass—what would the abolition movement have been without them? They stood as living examples of the possibilities of the Negro race, their own hard experiences and well-wrought culture said silently more than all the drawn periods of orators—they were the men who made American slavery impossible. As Maria Weston Chapman once said, from the school of anti-slavery agitation "a throng of authors, editors, lawyers, orators and accomplished gentlemen of color have taken their degree! It has equally implanted hopes and aspirations, noble thoughts, and sublime purposes, in the hearts of both races. It has prepared the white man for the freedom of the black man, and it has made the black man scorn the thought of enslavement, as does a white man, as far as its influence has extended. Strengthen that noble influence! Before its organization, the country only saw here and there in slavery some faithful Cudjoe or Dinah, whose strong natures blossomed even in bondage, like a fine plant beneath a heavy stone. Now, under the elevating and cherishing influence of the American Anti-slavery Society, the colored race, like the white, furnishes Corinthian capitals for the noblest temples."

Where were these black abolitionists trained? Some, like Frederick Douglass, were self-trained, but yet trained liberally; others like Alexander Crummell and McCune Smith, graduated from famous foreign universities. Most of them rose up through the colored schools of New York and Philadelphia and Boston, taught by college-bred men like Russwrom, of Dartmouth, and college-bred white men like Neau and Benezet.

After emancipation came a new group of educated and gifted leaders: Langston, Bruce and Elliot, Greener, Williams and Payne.

Through political organization, historical and polemic writing and moral regeneration, these men strove to uplift their people. It is now the fashion of to-day to sneer at them and to say that with freedom Negro leadership should have begun at the plow and not in the Senate—a foolish and mischievous lie; two hundred and fifty years that black serf toiled at the plow and yet that toiling was in vain till the Senate passed the war amendments; and two hundred and fifty years more the half-free serf of to-day may toil at his plow, but unless he have political rights and righteously guarded civic status, he will still remain the poverty-stricken and ignorant plaything of rascals, that he now is. This all sane men know even if they dare not say it.

And so now we come to the present—a day of cowardice and vacillation, of strident wide voiced wrong and faint hearted compromise; of double-faced dallying with Truth and Right. Who are to-day guiding the work of the Negro people? The "exceptions" of course. And yet so sure as this Talented Tenth is pointed out, the blind worshippers of the Average cry out in alarm: "These are the exceptions, look here at death, disease and crime—these are the happy rule." Of course they are the rule, because a silly nation made them the rule: Because for three long centuries this people lynched Negroes who dared to be brave, raped black women who dared to be virtuous, crushed dark-hued youth who dared to be ambitious, and encouraged and made to flourish servility and lewdness and apathy. But not even this was able to crush all manhood and chastity and aspiration from black folk. A saving remnant continually survives and persists, continually aspires, continually shows itself in thrift and ability and character. Exceptional it is to be sure, but this is its chiefest promise; it shows the capability of Negro blood, the promise of black men. Do Americans ever stop to reflect that there are in this land a million men of Negro blood, well-educated,

owners of homes, against the honor of whose womanhood no breath was ever raised, whose men occupy positions of trust and usefulness, and who, judged by any standard, have reached the full measure of the best type of modern European culture? Is it fair, is it decent, is it Christian to ignore these facts of the Negro problem, to belittle such aspiration, to nullify such leadership and seek to crush these people back into the mass out of which by toil and travail, they and their fathers have raised themselves?

Can the masses of the Negro people be in any possible way more quickly raised than by the effort and example of this aristocracy of talent and character? Was there ever a nation on God's fair earth civilized from the bottom upward? Never; it is, ever was and ever will be from the top downward that culture filters. The Talented Tenth rises and pulls all that are worth the saving up to their vantage ground. This is the history of human progress; and two historic mistakes which have hindered that progress were the thinking first that no more could ever rise save the few already risen; or second, that it would better the unrisen to pull the risen down.

How then shall the leaders of a struggling people be trained and the hands of the risen few be strengthened? There can be but one answer: The best and most capable of their youth must be schooled in the colleges and universities of the land. We will not quarrel as to just what the university of the Negro should teach or how it should teach it—I willingly admit that each soul and each race-soul needs its own peculiar curriculum. But this is true: A university is a human invention for the transmission of knowledge and culture from generation to generation, through the training of quick minds and pure hearts, and for this work no other human invention will suffice, not even trade and industrial schools.

All men cannot go to college but some men must; every isolated group or nation must have its yeast, must have for the talented few centers of training where men are not so mystified and befuddled by the hard necessary toil of earning a living, as to have no aims higher than their bellies, and no God greater than Gold. This is true training, and thus in the beginning were the favored sons of the freedmen trained. Out of the colleges of the North came, Cravath, Chase, Andrews, Bumstead and Spence to build the foundations of knowledge and civilization in the black South. Where ought they to have begun to build? At the bottom, of course, quibbles the mole with his eyes in the earth. Aye! truly at the bottom, at the very bottom; at the bottom of knowledge, down in the very depths of knowledge there where the roots of justice strike into the lowest soil of Truth. And so they did begin; they founded colleges, and up from the colleges shot normal schools, and out from the normal schools went teachers, and around the normal teachers clustered other teachers to teach the public schools; the colleges trained in Greek and Latin and mathematics, 2,000 men; and these men trained full 50,000 others in morals and manners and they in turn taught thrift and the alphabet to nine millions of men, who to-day hold $300,000,000 of property. It was a miracle—the most wonderful peace-battle of the nineteenth century, and yet to-day men smile at it, and in fine superiority tell us that it was all a strange mistake; that a proper way to found a system of education is first to gather the children and buy them spelling books and hoes; afterward men may look about for teachers, if haply they find them; or again they would teach men Work, but as for Life—why, what has Work to do with Life, they ask vacantly.

Was the work of these college founders successful; did it stand the test of time? Did the college graduates, with all their fine theories of life, really live? Are they useful men helping to civilize and elevate their less fortunate fellows? Let us see. Omitting all institutions which have not actually graduated students from college courses, there are to-day in the United States thirty-four institutions giving something above high school training to Negroes and designed especially for this race.

Three of these were established in the border States before the War; thirteen were planted by the Freedmen's Bureau in the years 1864–1869; nine were established between 1870 and 1880 by various church bodies; five were established after 1881 by Negro churches, and four are state institutions supported by United States' agricultural funds. In most cases the college departments are small adjuncts to high and common school work. As a matter of fact six institutions—Atlanta, Fisk, Howard, Shaw, Wilberforce and Leland, are the important Negro colleges so far as actual work and number of students are concerned. In all these institutions, seven hundred and fifty Negro college students are enrolled. In grade the best of these colleges are about a year behind the smaller New England colleges and a typical curriculum is that of Atlanta University. Here students from the grammar grades, after a three years' high school course, take a college course of 136 weeks. One-fourth of this time is given to Latin and Greek; one-fifth, to English and modern languages; one-sixth, to history and social science; one-seventh, to natural science; one-eighth to mathematics, and one-eighth to philosophy and pedagogy.

In addition to these students in the South, Negroes have attended Northern colleges for many years. As early as 1826 one was graduated from Bowdoin college, and from that time till to-day nearly every year has seen elsewhere, other such graduates. They have, of course, met much color prejudice. Fifty years ago very few colleges would admit them at all. Even to-day no Negro has ever been admitted to Princeton, and at some other leading institutions they are rather endured than encouraged. Oberlin was the great pioneer in the work of blotting out the color line in colleges, and has more Negro graduates by far than any other Northern college.

The total number of Negro college graduates up to 1899 (several of the graduates of that year not being reported), was as follows:

	Negro Colleges	White Colleges
Before '76	137	75
'75–80	143	22
'80–85	250	31
'85–90	413	43
'90–95	465	66
'95–99	475	88
Class Unknown	57	64
TOTAL	1,940	389

Of these graduates 1,079 were men and 250 were women; 50 per cent of Northern-born college men come South to work among the masses of their people, at a sacrifice which few people realize; nearly 90 per cent of the Southern-born graduates instead of seeking that personal freedom and broader intellectual atmosphere which their training has led them, in some degree, to conceive, stay and labor and wait in the midst of their black neighbors and relatives.

The most interesting question, and in many respects the crucial question, to be asked concerning college-bred Negroes, is: Do they earn a living? It has been intimated more than once that the higher training of Negroes has resulted in sending into the world of work, men who could find nothing to do suitable to their talents. Now and then there comes a rumor of a colored college man working at menial service, etc. Fortunately, returns as to occupations of college-bred Negroes, gathered by the Atlanta conference, are quite full—nearly 60 per cent of the total number of graduates.

This enables us to reach fairly certain conclusions as to the occupations of all college-bred Negroes. Of 1,312 persons reported, there were:

	Per Cent
Teachers,	53.4
Clergymen,	16.8
Physicians, etc.,	6.3
Students,	5.6
Lawyers,	4.7
In Govt.Service,	4.0
In Business,	3.6
Farmers and Artisans,	2.7
Editors, Secretaries and Clerks	2.4
Miscellaneous,	.5

Over half are teachers, a sixth are preachers, another sixth are students and professional men; over 6 per cent are farmers, artisans and merchants, and 4 per cent are in government service. In detail the occupations are as follows:

Occupations of College-Bred Men

TEACHERS:

Presidents and Deans,	19		
Teachers of Music,	7		
Professors, Principals and Teachers,	675	Total	701

CLERGYMEN:

Bishop,	1		
Chaplains, U.S. Army,	2		
Missionaries,	9		
Presiding Elders,	12		
Preachers,	197	Total	221

PHYSICIANS:

Doctors of Medicine,	76		
Druggists,	4		
Dentists,	3	Total	83

STUDENTS:	74
LAWYERS:	62

(Continued)

(Continued)

CIVIL SERVICE:

U.S. Minister Plenipotentiary,	1		
U.S. Consul,	1		
U.S. Deputy Collector,	1		
U.S. Gauger,	1		
U.S. Postmasters,	2		
U.S. Clerks,	44		
State Civil Service,	2		
City Civil Service,	1	Total	53

BUSINESS MEN:

Merchants, etc.,	30		
Managers,	13		
Real Estate Dealers,	4	Total	47
FARMERS,			26

CLERKS AND SECRETARIES:

Secretary of National Societies,	7		
Clerks, etc.	15	Total	22
ARTISANS:			9
EDITORS:			9
MISCELLANEOUS:			5

These figures illustrate vividly the function of the college-bred Negro. He is, as he ought to be, the group leader, the man who sets the ideals of the community where he lives, directs its thoughts and heads its social movements. It need hardly be argued that the Negro people need social leadership more than most groups; that they have no traditions to fall back upon, no long established customs, no strong family ties, no well defined social classes. All these things must be slowly and painfully evolved. The preacher was, even before the war, the group leader of the Negroes, and the church their greatest social institution. Naturally this preacher was ignorant and often immoral, and the problem of replacing the older type by better educated men has been a difficult one. Both by direct work and by direct influence on other preachers, and on congregations, the college-bred preacher has an opportunity for reformatory work and moral inspiration, the value of which cannot be overestimated.

It has, however, been in the furnishing of teachers that the Negro college has found its peculiar function. Few persons realize how vast a work, how mighty a revolution has been thus accomplished. To furnish five millions and more of ignorant people with teachers of their own race and blood, in one generation, was not only a very difficult undertaking, but a very important one, in that, it placed before the eyes of almost every Negro child an attainable ideal. It brought the masses of the blacks in contact with modern civilization, made black men the leaders of their communities and trainers of the new generation. In this work college-bred Negroes were first teachers, and then teachers of teachers. And here it is that the broad culture of college work has been of peculiar value. Knowledge of life and its wider meaning, has been the point of the Negro's deepest ignorance, and the sending out of teachers whose training has not been simply for bread winning, but also for human culture, has been of inestimable value in the training of these men.

In the earlier years the two occupations of preacher and teacher were practically the only ones open to the black college graduate. Of later years a larger diversity of life among his people has opened new avenues of employment. Nor have these college men been paupers and spendthrifts; 557 college-bred Negroes owned in 1899, $1,342,862.50 worth of real estate (assessed value), or $2,411 per family. The real value of the total accumulations of the whole group is perhaps about $10,000,000, or $5,000 apiece. Pitiful, is it not, beside the fortunes of oil kings and steel trusts, but after all is the fortune of the millionaire the only stamp of true and successful living? Alas! it is, with many, and there's the rub.

The problem of training the Negro is to-day immensely complicated by the fact that the whole question of the efficiency and appropriateness of our present systems of education, for any kind of child, is a matter of active debate, in which final settlement seems still afar off. Consequently it often happens that persons arguing for or against certain systems of education for Negroes have these controversies in mind and miss the real question at issue. The main question, so far as the Southern Negro is concerned, is: What under the present circumstance, must a system of education do in order to raise the Negro as quickly as possible in the scale of civilization? The answer to this question seems to me clear: It must strengthen the Negro's character, increase his knowledge and teach him to earn a living. Now it goes without saying, that it is hard to do all these things simultaneously or suddenly, and that at the same time it will not do to give all the attention to one and neglect the others; we could give black boys trades, but that alone will not civilize a race of ex-slaves; we might simply increase their knowledge of the world, but this would not necessarily make them wish to use this knowledge honestly; we might seek to strengthen character and purpose, but to what end if this people have nothing to eat or to wear? A system of education is not one thing, nor does it have a single definite object, nor is it a mere matter of schools. Education is that whole system of human training within and without the school house walls, which molds and develops men. If then we start out to train an ignorant and unskilled people with a heritage of bad habits, our system of training must set before itself two great aims—the one dealing with knowledge and character, the other part seeking to give the child the technical knowledge necessary for him to earn a living under the present circumstances. These objects are accomplished in part by the opening of the common schools on the one, and of the industrial schools on the other. But only in part, for there must also be trained those who are to teach these schools—men and women of knowledge and culture and technical skill who

understand modern civilization, and having the training and aptitude to impart it to the children under them. There must be teachers, and teachers of teachers, and to attempt to establish any sort of system of common and industrial school training, without *first* (and I say *first* advisedly) without *first* providing for the higher training of the very best teachers, is simply throwing your money to the winds. School houses do not teach themselves—piles of brick and mortar and machinery do not send out *men*. It is the trained, living human soul, cultivated and strengthened by long study and thought, that breathes the real breath of life into boys and girls and makes them human, whether they be black or white, Greek, Russian or American. Nothing, in these latter days, has so dampened the faith of thinking Negroes in recent educational movements, as the fact that such movements have been accompanied by ridicule and denouncement and decrying of those very institutions of higher training which made the Negro public school possible, and make the Negro industrial schools thinkable. It was Fisk, Atlanta, Howard and Straight, those colleges born of the faith and sacrifice of the abolitionists, that placed in the black schools of the South 30,000 teachers and more, which some, who depreciate the work of these higher schools, are using to teach their own new experiments. If Hampton, Tuskegee and the hundred other industrial schools prove in the future to be as successful as they deserve to be, then their success in training black artisans for the South will be due primarily to the white colleges of the North and the black colleges of the South, which trained the teachers who today conduct these institutions. There was a time when the American people believed pretty devoutly that a log of wood with a boy at one end and Mark Hopkins at the other, represented the highest ideal of human training. But in these eager days it would seem that we have changed all that and think it necessary to add a couple of saw-mills and a hammer to this outfit, and, at a pinch, to dispense with the services of Mark Hopkins.

I would not deny, or for a moment seem to deny, the paramount necessity of teaching the Negro to work, and to work steadily and skillfully; or seem to depreciate in the slightest degree the important part industrial schools must play in the accomplishments of these ends, but I *do* say, and insist upon it, that it is industrialism drunk with its vision of success, to imagine that its own work can be accomplished without providing for the training of broadly cultured men and women to teach its own teachers, and to teach the teachers of the public schools.

But I have already said that human education is not simply a matter of schools; it is much more a matter of family and group life—the training of one's home, of one's daily companions, of one's social class. Now the black boy of the South moves in a black world—a world with its own leaders, its own thoughts, its own ideals. In this world he gets by far the larger part of his life training, and through the eyes of this dark world he peers into the veiled world beyond. Who guides and determines the education which he receives in his world? His teachers here are the group-leaders of the Negro people—the physicians and clergymen, the trained fathers and mothers, the influential and forceful men about him of all kinds; here it is, if at all, that the culture of the surrounding world trickles through and is handed on by the graduates of the higher schools. Can such culture training of group-leaders be neglected? Can we afford to ignore it? Do you think that if the leaders of thought among Negroes are not trained and educated thinkers, that they will have no leaders? On the contrary a hundred half-trained demagogues will still hold the places they so largely occupy now, and hundreds of vociferous busy-bodies will multiply. You have no choice; either you must help furnish this race from within its own ranks with thoughtful men of trained leadership, or

you must suffer the evil consequences of a headless misguided rabble.

I am an earnest advocate of manual training and trade teaching for black boys, and for white boys, too. I believe that next to the founding of Negro colleges the most valuable addition to Negro education since the war, has been industrial training for black boys. Nevertheless, I insist that the object of all true education is not to make men carpenters, it is to make carpenters men; there are two means of making the carpenter a man, each equally important: the first is to give the group and community in which he works, liberally trained teachers and leaders to teach him and his family what life means; the second is to give him sufficient intelligence and technical skill to make him an efficient workman; the first object demands the Negro college and college-bred men—not a quantity of such colleges, but a few of excellent quality; not too many college-bred men, but enough to leaven the lump, to inspire the masses, to raise the Talented Tenth to leadership; the second object demands a good system of common schools, well-taught, conveniently located and properly equipped.

The Sixth Atlanta Conference truly said in 1901:

"We call the attention of the Nation to the fact that less than one million of the three million Negro children of school age, are at present regularly attending school, and these attend a session which lasts only a few months.

"We are to-day deliberately rearing millions of our citizens in ignorance, and at the same time limiting the rights of citizenship by educational qualifications. This is unjust. Half the black youth of the land have no opportunities open to them for learning to read, write and cipher. In the discussion as to the proper training of Negro children after they leave the public schools, we have forgotten that they are not yet decently provided with public schools.

"Propositions are beginning to be made in the South to reduce the already meagre school facilities of Negroes. We congratulate the South on resisting, as much as it has, this pressure, and on the many millions it has spent on Negro education. But it is only fair to point out that Negro taxes and the Negroes' share of the income from indirect taxes and endowments have fully repaid this expenditure, so that the Negro public school system has not in all probability cost the white taxpayers a single cent since the war.

"This is not fair. Negro schools should be a public burden, since they are a public benefit. The Negro has a right to demand good common school training at the hands of the States and the Nation since by their fault he is not in position to pay for this himself."

What is the chief need for the building up of the Negro public school in the South? The Negro race in the South needs teachers to-day above all else. This is the current testimony of all who know the situation. For the supply of this great demand two things are needed—institutions of higher education and money for school houses and salaries. It is usually assumed that a hundred or more institutions for Negro training are to-day turning out so many teachers and college-bred men that the race is threatened with an over-supply. This is sheer nonsense. There are to-day less than 3,000 living Negro college graduates in the United States, and less than a 1,000 Negroes in college. Moreover, in the 164 schools for Negroes, 95 per cent of their students are doing elementary and secondary work, work which should be done in the public schools. Over half of the remaining 2,157 students are taking high school studies. The mass of so-called "normal" schools for the Negro are simply doing elementary common school work, or, at most, high school work, with a little instruction in methods. The Negro colleges and the post-graduate courses at other institutions are the only agencies for the broader and more careful training of teachers. The work of these institutions is hampered for lack of funds. It is getting increasingly difficult to get funds for training teachers in the best modern methods, and yet all over the South, from State Superintendents, county officials, city boards and school principals comes the wail, "We need *teachers*!" and teachers must be trained. As the fairest minded of all white Southerners, Atticus G. Haygood, once said: "The defects of colored teachers are so great as to create an urgent necessity for training better ones. Their excellencies and their successes are sufficient to justify the best hopes of success in the effort, and to vindicate the judgment of those who make large investments of money and service, to give to colored students opportunity for thoroughly preparing themselves for the work of teaching children of their people."

The truth of this has been strikingly shown in the marked improvement of white teachers in the South. Twenty years ago the rank and file of white public school teachers were not as good as the Negro teachers. But they, by scholarships and good salaries, have been encouraged to thorough normal collegiate preparation, while the Negro teachers have been discouraged by starvation wages and the idea that any training will do for a black teacher. If carpenters are needed it is well and good to train men as carpenters. But to train men as carpenters, and then set them to teaching is wasteful and criminal; and to train men as teachers and then refuse them a living wage, unless they become carpenters, is rank nonsense.

The United States Commissioner of Education says in his report for 1900: "For comparison between the white and colored enrollment in secondary and higher education, I have added together the enrollment in high schools and secondary schools with the attendance in colleges and universities, not being sure of the actual grade of work done in the colleges and universities. The work done in the secondary schools is reported in such detail in this office, that there can be no doubt of its grade."

He then makes the following comparisons of persons in every million enrolled in secondary and higher education:

	Whole Country	*Negroes*
1880	4,362	1,289
1900	10,743	2,061

And he concludes: "While the number in colored high schools and colleges had increased somewhat faster than the population, it had not kept pace with the average of the whole country, for it had fallen from 30 per cent to 24 per cent of the average quota. Of all colored pupils, one (1) in one hundred was engaged in secondary and higher work, and that ratio has continued substantially for the past twenty years. If the ratio of colored population in secondary and higher education is to be equal to the average for the whole country, it must be increased to five times its present average." And if this be true of the secondary and higher education, it is safe to say that the Negro has not one-tenth his quota in college studies. How baseless, therefore, is the charge of too much training! We need Negro teachers for the Negro common schools, and we need first-class normal schools and colleges to train them. This is the work of higher Negro education and it must be done.

Further than this, after being provided with group leaders of civilization, and a foundation of intelligence in the public schools, the carpenter, in order to be a man, needs technical skill. This calls for trade school. Now trade schools are not nearly such simple things as people once thought. The original idea was that the "Industrial" school was to furnish education practically free, to those willing to work for it; it was to "do" things—i.e.: become a center of productive industry, it was to be partially, if not wholly, self-supporting, and it was to teach trades. Admirable as were

some of the ideas underlying this scheme, the whole thing simply would not work in practice; it was found that if you were to use time and material to teach trades thoroughly, you could not at the same time keep the industries on a commercial basis and make them pay. Many schools started out to do this on a large scale and went into virtual bankruptcy. Moreover, it was found also that it was possible to teach a boy a trade mechanically, without giving him the full educative benefit of the process, and, vice versa, that there was a distinctive educative value in teaching a boy to use his hands and eyes in carrying out certain physical processes, even though he did not actually learn a trade. It has happened, therefore, in the last decade that a noticeable change has come over the industrial schools. In the first place the idea of commercially remunerative industry in a school is being pushed rapidly to the background. There are still schools with shops and farms that bring in an income, and schools that use student labor partially for the erection of their buildings and the furnishing of equipment. It is coming to be seen, however, in the education of the Negro, as clearly as it has been seen in the education of the youths the world over, that it is the *boy* and not the material product, that is the true object of education. Consequently the object of the industrial school came to be the thorough training of boys regardless of the cost of the training, so long as it was thoroughly well done.

Even at this point, however, the difficulties were not surmounted. In the first place modern industry has taken great strides since the war, and the teaching of trades is no longer a simple matter. Machinery and the long processes of work have greatly changed the work of the carpenter, the iron worker and the shoemaker. A really efficient workman must be to-day an intelligent man who has had good technical training in addition to thorough common school, and perhaps even higher training. To meet this situation the industrial schools began a further development; they established distinct Trade Schools for the thorough training of better class artisans, and at the same time they sought to preserve for the purpose of general education, such of the simpler processes of the elementary trade learning as were best suited therefor. In this differentiation of the Trade School and manual training, the best of the industrial schools simply followed the plain trend of the present educational epoch. A prominent educator tells us that, in Sweden, "In the beginning the economic conception was generally adopted, and everywhere manual training was looked upon as a means of preparing the children of the common people to earn their living. But gradually it came to be recognized that manual training has a more elevated purpose, and one, indeed, more useful in the deeper meaning of the term. It came to be considered as an educative process for the complete moral, physical and intellectual development of the child."

Thus, again, in the manning of trade schools and manual training schools we are thrown back upon the higher training as its source and chief support. There was a time when any aged and worn-out carpenter could teach in a trade school. But not so to-day. Indeed the demand for college-bred men by a school like Tuskegee ought to make Mr. Booker T. Washington the firmest friend of higher training. Here he has as helpers the son of a Negro senator, trained in Greek and the humanities, and graduated at Harvard; the son of a Negro congressman and lawyer, trained in Latin and mathematics, and graduated at Oberlin; he has as his wife, a woman who read Virgil and Homer in the same class room with me; he has a college chaplain, a classical graduate of Atlanta University; as teacher of science, a graduate of Fisk; as teacher of history, a graduate of Smith—indeed some thirty of his chief teachers are college graduates, and instead of studying

French grammars in the midst of weeds, or buying pianos for dirty cabins, they are at Mr. Washington's right hand helping him in a noble work. And yet one of the effects of Mr. Washington's propaganda has been to throw doubt upon the expediency of such training for Negroes, as these persons have had.

Men of America, the problem is plain before you. Here is a race transplanted through the criminal foolishness of your fathers. Whether you like it or not the millions are here, and here they will remain. If you do not lift them up, they will pull you down. Education and work are the levers to uplift a people. Work will not do it unless inspired by the right ideals and guided by intelligence. Education must not simply teach work—it must teach life. The Talented Tenth of the Negro race must be made leaders of thought and missionaries of culture among their people. No others can do this work and the Negro colleges must train men for it. The Negro race, like all other races, is going to be saved by its exceptional men.

2. "Education"

Published in 1912 in *The Crisis*

Consider this argument: Education is the training of men for life. The best training is experience, but if we depended entirely upon this each generation would begin where the last began and civilization could not advance.

We must then depend largely on oral and written tradition and on such bits of typical experience as we can arrange for the child's guidance to life.

More than that, children must be trained in the technique of earning a living and doing their part of the world's work.

But no training in technique must forget that the object of education is the child and not the things he makes.

Moreover, a training simply in technique will not do because general intelligence is needed for any trade, and the technique of trades changes.

Indeed, by the careful training of intelligence and ability, civilization is continually getting rid of the hardest and most exhausting toil, and giving it over to machines, leaving human beings freer for higher pursuits and self-development.

Hence, colored people in educating their children should be careful.

First: To conserve and select ability, giving to their best minds higher college training.

Second: They should endeavor to give all their children the largest possible amount of general training and intelligence before teaching them the technique of a particular trade, remembering that the object of all true education is not to make men carpenters, but to make carpenters men.

Is not this reasoning sound? Could you imagine an educator of any experience who would take material exception to it? Would you call it revolutionary or in the nature of a "personal" attack?

Certainly not.

Yet this very argument, with illustrations and emphasis delivered to some seven hundred apparently well-pleased folk in Indianapolis, has had the most astounding results. The Indianapolis *Star* in a leading editorial denounced it as "dangerous"!

A leading white philanthropist of abolition forebears considered it not only "misleading" and "mischievous" but a covert and damaging personal attack!

The supervisor of the colored schools of Indianapolis wrote to express regret that the lecture had seemed to attack his school curriculum and ideals, and the assistant superintendent of schools in the District of Columbia hastens to give advice!

Yet where is the flaw in the argument?

There is no flaw, but there are serious flaws in the thinking of some of these critics.

The first flaw is the naive assumption that the paraphernalia of a school shows the education it is imparting. If some people see a Greek book and a cap and gown, they conclude that the boy between them is receiving higher education. But is he? That depends. If other people see a hammer, a saw, and a cook book, they conclude that the boy who uses them is being trained in intelligence, ability, and the earning of a living. But is he? That depends.

When the proud principal of a school shows workshop and kitchen, table and pie, one may be interested, but one is no more convinced than when another shows an array of Greek roots and rounded phrases. One must merely remark: the end of education is neither the table nor the phrase—it is the boy; what kind of boys are you training here? Are they boys quickened in intelligence, with some knowledge of the world they live in? Are they trained in such ways as to discover their true bent and ability, and to be intelligently guided to the choice of a life work? Then your system is right. Otherwise it is wrong, and not all the gingham dresses in Indiana will justify it.

The second flaw is the more or less conscious determination of certain folk to use the American public-school system for the production of laborers who will do the work they want done. To them Indianapolis exists for the sake of its factories and not the factories for the sake of Indianapolis. They want dinners, chairs, and motor cars, and they want them cheap; therefore use the public schools to train servants, carpenters, and mechanics. It does not occur to them to think of workingmen as existing for their own sakes. What with impudent maids, and half-trained workingmen, they are tired of democracy; they want caste; a place for everybody and everybody in his father's place with themselves on top, and "niggers" at the bottom where they belong. To such folk the problem of education is strikingly simple. To teach the masses to work; show them how to do things; increase their output; give them intelligence, of course; but this as a means, not as an end, and be careful of too much of it. Of course, if a meteoric genius bursts his birth's invidious bar, let him escape, but keep up the bars, and as most men are fools, treat them and train them as such.

It was such darkened counsels as these that brought the French Revolution. It is such mad logic as this that is at the bottom of the social unrest today.

The lecturer came to Indianapolis not to criticize, but to warn—not to attack, but to make straight the way of the Lord. He is no despiser of common humble toil; God forbid! He and his fathers before him have worked with their hands at the lowliest occupations and he honors any honest toilers at any task; but he makes no mistake here. It is the toilers that he honors, not the task—the man and not the thing. The thing may or may not be honorable—the man always is.

Yet the despising of men is growing and the caste spirit is rampant in the land; it is laying hold of the public schools and it has the colored public schools by the throat, North, East, South and West. Beware of it, my brothers and dark sisters; educate your children. Give them the broadest and highest education possible; train them to the limit of their ability, if you work your hands to the bone in doing it. See that your child gets, not the highest task, but the task best fitted to his ability, whether it be digging dirt or painting landscapes; remembering that our recognition as common folk by the world depends on the number of men of ability we produce—not great geniuses, but efficient thinkers and doers in all lines. Never forget that if we ever compel the world's respect, it will be by virtue of our heads and not our heels.

3. "Education"

Published in 1922 in *The Crisis*

There is a widespread feeling that a school is a machine. You insert a child at 9 a.m. and extract it at 4 p.m., improved and standardized with parts of Grade IV, first term. In truth, school is a desperate duel between new souls and old to pass on facts and methods and dreams from a dying world to a world in birth pains without letting either teacher or taught lose for a moment faith and interest. It is hard work. Often, most often, it is a futile failure. It is never wholly a success without the painstaking help of the parent.

Yet I know Negroes, thousands of them, who never visit the schools where their children go; who do not know the teachers or what they teach or what they are supposed to teach; who do not consult the authorities on matters of discipline—do not know who or what is in control of the schools or how much money is needed or received.

Oh, we have our excuses! The teachers do not want us around. They do not welcome co-operation. Colored parents especially may invite insult or laughter. All true in some cases. Yet the best schools and the best teachers pray for and welcome the continuous intelligent co-operation of parents. And the worst schools need it and must be made to realize their need.

There has been much recent discussion among Negroes as to the merits of mixed and segregated schools. It is said that our children are neglected in mixed schools. "Let us have our own schools. How else can we explain the host of colored High School graduates in Washington, and the few in Philadelphia?" Easily. In Washington, parents are intensely interested in their schools and have for years followed, watched and criticized them. In Philadelphia, the colored people have evinced no active interest save in *colored schools* and there is no colored High School.

Save the great principle of democracy and equal opportunity and fight segregation by wealth, class or race or color, not by yielding to it but by watching, visiting and voting in all school matters, organizing parents and children and bringing every outside aid and influence to co-operate with teachers and authorities.

In the North with mixed schools unless colored parents take intelligent, continuous and organized interest in the schools which their children attend, the children will be neglected, treated unjustly, discouraged and balked of their natural self-expression and ambition. Do not allow this. Supervise your children's schools.

In the South unless the parents know and visit the schools and keep up continuous, intelligent agitation, the teachers will be sycophants, the studies designed to make servant girls, and the funds stolen by the white trustees.

4. *"The Negro College"*

Delivered as a speech in 1933 at Fisk University

It has been said many times that a Negro University is nothing more and nothing less than a university. Quite recently one of the great leaders of education in the United States, Abraham Flexner, said something of that sort concerning Howard. As President of the Board of Trustees, he said he was seeking to build not a Negro university, but a University. And by those words he brought again before our eyes the ideal of a great institution of learning which becomes a center of universal culture. With all good will toward them that say such words—it is the object of this paper to insist that there can be no college for Negroes which is not a Negro college and that while an American Negro university, just like a German or Swiss university may rightly aspire to a universal culture unhampered by limitations of race and culture, yet it must start on the earth where we sit and not in the skies whither we aspire. May I develop this thought.

In the first place, we have got to remember that here in America, in the year 1933, we

have a situation which cannot be ignored. There was a time when it seemed as though we might best attack the Negro problem by ignoring its most unpleasant features. It was not and is not yet in good taste to speak generally about certain facts which characterize our situation in America. We are politically hamstrung. We have the greatest difficulty in getting suitable and remunerative work. Our education is more and more not only being confined to our own schools but to a segregated public school system far below the average of the nation with one-third of our children continuously out of school. And above all, and this we like least to mention, we suffer social ostracism which is so deadening and discouraging that we are compelled either to lie about it or to turn our faces to the red flag of revolution. It consists of studied and repeated and emphasized public insult of the sort which during all the long history of the world has led men to kill or be killed. And in the full face of any effort which any black man may make to escape this ostracism for himself, stands this flaming sword of racial doctrine which will distract his effort and energy if it does not lead him to spiritual suicide.

We boast and have right to boast of our accomplishment between the days that I studied here and this forty-fifth anniversary of my graduation. It is a calm appraisal of fact to say that the history of modern civilization cannot surpass if it can parallel the advance of American Negroes in every essential line of culture in these years. And yet, when we have said this we must have the common courage honestly to admit that every step we have made forward has been greeted by a step backward on the part of the American public in caste intolerance, mob law, and racial hatred.

I need but remind you that when I graduated from Fisk there was no "Jim Crow" car in Tennessee and I saw Hunter of '89 once sweep a brakeman aside at the Union Station and escort a crowd of Fisk students into the first-class seats for which they had paid. There was no legal disfranchisement and a black Fiskite sat in the Legislature; and while the Chancellor of the Vanderbilt University had annually to be reintroduced to the President of Fisk, yet no white Southern group presumed to dictate the internal social life of this institution.

Manifestly with all that can be said, pro and con, and in extenuation, and by way of excuse and hope, this is the situation and we know it. There is no human way by which these facts can be ignored. We cannot do our daily work, sing a song or write a book or carry on a university and act as though these things were not.

If this is true, then no matter how much we may dislike the statement, the American Negro problem is and must be the center of the Negro American university. It has got to be. You are teaching Negroes. There is no use pretending that you are teaching Chinese, or that you are teaching white Americans or that you are teaching citizens of the world. You are teaching American Negroes in 1933, and they are the subjects of a caste system in the Republic of the United States of America and their life problem is primarily this problem of caste.

Upon these foundations, therefore, your university must start and build. Nor is the thing so entirely unusual or unheard of as it sounds. A university in Spain is not simply a university. It is a Spanish university. It is a university located in Spain. It uses the Spanish language. It starts with Spanish history and makes conditions in Spain the starting point of its teaching. Its education is for Spaniards— not for them as they may be or ought to be, but as they are with their present problems and disadvantages and opportunities.

In other words, the Spanish university is founded and grounded in Spain, just as surely as a French university is French. There are some people who have difficulty in apprehending this very clear truth. They assume, for instance, that the French university is in a singular sense universal, and is based on a comprehension and inclusion of all mankind and of their problems. But it is not so, and the assumption that it is arises simply because so much of French culture has been built into universal civilization. A French university is founded in France; it uses the French language and assumes a knowledge of French history. The present problems of the French people are its major problems and it becomes universal only so far as other peoples of the world comprehend and are at one with France in its mighty and beautiful history.

In the same way, a Negro university in the United States of America begins with Negroes. It uses that variety of the English idiom which they understand; and above all, it is founded or it should be founded on a knowledge of the history of their people in Africa and in the United States, and their present condition. Without whitewashing or translating wish into fact, it begins with that; and then it asks how shall these young men and women be trained to earn a living and live a life under the circumstances in which they find themselves or with such changing of those circumstances as time and work and determination will permit.

Is this statement of the field of a Negro university a denial of aspiration or a change from older ideals? I do not think it is, although I admit in my own mind some change of thought and modification of method. The system of learning which bases itself upon the actual condition of certain classes and groups of human beings is tempted to suppress a minor premise of fatal menace. It proposes that the knowledge given and the methods pursued in such institutions of learning shall be for the definite object of perpetuating present conditions or of leaving their amelioration in the hands of and at the initiative of other forces and other folk. This was the great criticism that those of us who fought for higher education of Negroes thirty years ago, brought against the industrial school.

The industrial school founded itself and rightly upon the actual situation of American Negroes and said: "What can be done to change this situation?" And its answer was: "A training in technique and method such as would incorporate the disadvantaged group into the industrial organization of the country," and in that organization the leaders of the Negro had perfect faith. Since that day the industrial machine has cracked and groaned. Its technique has changed faster than any school could teach; the relations of capital and labor have increased in complication and it has become so clear that Negro poverty is not primarily caused by ignorance of technical knowledge that the industrial school has almost surrendered its program.

In opposition to that, the opponents of college training in those earlier years said: "What black men need is the broader and more universal training so that they can apply the general principle of knowledge to the particular circumstances of their condition."

Here again was the indubitable truth but incomplete truth. The technical problem lay in the method of teaching this broader and more universal truth and here just as in the industrial program, we must start where we are and not where we wish to be. As I said a few years ago at Howard University, both these positions had thus something of truth and right. Because of the peculiar economic situation in our country the program of the industrial school came to grief first and has practically been given up. Starting even though we may with the actual condition of the Negro peasant and artisan, we cannot ameliorate his condition simply by learning a trade which is the technique of a passing era. More vision and knowledge are needed than that. But on the other hand, while the Negro college of a generation ago set down a defensible and true program of applying knowledge to facts, it unfortunately could not completely carry it out, and it did not carry it out, because the one

thing that the industrial philosophy gave to education, the Negro college did not take and that was that the university education of black men in the United States must be grounded in the condition and work of those black men!

On the other hand, it would be of course idiotic to say, as the former industrial philosophy almost said, that so far as most black men are concerned education must stop with this. No, starting with present conditions and using the facts and the knowledge of the present situation of American Negroes, the Negro university expands toward the possession and the conquest of all knowledge. It seeks from a beginning of the history of the Negro in America and in Africa to interpret all history; from a beginning of social development among Negro slaves and freedmen in America and Negro tribes and kingdoms in Africa, to interpret and understand the social development of all mankind in all ages. It seeks to reach modern science of matter and life from the surroundings and habits and aptitudes of American Negroes and thus lead up to understanding of life and matter in the universe.

And this is a different program than a similar function would be in a white university or in a Russian university or in an English university, because it starts from a different point. It is a matter of beginnings and integrations of one group which sweep instinctive knowledge and inheritance and current reactions into a universal world of science, sociology, and art. In no other way can the American Negro college function. It cannot begin with history and lead to Negro history. It cannot start with sociology and lead to Negro sociology.

Why was it that the Renaissance of literature which began among Negroes ten years ago has never taken real and lasting root? It was because it was a transplanted and exotic thing. It was a literature written for the benefit of white people and at the behest of white readers, and starting out privately from the white point of view. It never had a real Negro constituency and it did not grow out of the inmost heart and frank experience of Negroes; on such an artificial basis no real literature can grow.

On the other hand, if starting in a great Negro university you have knowledge, beginning with the particular, and going out to universal comprehension and unhampered expression, you are going to begin to realize for the American Negro the full life which is denied him now. And then after that comes a realization of the older object of our college—to bring this universal culture down and apply it to the individual life and individual conditions of living Negroes.

The university must become not simply a center of knowledge but a center of applied knowledge and guide of action. And this is all the more necessary now since we easily see that planned action especially in economic life, is going to be the watchword of civilization. If the college does not thus root itself in the group life and afterward apply its knowledge and culture to actual living, other social organs must replace the college in this function. A strong, intelligent family life may adjust the student to higher culture; and, too, a social clan may receive the graduate and induct him into life. This has happened and is happening among a minority of privileged people. But it costs society a fatal price. It tends to hinder progress and hamper change; it makes education propaganda for things as they are. It leaves the mass of those without family training and without social standing misfits and rebels who despite their education are uneducated in its meaning and application. The only college which stands for the progress of all, mass as well as aristocracy, functions in root and blossom as well as in the overshadowing and heaven-filling tree. No system of learning—no university can be universal before it is German, French, Negro. Grounded in inexorable fact and condition, in Poland, Italy, or elsewhere, it may seek the universal and happily it may find it—and finding it, bring it down to earth and us.

We have imbibed from the surrounding white world a childish idea of progress. Progress means bigger and better results always and forever. But there is no such rule of life. In six thousand years of human culture, the losses and retrogressions have been enormous. We have no assurance this twentieth century civilization will survive. We do not know that American Negroes will survive. There are sinister signs about us, antecedent to and unconnected with the Great Depression. The organized might of industry North and South is relegating the Negro to the edge of survival and using him as a labor reservoir on starvation wage. No secure professional class, no science, literature, nor art can live on such a subsoil. It is an insistent, deep-throated cry for rescue, guidance, and organized advance that greets the black leader today, and the college that trains him has got to let him know at least as much about the great black miners' strike in Alabama as about the age of Pericles.

We are on the threshold of a new era. Let us not deceive ourselves with outworn ideals of wealth and servants and luxuries, reared on a foundation of ignorance, starvation, and want. Instinctively, we have absorbed these ideals from our twisted white American environment. This new economic planning is not for us unless we do it. Unless the American Negro today, led by trained university men of broad vision, sits down to work out by economics and mathematics, by physics and chemistry, by history and sociology, exactly how and where he is to earn a living and how he is to establish a reasonable Life in the United States or elsewhere—unless this is done, the university has missed its field and function and the American Negro is doomed to be suppressed and inferior caste in the United States for incalculable time.

Here, then, is a job for the American Negro university. It cannot be successfully ignored or dodged without the growing menace of disaster. I lay the problem before you as one which you must not ignore.

To carry out this plan, two things and only two things are necessary—teachers and students. Buildings and endowments may help, but they are not indispensable. It is necessary first to have teachers who comprehend this program and know how to make it live among their students. This is calling for a good deal, because it asks that teachers teach that which they have learned in no American school and which they never will learn until we have a Negro university of the sort that I am envisioning. No teacher, black or white, who comes to a university like Fisk, filled simply with general ideas of human culture or general knowledge of disembodied science, is going to make a university of this school. Because a university is made of human beings, learning of the things they do not know from the things they do know in their own lives.

And secondly, we must have students. They must be chosen for their ability to learn. There is always the temptation to assume that the children of the privileged classes—the rich, the noble, the white—are those who can best take education. One has but to express this to realize its utter futility. But perhaps the most dangerous thing among us is for us, without thought, to imitate the white world and assume that we can choose students at Fisk because of the amount of money which their parents have happened to get hold of. That basis of selection is going to give us an extraordinary aggregation. We want, by the nicest methods possible, to seek out the talented and the gifted among our constituency, quite regardless of their wealth or position, and to fill this university and similar institutions with persons who have got brains enough to take fullest advantage of what the university offers. There is no other way. With teachers who know they are teaching and whom they are teaching, and the life that surrounds both acknowledge and the knower, and with students who have the capacity and the will to absorb this knowledge, we can build the sort

of Negro university which will emancipate not simply the black folk of the United States, but those white folk who in their effort to suppress Negroes have killed their own culture.

Men in their desperate effort to replace equality with caste and to build inordinate wealth on a foundation of abject poverty have succeeded in killing democracy, art, and religion.

Only a universal system of learning rooted in the will and condition of the masses and blossoming from that manure up toward the stars is worth the name. Once built it can only grow as it brings down sunlight and starshine and impregnates the mud.

The chief obstacle in this rich land endowed with every national resource and with the abilities of a hundred different peoples—the chief and only obstacle on the coming of that kingdom of economic equality which is the only logical end of work, is the determination of the white world to keep the black world poor and make themselves rich. The disaster which this selfish and shortsighted policy has brought lies at the bottom of this present depression, and too, its cure lies beside it. Your clear vision of a world without wealth, of capital without profit, of income based on work alone, is the path out not only for you but for all men.

Is not this a program of segregation, emphasis of race, and particularism as against national unity and universal humanity? It is and it is not by choice but by force; you do not get humanity by wishing it nor do you become American citizens simply because you want to. A Negro university, from its high ground of unfaltering facing of the truth, from its unblinking stare at hard facts does not advocate segregation by race; it simply accepts the bald fact that we are segregated, apart, hammered into a separate unity by spiritual intolerance and legal sanction backed by mob law, and that this separation is growing in strength and fixation; that it is worse today than a half century ago and that no character, address, culture, or desert is going to change it in our day or for centuries to come. Recognizing this brute fact, groups of cultured, trained and devoted men gathering in great institutions of learning proceed to ask, What are we going to do about it? It is silly to ignore the gloss of truth; it is idiotic to proceed as though we were white or yellow, English or Russian. Here we stand. We are American Negroes. It is beside the point to ask whether we form a real race. Biologically we are mingled of all conceivable elements, but race is psychology, not biology; and psychologically we are a unified race with one history, one red memory, and one revolt. It is not ours to argue whether we will be segregated or whether we ought to be a caste. We are segregated; we are a caste. This is our given and at present unalterable fact. Our problem is how far and in what we can consciously and scientifically guide our future so as to ensure our physical survival, our spiritual freedom and our social growth? Either we do this or we die. There is no alternative. If America proposed the murder of this group, its moral descent into imbecility and crime and its utter loss of manhood, self-assertion, and courage, the sooner we realize this the better. By that great line of McKay:

"If we must die, let it not be like hogs."

But the alternative of not dying like hogs is not that of dying or killing like snarling dogs. It is rather conquering the world by thought and brain and plan; by expression and organized cultural ideals. Therefore let us not beat futile wings in impotent frenzy, but carefully plan and guide our segregated life, organize in industry and politics to protect it and expand it and above all to give it unhampered spiritual expression in art and literature. It is the counsel of fear and cowardice to say this cannot be done. What must be can be and it is only a question of science and sacrifice to bring the great consummation.

What that will be, no one knows. It may be a great physical segregation of the world along the color line; it may be an economic rebirth which ensures spiritual and group integrity amid physical diversity. It may be utter annihilation of class and race and color barriers in one ultimate mankind differentiated by talent, susceptibility and gift—but any of these ends are matters of long centuries and not years. We live in years, swift-flying, transient years. We hold the possible future in our hands but not by wish and will, only by thought, plan, knowledge, and organization. If the college can pour into the coming age an American Negro who knows himself and his plight and how to protect himself and fight race prejudice, then the world of our dream will come and not otherwise.

5. "The Freedom to Learn"

Published in 1949 in *The Midwest Journal*

This is a time when any man who sincerely questions the efficiency of industrial organization in the United States is liable to be called a revolutionist, a traitor, and a liar, and to be accused of having selfish and unfair designs upon the progress and well-being of the people of this nation.

If he is so accused, no matter by whom or under what circumstances, anonymously, by rumor or innuendo, he is going to find it difficult to make answer or to prove his sincerity. He will find newspapers and radio filled with false interpretation of facts to such an extent that it is practically impossible for him to explain his belief or defend his conclusions. If he attempts to defend his position he may lose his friends, his influence, and what is more important, he may lose his chance to earn a decent living. Such a situation is one of the greatest dangers, not only to the person himself but even more to his family, his nation, and the civilization in which he lives.

What can we do about it? It is the temptation of every civilization to think of itself as supremely modern; as the last word of accomplishment; as having reached such perfection and efficiency that any change in object or method must be regarded with fear and suppressed by force. This is the all-too-natural conclusion of those who are comfortable and reasonably content under present conditions. But for those who suffer discomfort, the poor, the ignorant and sick, this restriction upon education is not only unfair for them but fatal for their children.

The present organization of industry in the United States fears for the future, lest the great advances which we have undoubtedly made in technique and production, in transportation and distribution should be disturbed and ruined by new untried and unproven plans and doctrines. Nevertheless, it seems to wise men that now all the more it is necessary to know, to open as widely as possible the opportunity for careful study of our situation and careful training of youth to seek truth, and to judge it.

If, for instance, the United States fears the doctrines of Karl Marx and Frederick Engels; if Americans do not believe in the work and thought of Lenin and Stalin; if they regard Communism as not only dangerous but malevolent, then what this nation needs most of all is the free and open curriculum of a school where people may study and read Marx, know what Communism is or proposes to be, and learn actual facts and accomplishments.

I should think that the greatest disservice that this nation or any people could do to the United States would be to stop the study of economic change; to prevent people from pursuing knowledge of Marx and Communism, and to try not to answer the great arguments for change. But instead, to let our children believe that none of the great minds of the eighteenth, nineteenth, and twentieth centuries have advocated programs of fundamental change in our economic organization.

It is all the more dangerous to stop the education of youth and the pursuit of knowledge in any direction because of the fact that practically always some persons, some classes, and some nations are enjoying great advantage in any current situation. Naturally, today those persons who own the capital and control the production and distribution of wealth enjoy distinct advantage, as compared with those who own little money or property, who are employees and not employers, and who have small voice in the organization or conduct of industry.

Of course, it is possible that persons who have the advantage in any particular social organization will, nevertheless, do the right thing, as far as they see it, and that the results of their actions will inure to the common good. But it is even more probable that power and influence will mislead them and work for the disadvantage of the nation. The question whether this is true or not can only be determined by honest study, by the encouragement of inquiry and argument, and by wide knowledge of the facts. To prevent this is, in the long run, to prevent progress.

What we need today, then, to ward off the threatened collapse of the civilization in which we live, is not only opposition to war as a method of human progress, but also a determination to keep the civil rights which modern civilization has gained at so vast a cost, and the possession of which is the surest preventive of war: the right to think, the right to express one's thought, the right to act in accordance with one's conclusions. Especially we should insist upon the right to learn, upon the right to have our children learn, and upon keeping our schools, uncoerced by the dominant forces of the present world, free to exercise the right to join with the great Goethe in a worldwide cry for "light, more light."

Of all the civil rights for which the world has struggled and fought for five thousand years, the right to learn is undoubtedly the most fundamental. If a people has preserved this right, then no matter how far it goes astray, no matter how many mistakes it makes, in the long run, in the unfolding of generations, it is going to come back to the right. But if at any time, or for any long period, people are prevented from thinking, children are indoctrinated with dogma, and they are made to learn not what is necessarily true but what the dominant forces in their world want them to think is true, then there is no aberration from truth and progress of which such a people may not be guilty.

We have had example upon example of this sort of thing. We have seen great priesthoods in Egypt and Babylon monopolize learning and keep the mass of people in ignorance. We have seen the Inquisition seek to make people righteous by fear and death. We have seen in the last one hundred and fifty years attempts to keep even elementary learning away from children, away from women, and away from certain classes and races.

The freedom to learn, curtailed even as it is today, has been bought by bitter sacrifice. And whatever we may think of the curtailment of other civil rights, we should fight to the last ditch to keep open the right to learn, the right

to have examined in our schools not only what we believe, but what we do not believe; not only what our leaders say, but what the leaders of other groups and nations, and the leaders of other centuries have said. We must insist upon this in order to give our children the fairness of a start which will equip them with such an array of facts and such an attitude toward truth that they can have a real chance to judge what the world is and what its greater minds have thought it might be.

It is astonishing in days of crisis or disaster how quickly we turn toward the schools and assume that through them we can make people believe anything. This, of course, is a great compliment to learning, but it is an unfortunate comment upon our belief in current patterns of culture. If the school is so great an instrument of progress, then we ought at least to have the breadth of conviction that would allow us to make it the freest of our institutions and oppose bitterly any attempt to curtail learning or discussion.

Freedom always entails danger. Complete freedom never exists. But of all the freedoms of which we think, the freedom to learn is in the long run the least dangerous and the one that should be curtailed last.

Index

Note: "Negro" and "black" are used in this index according to Du Bois's usage.

About the Author

Phil Zuckerman is Assistant Professor of Sociology at Pitzer College, where he teaches various courses in social theory, sociology of religion, and sociology of deviance. He has written extensively on W. E. B. Du Bois; he wrote the introduction for and edited *Du Bois on Religion,* cowrote the introduction for the 100th anniversary republication of Du Bois's *The Negro Church,* and has written several articles on Du Bois for various scholarly journals. In addition to his work on Du Bois, he is the author of *Invitation to the Sociology of Religion* and *Strife in the Sanctuary.*

Professor Zuckerman was born and raised in southern California. He attended the University of Oregon for undergraduate as well as graduate school, earning B.A., M.A., and Ph.D. degrees in sociology. He lives in Claremont, California, with his wife and two daughters. Along with his passion for sociology, he is interested in psychedelic folk music, Scandinavian culture, and cultivating apple trees.